Cybersecurity Essentials for Businesses: Practical Solutions to Protect Your Business Against Digital Threats

Andrew N. Gonzalez

Preface

In today's world, cyber threats are a constant and growing concern. No longer reserved for large enterprises or high-profile organizations, cyberattacks are increasingly targeting small and medium-sized businesses (SMBs) that may lack the robust defenses of their larger counterparts. In fact, small businesses are often seen as **low-hanging fruit** by cybercriminals, given their limited resources to invest in security.

But here's the good news: **Cybersecurity doesn't have to be overwhelming,** and it certainly doesn't require a large IT department or a massive budget. Whether you're running a startup, managing a growing small business, or leading a team within a larger organization, you can **take practical, cost-effective steps to protect your business** from digital threats. And that's exactly what this book is all about.

As someone who has worked in the cybersecurity field for years, I've seen firsthand the devastating consequences of a breach—and I've also seen how businesses, with the right strategies and tools, can significantly reduce their risk and recover quickly from attacks. **This book is designed to empower you**, regardless of your level of experience with cybersecurity, with the knowledge and tools to secure your business's digital assets, data, and reputation.

Why Cybersecurity Matters for Businesses

You might be wondering, **"Why should I care about cybersecurity?"** Perhaps you're a small business owner, a manager, or even an entrepreneur who is primarily focused on **growth** and **day-to-day operations**. I get it. It's easy to prioritize other aspects of running your business—like increasing sales, improving customer service, or launching new products—over securing your digital infrastructure. But let me share some quick facts that may change your perspective:

- **43% of cyberattacks target small businesses**, and about **60% of small businesses** that are hacked go out of business within six months.

- **SMBs are more likely to face ransomware attacks** because cybercriminals know they are often less prepared than larger organizations.
- The **average cost of a data breach** for a small business is over **$100,000**—a significant amount for any organization to absorb.

What makes this particularly concerning is that many small business owners don't even realize the threat until it's too late. Often, these attacks exploit common **vulnerabilities**—like outdated software, weak passwords, or lack of employee training—that are easily preventable. This book will walk you through these common mistakes and provide practical solutions you can implement immediately to protect your business.

What You Can Expect From This Book

The goal of this book is simple: to **equip you with practical, actionable cybersecurity strategies** that will help you identify, mitigate, and respond to digital threats in a manageable way. While cybersecurity can seem like an intimidating, highly technical field, this book is written to break it down in an **easy-to-understand, step-by-step format**. You don't need to be a tech expert to get value from this content.

Here's a quick breakdown of what you can expect:

1. **Understanding the Basics**:
   We begin by demystifying cybersecurity. From understanding why it matters for small businesses to learning about common threats, we'll make sure you understand the foundational concepts without overwhelming you with jargon.
2. **Building a Strong Cybersecurity Foundation**:
   We cover practical steps you can take to secure your business right now—things like **password management, firewalls, encryption**, and **regular software updates**. These may seem like small steps, but they can significantly reduce your vulnerability to attacks.
3. **Implementing Security Policies**:
   Creating clear **cybersecurity policies** for your team is crucial. We'll walk you through how to build policies that address **data protection, access control, incident response**, and more.

4. **Preparing for the Worst**:
   Even the best defenses can sometimes be breached. That's why we'll cover the importance of creating an **incident response plan** and a **business continuity plan** so that, in case of a breach, your business can recover quickly with minimal damage.
5. **Staying Up-to-Date**:
   The digital landscape is constantly changing, which means cybersecurity is never a one-time task. We'll discuss how to **stay informed** about emerging threats and make continuous improvements to your defenses.

A Personal Journey in Cybersecurity

As someone who has spent years in the trenches of cybersecurity, I've seen firsthand how small businesses often struggle with security, simply because they don't know where to start or don't have the resources to manage complex systems. In fact, much of the content in this book stems from conversations I've had with small business owners who were overwhelmed by the idea of cybersecurity. Many of them just wanted a **simple guide**—something that would help them understand what they were up against and offer a roadmap to securing their business.

Through these conversations, I realized that small business owners needed to feel **empowered**, not intimidated. Cybersecurity doesn't need to be an obstacle to your success—it should be a foundation for it. By integrating simple security measures into your business practices, you are **future-proofing** your organization and **building customer trust** at the same time.

A Practical Approach: Why This Book Is Different

While other cybersecurity books can feel dense or overly technical, this one is focused on **actionable advice** that's easy to implement. You won't find complicated algorithms or exhaustive technical jargon here. Instead, you'll find clear, concise steps that you can start using immediately.

- **Step-by-Step Guidance**: We break down complex cybersecurity tasks into simple steps. You can take one action today and another tomorrow without feeling overwhelmed.
- **Real-World Case Studies**: We've included practical examples from businesses of various sizes to help you relate the advice to your own organization.
- **Easy-to-Implement Tools**: We provide recommendations for **affordable** and **user-friendly tools** that you can begin using without requiring a dedicated IT team.

An Invitation to Get Started

I want to encourage you to view cybersecurity as an ongoing journey, not a destination. The digital world can be unpredictable, but by taking a few key steps now, you'll be better prepared for whatever comes your way.

Whether you're looking to **secure your business's data**, **protect your customers**, or simply **understand** how to prevent common threats, this book will guide you in the right direction. Let's begin by starting with the basics and building your security foundation, one step at a time.

My Promise to You

By the end of this book, you will have a clear understanding of the cybersecurity threats that face businesses today, and more importantly, the tools and strategies to defend against them. **I am confident that with the insights, tips, and best practices you'll learn here, you'll be well on your way to securing your business's digital future.**

Let's get started. Secure your business today, and be prepared for the challenges of tomorrow.

Table of Contents

Part 1: Cybersecurity Fundamentals and Risk Awareness (Beginner Level)

Chapter 1: What is Cybersecurity and Why Does It Matter?

1.1: Defining Cybersecurity

Imagine for a moment that your business is a house. You have valuable items inside—your intellectual property, financial records, customer data, and even your business's reputation. Now, picture that house without any locks on the doors or windows, and with no security system in place. Would you feel safe?

This is essentially what it's like to run a business without cybersecurity.

Cybersecurity refers to the practice of protecting your business's digital assets—data, systems, and networks—against malicious threats. These threats could come in many forms: cyberattacks, hacking, data breaches, or even simple human errors that leave your business vulnerable. But it's not just about preventing the bad guys from getting in; it's about ensuring that your systems function properly, your data remains confidential, and your business can keep running smoothly.

In the digital world, your business operates like an intricate network of systems, devices, and connections. Cybersecurity ensures that each of these components is secure, safeguarding your operations from external threats and internal vulnerabilities. It's much like setting up a security system for your house but in the virtual world—protecting both your business and your customers.

Think of cybersecurity as your business's first line of defense. But just like a security system, it's not foolproof on its own. You need to maintain it, update it, and remain vigilant about new risks and vulnerabilities.

1.2: The Importance of Cybersecurity for Businesses

Now, you might be thinking, *"I'm a small business. Why would anyone target me?"*

Here's the reality: small businesses are actually **prime targets** for cybercriminals. Why? Because many small businesses think they're too small to be attacked, or they believe they lack valuable data. This is far from true.

In fact, small businesses are often **less prepared** and have weaker defenses compared to larger companies, making them more vulnerable. Cybercriminals know this, which is why they target businesses like yours. In fact, according to a report by the **National Cyber Security Alliance**, **43% of cyberattacks** target small businesses. And the impact can be devastating. A single breach can cost thousands—or even millions—in lost revenue, customer trust, and reputational damage.

But that's not all. The **costs** of a cyberattack don't just come from the immediate damage. There's also the aftermath:

- **Ransom payments** (if you get hit with ransomware)
- **Legal fees** if customer data is compromised
- **Regulatory fines** for non-compliance with data protection laws like GDPR
- **Downtime** in operations, meaning no sales or services for an extended period

The bottom line: cybersecurity is not optional. It's a **critical part** of your business's success and longevity. Whether you're a startup or an established small business, investing in cybersecurity protects your hard-earned reputation, customer loyalty, and overall business health.

1.3: The Digital Threat Landscape

In today's world, threats to your business are **everywhere**. Cyberattacks come in many forms, and they're becoming more sophisticated by the day. Let's take a look at some of the most common and dangerous threats you might face:

- **Phishing:** Phishing attacks are the digital equivalent of a scam phone call. A hacker impersonates a trusted source—like your bank, a vendor, or even a colleague—and asks for sensitive information (login details, financial data, etc.). The hacker usually tricks you into clicking on a link or opening an attachment, which then installs malware or steals your data.
- **Ransomware:** This is when a hacker encrypts your business's data and demands payment (usually in cryptocurrency) to release it. If you don't pay, your business could lose access to crucial data forever. Ransomware attacks can be incredibly disruptive and financially devastating for small businesses.
- **Malware:** Short for "malicious software," malware includes viruses, worms, and trojans that can infect your business's devices. Malware can steal data, damage files, or even take control of your systems. A single infected device can cause a domino effect across your entire network.
- **Man-in-the-Middle (MitM) Attacks:** This happens when a hacker intercepts the communication between you and your customer, vendor, or any other business partner. The attacker can then steal data, inject malicious code, or impersonate one of the parties involved. This is often done when businesses use unsecured networks, like public Wi-Fi.
- **Social Engineering:** Social engineering attacks rely on human behavior rather than technology. These attacks manipulate people into divulging confidential information. Hackers might call your employees and impersonate IT staff, asking for passwords or access to systems.
- **Denial-of-Service (DoS) Attacks:** A DoS attack floods your website or systems with more traffic than they can handle, causing them to crash. For businesses that rely on online sales or digital operations, this can be disastrous, leaving customers frustrated and unable to access your services.

Cybercriminals are constantly evolving their tactics, often staying one step ahead of businesses trying to protect themselves. For example, in recent years, **AI-powered cyberattacks** have started to emerge, where bots learn to bypass traditional security systems. The reality is that cyber threats are complex and evolving, and it's essential to stay ahead of them.

Personal Insight: A Real-Life Example

Let me tell you a quick story about a small bakery I once worked with. They had an adorable website where customers could place orders online. One day, they received an email that appeared to come from their payment processing company. The email told them that they needed to "verify" their account to prevent fraud, and the link in the email looked legitimate. Unfortunately, the link was a phishing attempt. The bakery's account was compromised, and thousands of dollars in orders were stolen before they even knew what hit them.

Had they been aware of cybersecurity risks and understood the importance of verifying emails and links, they could have prevented this breach. The bakery learned the hard way that cybersecurity isn't something you can ignore, no matter how small your business is.

Why Cybersecurity Matters

Cybersecurity is the **backbone** of your business's online and offline operations. In an era where so much of our personal and business lives are conducted online, it's crucial to take proactive steps in protecting what matters most. Cybercriminals don't care if you're a small business, they just care about finding vulnerable targets. So, don't wait until it's too late.

At the end of the day, the **cost of doing nothing** is far higher than the cost of setting up the necessary safeguards. Whether you're just starting out or you've been in business for years, now is the time to take action. In the following chapters, we'll dive into practical steps to protect your business, from simple actions like using strong passwords to more advanced measures like creating comprehensive security policies and responding to incidents.

Chapter 2: Building Awareness – Identifying Digital Threats

2.1: Common Digital Threats (Phishing, Malware, Ransomware)

In today's digital landscape, small businesses are under constant threat from cybercriminals. These criminals often target businesses with weak security measures or a lack of awareness about the dangers lurking in cyberspace. Three of the most prevalent threats to your business are **phishing**, **malware**, and **ransomware**. Understanding these threats and how they work is the first step in defending your business from costly breaches and disruptions. In this guide, we will break down each of these threats, provide practical tips for protecting your business, and offer real-life examples to show just how dangerous these attacks can be.

Phishing: The Social Engineer's Favorite Tool

Phishing is one of the oldest and most effective digital threats. It's an attack where cybercriminals impersonate a trusted entity (like your bank, a vendor, or even a colleague) to deceive you into revealing sensitive information such as login credentials, financial details, or personal data. Unlike many cyberattacks, phishing relies on human error, making it one of the easiest and most effective ways for hackers to gain unauthorized access to systems.

How Phishing Works

Phishing attacks often take the form of **email**, but they can also appear through **SMS**, **social media**, or **phone calls**. A typical phishing email might look like it's coming from a trusted source, with the message urging you to click on a link or download an attachment. When you do, the attacker either collects your personal information or installs malware on your system.

Practical Examples:

1. **Fake Invoice**: You might receive an email that looks like an invoice from a supplier, asking you to open an attachment to view the details. The attachment contains malicious code that, once opened, infects your system with malware.
2. **Account Verification**: A "security alert" might prompt you to log into your bank account through a link. The link takes you to a fake login page where you enter your credentials, which are then captured by the attacker.

How to Protect Against Phishing

- **Check the sender's email address**: Even if the email looks official, a quick check of the sender's email can reveal discrepancies (e.g., "*support@paypa1.com*" *instead of* "*support@paypal.com*").
- **Don't click on links**: If you receive an unsolicited email with a link, don't click on it. Instead, go directly to the website by typing the URL into your browser.
- **Enable multi-factor authentication (MFA)**: MFA adds an extra layer of security, making it harder for attackers to use stolen credentials.
- **Educate employees**: Train staff on the dangers of phishing and how to recognize suspicious emails.

Malware: The Silent Intruder

Malware (short for "malicious software") is a catch-all term for any software designed to damage or disrupt systems. It can range from relatively harmless viruses to highly sophisticated spyware. The primary purpose of malware is to either steal data, disrupt business operations, or gain unauthorized access to systems.

How Malware Works

Malware is typically spread via **email attachments**, **infected software downloads**, **compromised websites**, or **USB drives**. Once installed, it can spread throughout your network, stealing sensitive information or damaging files. Some types of malware, like **keyloggers**, silently record what you type, including passwords and credit card numbers, sending this information back to the attacker.

Types of Malware:

- **Viruses**: These attach themselves to clean files and spread throughout a system, damaging files and programs.
- **Trojans**: Malicious software disguised as legitimate software, often used to gain unauthorized access to a system.
- **Worms**: These self-replicating programs can spread from one device to another, often over a network.
- **Spyware**: Designed to secretly gather information from your system without your knowledge.

Practical Example:

Let's say your company downloads a software update from a website that appears to be legitimate. However, the software was compromised and now contains malware. Once installed, the malware starts sending confidential data (like customer information) to the attacker. Over time, this data leak can result in a significant security breach and potential loss of customer trust.

How to Protect Against Malware

- **Install and regularly update antivirus software**: This helps detect and remove malware before it can cause damage.
- **Avoid downloading from untrusted sources**: Only download software from official or trusted websites.
- **Enable automatic updates**: Ensure that your operating system and software are always up to date to patch vulnerabilities.
- **Be cautious with email attachments**: Don't open attachments from unknown senders.

Ransomware: The Digital Extortionist

Ransomware is one of the most dangerous and disruptive cyberattacks because it completely locks you out of your own systems or data, and demands a ransom for its release. In many cases, ransomware attackers threaten to delete your data or release it publicly unless you pay them.

How Ransomware Works

Ransomware typically enters your system through phishing emails or **exploited vulnerabilities** in your network. Once the ransomware infects your computer, it encrypts your files, rendering them inaccessible. You are then presented with a ransom note demanding payment, usually in **cryptocurrency**, in exchange for the decryption key.

Practical Example:

A small law firm receives an email that looks like an invoice from a vendor. After the employee opens the attachment, ransomware installs itself on the system. The attacker encrypts the firm's database, which contains sensitive client information. The attacker demands a ransom of $50,000, threatening to delete the data if the payment isn't made within 72 hours.

How to Protect Against Ransomware

- **Backup data regularly**: Use a reliable and secure backup system to ensure you can restore your data if it's encrypted or deleted.
- **Keep software up to date**: Many ransomware attacks exploit known vulnerabilities in software. Regular updates can help patch these security gaps.
- **Educate employees**: Ensure your staff is aware of phishing scams and the dangers of downloading untrusted attachments.
- **Use advanced email filtering**: A good email filtering system can block phishing emails and other potentially harmful messages.
- **Implement network segmentation**: Divide your network into segments to limit the spread of ransomware if an infection occurs.

Case Study: A Real-Life Ransomware Attack on a Small Business

Let's take the example of a **local healthcare clinic** that suffered a ransomware attack. The clinic stored patient records digitally, and when the ransomware encrypted their files, they were unable to access crucial patient information for several days. The attackers demanded $10,000 in Bitcoin to restore the data.

The clinic was forced to **shut down temporarily**, resulting in loss of revenue and a severe hit to their reputation. While they did eventually restore the data from backups, the attack cost them a significant amount in lost business, plus legal fees due to regulatory requirements for breach notification.

What Could They Have Done Differently?

- **Regular backups**: The clinic's backups were not up to date, which slowed down their recovery process.
- **Employee training**: The clinic's staff weren't fully trained to spot phishing emails, which is how the ransomware first entered the system.

---

2. Suspicious Email Activity

What to Look For:

Phishing emails are one of the most common ways cybercriminals gain access to systems. Suspicious email activity often indicates an attempt to deceive your team into revealing confidential information.

Key Warning Signs:

- **Unsolicited Emails with Attachments or Links**: Unexpected emails with links or attachments, especially from unverified senders, can be dangerous. Hackers use these emails to install malware or steal credentials.

- **Fake "Urgent" Requests**: Cybercriminals create urgency in their emails, asking for sensitive information or immediate action. They may impersonate a trusted source, such as your bank or a vendor.
- **Misspelled or Odd Sender Email Addresses**: Pay close attention to the sender's email address. Often, phishing emails will use slight variations in the domain name (e.g., "amazon.com" vs. "amaz0n.com").

Practical Advice:

- **Verify Suspicious Emails**: Always verify requests via alternate channels (e.g., a phone call or official website).
- **Install Anti-Phishing Software**: Use email filters to block suspicious emails before they reach your inbox.
- **Educate Your Team**: Provide training on how to spot phishing attempts and respond appropriately.

Phishing, malware, and ransomware are real and growing threats that every business, regardless of size, must take seriously. By understanding how these attacks work and implementing the steps we've outlined—such as employee education, regular software updates, and secure backups—you can dramatically reduce your risk.

Cybersecurity isn't just about installing software or buying the latest security tools; it's about creating a culture of awareness and vigilance within your business. Start by educating your team, investing in the right tools, and putting strong security practices in place.

2.2: Real-Life Examples of Cyberattacks on Small Businesses

When it comes to cyberattacks, small businesses are often the most vulnerable targets. Many assume that hackers only go after large corporations, but the truth is that small businesses are prime targets due to their often weak security defenses and lack of resources to implement sophisticated cybersecurity measures. Cyberattacks on small businesses are not just hypothetical—they happen every day, and the consequences can be devastating.

In this guide, we will delve into **real-life examples** of cyberattacks on small businesses. We will analyze how the attacks occurred, the impact they had, and how the businesses involved could have prevented or minimized the damage. Through these examples, we will also provide you with **practical advice** on how you can protect your own business from similar attacks.

Case Study 1: Phishing Attack on a Small Retail Business

The Situation

A small retail business received an email that appeared to come from a trusted supplier, requesting an immediate payment to settle an overdue invoice. The email contained a link to a payment portal that looked nearly identical to the supplier's legitimate website. The business owner clicked on the link, entered their payment details, and made the payment.

What Went Wrong? It turns out that the email was a **phishing attempt**, and the payment portal was a fake site designed to steal sensitive financial information. As a result, the business owner unknowingly transferred a large sum of money to the hacker's account.

How the Attack Happened

1. **Phishing Email**: The hacker sent an email disguised as a payment request from a trusted supplier.
2. **Fake Payment Portal**: The email included a link to a fake website that appeared identical to the real supplier's website.
3. **Credential Theft**: After the business owner entered the payment details, the hacker intercepted and stole the financial information.

Impact

The business lost $50,000 due to the fraudulent transaction. Beyond the immediate financial loss, the business also faced reputational damage, as they had to notify customers about the breach and reassure them that their information was secure.

How It Could Have Been Prevented

- **Verify Requests**: The business could have verified the payment request by contacting the supplier directly using a phone number from their official website, not the one in the email.
- **Phishing Awareness**: Educating employees about the risks of phishing and how to spot suspicious emails would have helped them identify the scam.
- **Multi-Factor Authentication (MFA)**: Implementing MFA on all financial accounts would have added an extra layer of security to prevent unauthorized transactions.

Case Study 2: Malware Infection in a Law Firm

The Situation

A small law firm specializing in family law was targeted by cybercriminals using **malware**. The attacker sent a fraudulent email to one of the firm's paralegals with an attachment disguised as a legal document. The paralegal opened the attachment, inadvertently installing malware onto the firm's system.

What Went Wrong? The malware was designed to **steal sensitive client data** and send it back to the attacker. This breach included personal details about clients, legal case files, and confidential information.

How the Attack Happened

1. **Malicious Email**: The cybercriminal sent an email containing an attachment, pretending to be a colleague or another trusted person within the industry.

2. **Malware Installation**: When the paralegal opened the attachment, it activated the malware on the firm's network.
3. **Data Theft**: The malware began transmitting sensitive client data back to the attacker, including confidential legal documents.

Impact

- **Data Breach**: Sensitive client information was compromised, putting both the firm and its clients at risk.
- **Reputation Damage**: The law firm's reputation was severely damaged, and clients lost trust in their ability to protect sensitive data.
- **Regulatory Fines**: The firm faced fines for failing to properly secure client data in accordance with data protection regulations.

How It Could Have Been Prevented

- **Antivirus and Anti-malware Software**: The firm could have installed and regularly updated antivirus and anti-malware software to detect and block malicious files.
- **Employee Training**: Educating staff about the dangers of opening unsolicited email attachments would have prevented the malware from being installed.
- **Network Segmentation**: The firm could have used network segmentation to isolate sensitive data, making it harder for malware to spread across their entire system.

Case Study 3: Ransomware Attack on a Healthcare Clinic

The Situation

A small healthcare clinic that provides dental and medical services was hit by a **ransomware attack**. The clinic's staff received an email with an attachment labeled "Patient Payment Record." When the attachment was opened, ransomware encrypted the clinic's database, locking them out of all patient records.

What Went Wrong? The ransomware locked the clinic's data, and the attacker demanded a **ransom payment** in cryptocurrency to decrypt the files. The clinic was unable to access important patient information, and as a result, they had to cancel appointments and temporarily suspend operations.

How the Attack Happened

1. **Phishing Email**: The attacker sent a seemingly innocent email that appeared to be from a billing system or payment service.
2. **Ransomware Execution**: When the clinic's staff opened the email attachment, the ransomware began encrypting the clinic's entire database of patient records.
3. **Ransom Demand**: The attacker demanded a ransom of $100,000 in cryptocurrency to decrypt the clinic's data and restore access.

Impact

- **Financial Loss**: The clinic was forced to pay the ransom (despite the uncertainty of getting the data back) to prevent further disruption.
- **Operational Downtime**: The clinic's operations were halted for several days while they restored data from backups and decrypted their files.
- **Loss of Reputation**: Patients were unable to access care for several days, and the clinic lost clients due to concerns about the security of their medical records.

How It Could Have Been Prevented

- **Regular Backups**: The clinic could have regularly backed up their data to a secure, offline system, allowing them to restore their records without paying the ransom.
- **Email Filtering and Anti-ransomware Software**: The clinic could have used advanced email filtering systems to detect and block phishing emails and ransomware before they reached the inbox.
- **Staff Education**: Training staff to be cautious with email attachments and links would have helped prevent the ransomware from being installed in the first place.

How Small Businesses Can Protect Themselves from Cyberattacks

After analyzing these real-life examples, it's clear that many of these attacks could have been prevented with some basic cybersecurity practices. Here are the key takeaways:

1. **Employee Awareness**: Train your employees to recognize phishing attempts, suspicious emails, and unsafe links. Encourage them to verify any requests for sensitive information through alternate channels (e.g., phone calls).
2. **Multi-Factor Authentication (MFA)**: Implement MFA on all accounts that store or access sensitive information, including financial and customer data. This adds an extra layer of protection against unauthorized access.
3. **Data Backup**: Regularly back up your business's data to an **offline or cloud-based backup system**. This ensures that you can quickly restore operations in the event of a ransomware attack or data breach.
4. **Antivirus and Anti-malware Software**: Keep your devices and systems protected by installing and regularly updating antivirus and anti-malware software.
5. **Network Segmentation**: Divide your network into smaller segments to limit the spread of malware in case of an infection. This is especially important for businesses that handle sensitive data, like healthcare or legal firms.
6. **Regular Software Updates**: Ensure that all software, including operating systems, firewalls, and antivirus programs, are regularly updated to protect against known vulnerabilities.
7. **Incident Response Plan**: Develop and regularly test an incident response plan to quickly and effectively address any cyberattacks. This should include steps for identifying, containing, and recovering from a breach.

The Importance of Proactive Cybersecurity

The real-life examples above highlight the devastating impact that cyberattacks can have on small businesses. But they also show that with the right precautions, these attacks can be prevented or minimized. Small businesses must prioritize cybersecurity by adopting best practices, educating employees, and investing in the right tools to protect their data and reputation.

2.3: Recognizing the Warning Signs of a Cyberattack

Cyberattacks are not always as dramatic as they seem in movies; in fact, they are often very subtle at first. Many cybercriminals move slowly, testing your defenses, looking for weaknesses, and gathering information before striking. As a small business owner, it is critical to recognize the early signs of an attack so you can take action quickly, minimizing the damage.

In this section, we will explore the most common warning signs that indicate your business might be under attack. Recognizing these signs early can help you implement **preventative measures** or respond rapidly when the worst happens.

Key Warning Signs of a Cyberattack

Let's go through the key indicators that your business may be the target of a cyberattack. These warning signs will help you spot trouble before it escalates.

1. Unusual Network Activity

Your network is the lifeblood of your business, and any unusual activity on it can indicate something is wrong. Cybercriminals often use your network to move undetected, sending data back to their servers or accessing unauthorized resources.

Key Warning Signs:

- **Slowdowns in Network Speed**: Sudden, unexplained network slowdowns could indicate that malware is using your bandwidth for unauthorized communication.
- **Large Amounts of Data Transfer**: If your network is transferring more data than usual, it could be a sign that cybercriminals are trying to exfiltrate your business's sensitive information.
- **Unrecognized Devices on the Network**: If you notice unfamiliar devices or IP addresses accessing your systems, it might mean that someone is trying to infiltrate your network.

Practical Advice:

- **Implement Network Monitoring**: Utilize network monitoring tools to track traffic and detect anomalies.
- **Limit Network Access**: Restrict access to sensitive areas of the network to only authorized devices.
- **Act Quickly**: If you detect unusual activity, isolate the affected systems from the network and investigate further.

---

3. System Errors or Crashes

What to Look For:

If your systems are crashing unexpectedly or showing error messages, it could be a sign of an active cyberattack. Malware and viruses can destabilize your system by corrupting files or consuming system resources.

Key Warning Signs:

- **Frequent System Crashes**: If software applications or your system crashes for no apparent reason, this could indicate that malicious software is interfering with normal operations.
- **Unexplained Error Messages**: If you start seeing new error messages or if files suddenly become corrupted or inaccessible, malware may be the culprit.
- **Strange System Behavior**: Unusual actions such as programs opening on their own or files being renamed without your knowledge could point to unauthorized access.

Practical Advice:

- **Run System Diagnostics**: Regularly run diagnostic tests to check for system issues or malware.
- **Back Up Important Files**: Always have up-to-date backups in case files are corrupted or lost.
- **Segment Your Network**: Isolate compromised devices to stop malware from spreading.

4. Unexplained Login Attempts or Account Access

What to Look For:

A sudden increase in login attempts, especially from unfamiliar locations, is a classic sign of a brute-force attack or unauthorized access attempt.

Key Warning Signs:

- **Multiple Failed Login Attempts**: If your systems report multiple failed login attempts or incorrect password entries, someone may be trying to break into your accounts.
- **Logins from Unknown Locations or Devices**: If you notice logins from IP addresses or devices that are not recognized, this could indicate a hacker is trying to gain access to your network.
- **Off-Hours Access**: Login attempts during non-business hours, particularly when no one is in the office, should raise a red flag.

- **Enable Multi-Factor Authentication (MFA)**: MFA adds an additional layer of security to prevent unauthorized access.
- **Lock Accounts After Failed Attempts**: Implement automatic account lockout after a set number of failed login attempts.
- **Review Access Logs Regularly**: Regularly check the access logs for any unusual login activity.

5. Sudden Data Loss or Corruption

What to Look For:

The loss or corruption of files and data can be a strong indicator of a cyberattack. This is especially true in cases of ransomware attacks, where hackers deliberately lock or destroy your data.

Key Warning Signs:

- **Files Are Missing or Corrupted**: If you notice files that have been deleted or corrupted without explanation, it could be a sign of an active attack.
- **Inability to Access Files**: If you are locked out of files and unable to access your important data, ransomware might be the cause.
- **Strange File Behavior**: Files that are renamed, moved, or modified without any user intervention could indicate an attacker has gained control of your systems.

Practical Advice:

- **Backup Your Data Regularly**: Ensure your data is backed up to a secure location so you can restore it in case of an attack.
- **Use Encryption**: Encrypt sensitive data both at rest and in transit to prevent unauthorized access.
- **Implement Access Controls**: Restrict who has access to sensitive files and systems within your organization.

Flowchart: Recognizing the Warning Signs of a Cyberattack

Now, let's take a step-by-step look at the flowchart format for recognizing and responding to these warning signs.

```
                        Start
                          |
                          V
                [Unusual Network Activity?]
                          |
                          V
            [Slowdowns or Large Data Transfers?]
                          |       No
                          V       |
                [Unrecognized Devices on Network?]
                        | Yes |   No
                        V         V
            [Verify Network Access] [Continue Monitoring]
                          |
                          V
                [Suspicious Email Activity?]
                          |
                          V
            [Unsolicited Email or Attachment?]
                        | Yes |   No
                        V         V
            [Verify Emails and Links] [Continue Monitoring]
                          |
                          V
                [System Crashes or Errors?]
                          |
                          V
            [Frequent Crashes or Error Messages?]
                        | Yes |   No
                        V         V
            [Run System Diagnostics] [Continue Monitoring]
                          |
                          V
                [Unexplained Login Attempts?]
                          |
                          V
            [Failed Login Attempts or Unknown Devices?]
                        | Yes |   No
                        V         V
        [Enable MFA or Lock Account] [Continue Monitoring]
                          |
                          V
```

```
            [Data Loss or Corruption?]
                       |
                       V
          [Missing or Corrupted Files?]
                  | Yes | No
                  V       V
       [Restore from Backup] [Continue Monitoring]
                       |
                       V
             Prevention is Crucial!
```

Stay Alert and Be Proactive

Recognizing the warning signs of a cyberattack is essential to staying
ahead of cybercriminals. Early detection can help you act quickly,
minimizing the damage and protecting your business's data and reputation.
It's important to remain vigilant, regularly monitor your systems, and
continuously educate your team about the potential threats.

By implementing the preventive measures outlined in this guide, such as
monitoring network activity, verifying suspicious emails, using strong
authentication methods, and keeping backups, you can significantly reduce
the risk of a successful cyberattack. Remember, cybersecurity is a
continuous process, and staying alert is key to maintaining a secure
environment.

Chapter 3: The Importance of Security Mindset

As a business owner, you've probably heard that "cybersecurity is everyone's responsibility." But what does that really mean in practice? How can you get your team to think about security every day—not just when there's a potential breach?

In this chapter, we'll explore how cultivating a **security-first mindset** within your business is critical to ensuring the safety and success of your operations. Cybersecurity isn't just about installing firewalls or running antivirus software—it's about creating a culture where every decision, action, and behavior is driven by an awareness of the digital threats that exist.

The foundation of a strong cybersecurity defense is in how your team thinks about and reacts to security challenges. A **security-first mindset** goes beyond the tools and technology you use; it's about how every person in your organization views cybersecurity as a priority and makes decisions accordingly.

3.1: Cultivating a Security-First Mindset in Your Business

In today's increasingly digital world, cybersecurity isn't just a technical concern—it's a business priority. Yet, many small businesses treat security as a set of tools, policies, and procedures, focusing on the tactical aspects of defense rather than the **mindset** needed to ensure long-term success. A **security-first mindset** goes beyond firewalls, encryption, or antivirus software—it's about **integrating security into the culture** of your business from the very top to the very bottom.

As a small business owner, you have the opportunity to build a security-conscious environment from the ground up. But what does it mean to have a security-first mindset, and how can you cultivate this within your team? This chapter will explore the key elements of creating a security-first mindset and provide practical advice on implementing it in your business.

What is a Security-First Mindset?

A security-first mindset is a philosophy that places the concept of security at the heart of all business operations. It means treating security as an ongoing responsibility that influences **every decision, process, and action** within the organization, not just something for the IT department to handle. It's a shift from thinking of cybersecurity as a collection of tools to understanding it as a culture of **vigilance** and **proactive defense**.

Having a security-first mindset means:

- **Prioritizing security in decision-making**: Always considering how actions and decisions could impact the security of your data, systems, and people.
- **Building a company-wide understanding of security risks**: Ensuring that every employee, from leadership to entry-level staff, is aware of potential cyber threats and how they contribute to protecting the organization.
- **Adopting a "zero-trust" approach**: Operating under the assumption that no one inside or outside the organization can be fully trusted, requiring verification at every point.

A security-first mindset isn't just about technology; it's about creating a **culture** where security is everyone's responsibility.

Why a Security-First Mindset Matters

1. Proactive Defense Rather Than Reactive Response

Many businesses only take action after they experience a cyberattack—by then, it might be too late. A security-first mindset ensures that you aren't waiting for something bad to happen before you take action. Instead, your business is continuously **assessing and mitigating risks**, adapting to new threats as they arise.

2. Reduced Risk of Human Error

Humans are often the weakest link in cybersecurity. The best technology in the world won't protect your business if employees aren't aware of the threats around them or if they make basic security mistakes. A security-first mindset ensures that all employees are trained to spot threats, follow security best practices, and contribute to the company's defense.

3. Greater Resilience Against Cyber Threats

With a security-first mindset, your organization is constantly improving its defense strategies, staying ahead of cybercriminals, and quickly adapting to new threats. This helps create a more resilient organization, better equipped to handle whatever challenges arise.

4. Protection of Reputation and Customer Trust

Your customers trust you with their data, and a data breach can significantly harm that trust. A business that emphasizes security shows customers that you take their privacy seriously and are committed to protecting their information, which in turn can foster customer loyalty.

How to Cultivate a Security-First Mindset in Your Business

Building a security-first mindset is a **gradual process**. It's not something that happens overnight but requires ongoing commitment from leadership and the involvement of everyone in your organization. Here's a step-by-step guide to help you cultivate a security-first mindset in your business.

Step 1: Lead by Example

As a leader, your attitude toward cybersecurity will set the tone for the rest of your organization. Employees look to you for direction, and if you downplay the importance of security, they'll follow suit. On the other hand, if you make security a visible and active priority, your team will understand that security is integral to the organization's success.

Practical Actions:

- **Communicate the importance of security regularly**: Don't just mention security during IT meetings—talk about it in regular team meetings, emails, and even during performance reviews. Make it clear that it's a key value of your business.
- **Allocate resources for cybersecurity**: Show your commitment by investing in the necessary tools, software, and training to protect your business.
- **Be a role model**: Follow best practices yourself, such as using strong passwords, enabling two-factor authentication, and being cautious with sensitive information. Your behavior will influence your employees' actions.

Step 2: Educate Your Employees

A strong security-first mindset starts with **education**. It's essential to regularly train your employees on the latest security threats and practices. The most common attack methods, such as phishing, ransomware, and social engineering, rely on **human error**—so the more informed your employees are, the more likely they are to recognize these threats and avoid falling victim to them.

Practical Actions:

- **Conduct regular training**: Provide ongoing training sessions that cover topics like how to identify phishing emails, the importance of strong passwords, and how to handle sensitive data securely.
- **Phishing simulations**: Run simulated phishing attacks to test your employees' ability to recognize suspicious emails. Reward employees who successfully identify the phishing attempts.
- **Create easy-to-follow guidelines**: Simplify complex security concepts into actionable steps and make them easily accessible,

whether through a quick reference guide, an intranet portal, or employee handbooks.

Step 3: Establish Clear Security Policies and Procedures

One of the cornerstones of a security-first mindset is having clear, well-communicated security policies and procedures that employees can follow. These policies should cover everything from password management and device security to how to handle confidential data and respond to potential threats.

Practical Actions:

- **Create a security policy**: Outline the security measures that must be followed, including password protocols, data protection practices, and acceptable use policies.
- **Make policies accessible**: Ensure that your security policies are readily available to employees and that they are updated regularly to reflect the latest security practices and threat intelligence.
- **Enforce accountability**: Hold employees accountable for following security protocols. For example, regularly audit their compliance with password policies and data protection guidelines.

Step 4: Foster a Culture of Security Awareness and Responsibility

Security should never feel like an afterthought. It should be part of every conversation, decision, and action taken in the organization. When employees understand that they are **active participants in the security process**, they will feel more responsible for keeping the business secure.

Practical Actions:

- **Encourage open communication**: Make sure employees feel comfortable reporting security concerns or incidents, whether they're related to suspicious emails or weak passwords. Create a clear and anonymous way for them to report issues.

- **Celebrate security successes**: Recognize and reward employees who go above and beyond in following security protocols or identifying potential threats. This encourages everyone to take security seriously.
- **Engage employees regularly**: Keep security top of mind through internal newsletters, security tips, or monthly meetings dedicated to cybersecurity discussions.

Step 5: Continuously Improve Your Security Practices

The digital landscape is constantly changing, and your business must continuously adapt to new threats. A security-first mindset means **always evaluating** and improving your security measures.

Practical Actions:

- **Regular audits and assessments**: Conduct regular security assessments to identify vulnerabilities and address them before they're exploited.
- **Stay informed**: Keep up with the latest trends and threats in cybersecurity. Subscribe to security blogs, attend webinars, and network with industry professionals to stay ahead of emerging risks.
- **Test your defenses**: Use penetration testing or vulnerability scanning tools to test your systems' resilience against potential attacks.

Case Study: A Retail Business Protects Customer Data

Let's look at a real-world example of a small retail business that successfully cultivated a security-first mindset.

The Challenge:
A small retail business that sells products online began noticing a slight

uptick in attempted fraudulent transactions. While they initially brushed off these incidents, they soon realized that their website and payment systems were not fully secured. The business relied heavily on customer trust to thrive, and a data breach could lead to a **loss of reputation** and customer loyalty.

The Solution:
The business owner decided to adopt a security-first mindset across the entire company. They implemented multi-factor authentication for both customer accounts and employee access to systems. Employees were trained on spotting phishing emails and securing their devices with strong passwords.

They also conducted a security audit and found several vulnerabilities in their website. They quickly hired a cybersecurity firm to patch the weaknesses, ensuring that customer data was encrypted and transactions were secure.

The Outcome:
By adopting a security-first mindset and implementing these changes, the business reduced fraudulent transactions, **maintained customer trust**, and avoided the financial and reputational damage of a potential breach. Employees were more vigilant and proactive in identifying potential security threats, creating a safer environment for both the business and its customers.

Cultivating a **security-first mindset** in your business is an ongoing journey. It's not just about tools and policies, but about fostering a culture where every person in your organization is committed to keeping your business secure. By leading by example, educating your employees, establishing clear policies, and fostering a culture of continuous improvement, you create an environment where security is embedded in every aspect of your operations.

3.2: Employee Awareness and Training

No matter how robust your technology is, or how many firewalls and antivirus tools you have in place, your employees remain your first line of defense when it comes to cybersecurity. Why? Because **human error** is the **leading cause** of cybersecurity breaches. Whether it's clicking on a malicious link, using weak passwords, or falling for a social engineering scam, employees can unknowingly compromise your business's security.

The good news is that **training** and **awareness** can significantly reduce these risks. Cybersecurity isn't just about the tools you use; it's about empowering your team with the knowledge and skills they need to recognize and respond to threats. In this chapter, we'll explore the importance of employee awareness and training, provide actionable advice on how to train your team effectively, and show how you can create a security-conscious culture that keeps your business safe.

Why Employee Awareness is Critical

While security software, firewalls, and encryption are all important parts of your cybersecurity strategy, they only cover part of the equation. Cybercriminals often rely on **social engineering**, exploiting human emotions like fear, curiosity, or urgency to trick employees into taking dangerous actions. Whether it's a phishing email that looks like it's from the CEO or a seemingly harmless link that downloads malware, these tactics are only effective when your employees aren't prepared to recognize them.

The Cost of Ignoring Employee Training:

- **Phishing Attacks**: One of the most common methods cybercriminals use to breach a business is **phishing**. If employees aren't trained to recognize suspicious emails, they might inadvertently hand over sensitive information, like login credentials or financial details, to hackers.
- **Data Breaches**: Poor employee practices, like sharing passwords or leaving sensitive information exposed, can lead to **data breaches**. When employees aren't aware of the risks, your business's data, customer information, and intellectual property are at greater risk.
- **Loss of Reputation**: A single cyberattack can severely damage your company's reputation. If customer data is compromised, or if

operations are disrupted by an attack, it can take years to rebuild trust and loyalty.

The **financial cost** of a breach can be substantial too. According to a study by IBM, the average cost of a **data breach** is over **$3.8 million**. By investing in employee training, you are actively protecting your business from these avoidable risks.

Creating a Comprehensive Employee Awareness Program

A successful employee awareness program focuses on education, engagement, and continuous improvement. Cybersecurity training isn't a one-time event—it needs to be **ongoing** to keep up with new threats and best practices. Here's how to implement an effective training program:

Step 1: Understand Your Employees' Needs

Before launching any training program, it's essential to understand the **current level of knowledge** among your employees. Are they familiar with basic cybersecurity concepts, or are they new to the idea of cybersecurity? Do they know the difference between a phishing email and a legitimate message?

Practical Action:

- **Survey Your Employees**: Conduct a simple survey to assess the general level of cybersecurity awareness among your employees. This will help you tailor the training to their needs.
- **Identify High-Risk Roles**: Some employees, such as those in finance or customer support, may be more likely to be targeted by phishing attacks. Ensure that employees in high-risk roles receive more in-depth, role-specific training.

Step 2: Develop Easy-to-Understand Training Modules

Cybersecurity can be complex, but **training doesn't have to be**. To make it accessible and engaging, break down the concepts into **easy-to-understand modules**. Training should cover everything from **basic concepts** to **practical, day-to-day actions**.

Essential Training Topics:

1. **Password Management**: Teach employees how to create strong, unique passwords, and emphasize the importance of using **password managers**. Encourage them to **enable multi-factor authentication (MFA)** wherever possible.
2. **Phishing Awareness**: Explain what phishing is, how to spot a phishing email, and what to do if they receive one. Use real-life examples of phishing attempts to help employees recognize the signs.
3. **Data Protection**: Teach employees how to handle sensitive data securely, including **encrypting files**, **avoiding public Wi-Fi**, and **storing files in secure, company-approved locations**.
4. **Safe Web Browsing**: Explain the risks of downloading software from untrusted websites and opening attachments from unknown sources.
5. **Incident Reporting**: Ensure that employees know how to report suspicious activity or potential security incidents without fear of retribution.

Practical Action:

- **Use Bite-Sized Content**: Break up your training into short, manageable segments—this helps ensure employees don't feel overwhelmed and that they retain the information.
- **Interactive Training**: Use quizzes, interactive games, or simulations to keep employees engaged and help reinforce key concepts.

Step 3: Simulate Real-World Scenarios

One of the most effective ways to train employees is to simulate real-world cyber threats. **Phishing simulations** are a great example. By sending simulated phishing emails, you can gauge how well employees can spot suspicious messages. This not only tests their knowledge but also reinforces the importance of remaining vigilant.

Practical Action:

- **Run Phishing Tests**: Use tools like **KnowBe4** or **PhishMe** to run regular phishing simulations. After each test, provide feedback and additional training on how to recognize phishing attempts.
- **Simulate a Cyberattack**: Conduct tabletop exercises where employees walk through what they would do in the event of a cybersecurity incident, like a ransomware attack. This helps them understand their role and how to respond effectively under pressure.

Step 4: Create a Culture of Continuous Learning

Cybersecurity is **always evolving**, with new threats emerging daily. To maintain a strong defense, your training program should be **ongoing**. This means providing continuous opportunities for employees to learn, adapt, and stay up-to-date on the latest security practices.

Practical Action:

- **Regular Refresher Courses**: Offer periodic refresher courses or **cybersecurity newsletters** that keep employees informed about the latest trends, threats, and best practices.
- **Recognize Cybersecurity Champions**: Identify employees who excel at cybersecurity practices and encourage others to follow their example. Consider offering incentives or recognition for those who go above and beyond in following best practices.
- **Gamify the Learning Process**: Use quizzes, badges, or friendly competitions to keep employees engaged and motivated to stay on top of cybersecurity training.

Step 5: Build an Open and Supportive Environment

The key to a successful cybersecurity culture is **open communication**. Employees should feel comfortable reporting potential security issues or seeking help when they are unsure about a threat. Creating a **non-punitive reporting system** encourages employees to take action rather than ignore potential risks.

Practical Action:

- **Establish a Clear Reporting Process**: Ensure that employees know how to report suspicious activity. Use tools like **ticketing systems** or internal chat platforms to facilitate easy and anonymous reporting.
- **Reward Employees for Reporting**: Publicly recognize employees who report potential security risks or take proactive steps to enhance security. This fosters a sense of **shared responsibility** for cybersecurity.

Case Study: A Financial Firm's Successful Employee Awareness Program

The Challenge:
A small financial firm was struggling with **security breaches** due to employee negligence. Employees were frequently falling for phishing emails, and there were instances where sensitive client data was improperly shared due to weak passwords.

The Solution:
The firm decided to launch a **comprehensive cybersecurity training program**. The program included:

1. **Onboarding Security Training**: New hires were given thorough security training during their onboarding process.
2. **Regular Phishing Simulations**: Employees received simulated phishing emails, and those who fell for the scam had to undergo additional training.

3. **Monthly Security Newsletters**: Employees received monthly updates on new threats and best practices.

The Outcome:
After six months of consistent training, the firm saw a **90% reduction in successful phishing attempts** and improved adherence to **password management policies**. Employees became more **vigilant**, and the overall security culture in the firm strengthened.

Flowchart: A Step-by-Step Approach to Employee Training

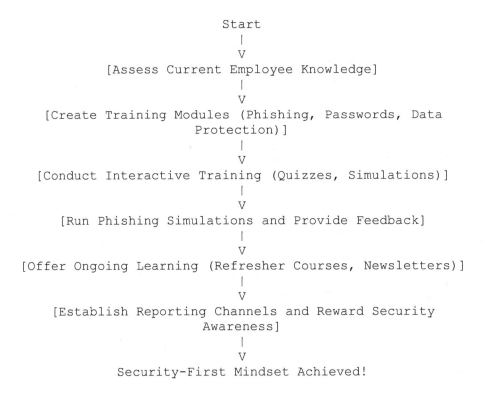

```
                          Start
                            |
                            V
             [Assess Current Employee Knowledge]
                            |
                            V
       [Create Training Modules (Phishing, Passwords, Data
                         Protection)]
                            |
                            V
       [Conduct Interactive Training (Quizzes, Simulations)]
                            |
                            V
          [Run Phishing Simulations and Provide Feedback]
                            |
                            V
     [Offer Ongoing Learning (Refresher Courses, Newsletters)]
                            |
                            V
          [Establish Reporting Channels and Reward Security
                         Awareness]
                            |
                            V
                Security-First Mindset Achieved!
```

Employee awareness and training are not optional—they are crucial to the success of your business's cybersecurity strategy. By continuously educating your employees, simulating real-world threats, and fostering a culture of vigilance, you are equipping your team with the tools they need to defend against cyberattacks. Remember, employees are your first line of defense. Make sure they are properly trained, supported, and engaged in the fight to protect your business from cybercriminals.

3.3: How to Build a Culture of Cybersecurity

In today's interconnected world, where almost everything is digital, building a culture of cybersecurity is no longer a luxury—it's a necessity. As a small business owner, you may think that cybersecurity is just a technical issue that your IT team should handle. But the reality is that **cybersecurity is a company-wide concern**, and it needs to be ingrained in your business culture.

A culture of cybersecurity means that **everyone** in your business, from leadership to staff, understands the importance of protecting sensitive information and is actively involved in ensuring the security of your digital assets. It's a **shared responsibility**, and creating a culture that prioritizes security is the most effective way to protect your business from cyber threats.

In this chapter, we will explore how to build a **culture of cybersecurity** within your organization. We'll provide practical advice, step-by-step implementation, and share real-world examples to help you make cybersecurity a core value that is embedded in everything your business does.

Why is a Culture of Cybersecurity Important?

A culture of cybersecurity is essential for several reasons:

1. **Human Error**: Even with the best technology, people are often the weakest link in the cybersecurity chain. A culture of cybersecurity makes employees more vigilant and aware of their actions, reducing the chances of them falling victim to phishing scams, weak passwords, or other threats.

2. **Rapid Response**: When cybersecurity is part of your organizational culture, employees are more likely to notice potential threats and report them quickly. This reduces response time and mitigates the risk of a full-blown security breach.
3. **Customer Trust**: Customers want to know their data is safe. A business that fosters a culture of cybersecurity demonstrates to clients that their security is a top priority, thereby building trust and credibility.
4. **Regulatory Compliance**: Many industries are governed by regulations that require certain cybersecurity practices (e.g., GDPR, HIPAA). A strong cybersecurity culture helps ensure compliance with these regulations, avoiding fines and legal issues.

How to Build a Culture of Cybersecurity

Building a culture of cybersecurity is not something that happens overnight, but with the right approach, it can be successfully integrated into the fabric of your business. Here's a **step-by-step approach**:

Step 1: Lead by Example

As a business owner or leader, your behavior and attitude toward cybersecurity will set the tone for the rest of your organization. If you make security a priority, your team will follow your lead.

Practical Actions:

- **Model Good Security Practices**: Use strong passwords, enable multi-factor authentication (MFA), and be mindful of phishing attempts. Your team is more likely to adopt these practices if they see you doing it.
- **Make Cybersecurity Part of Your Business Strategy**: Mention security in your meetings and plans, just like any other critical business function. When employees see that you're serious about security, they will take it more seriously too.

- **Prioritize Security in Resource Allocation**: Allocate the necessary budget for cybersecurity tools, training, and personnel. When security is properly resourced, it demonstrates its importance.

Step 2: Educate and Train Your Employees Regularly

Training is key to building a cybersecurity culture. It's essential that all employees, from the CEO to the intern, understand the risks associated with cybersecurity and know how to protect themselves and the company.

Practical Actions:

- **Regular Training and Awareness Programs**: Conduct training sessions that cover topics like phishing, password management, data protection, and secure browsing. Make sure the training is **interactive** and **ongoing**, not just a one-time event.
- **Create Role-Based Training**: Different departments or job roles may face different types of cybersecurity threats. Tailor the training to the needs of each team. For example, your finance team may need training on securing payment systems, while your customer service team may need guidance on handling customer data securely.
- **Test Employees with Simulations**: Run **phishing tests** and **social engineering exercises** to assess how well your employees can identify and respond to threats. Provide feedback and additional training for those who fall for the simulations.

Step 3: Make Security Part of the Daily Workflow

Cybersecurity shouldn't be a once-a-month topic; it should be embedded in your team's daily activities. When employees understand that security is something they need to consider in every action, it becomes second nature.

Practical Actions:

- **Incorporate Security into Meetings**: Discuss security in regular team meetings, not just during quarterly reviews. It can be as simple as asking, "Are there any security risks we need to be aware of this week?"
- **Create Clear Security Guidelines**: Develop easy-to-follow security protocols, and ensure they are easily accessible. These guidelines should cover everything from how to handle sensitive data to the steps for reporting a suspicious email.
- **Embed Security in the Development Process**: If your business involves any software development, ensure that security is embedded in the development process (a practice known as **secure by design**). Encourage developers to adopt **security best practices** such as code reviews and secure coding standards.

Step 4: Promote Open Communication and Reporting

A critical part of building a security culture is ensuring employees feel comfortable reporting security incidents or concerns. A **blame-free environment** helps ensure that employees don't hesitate to speak up if they spot something suspicious.

Practical Actions:

- **Establish Clear Reporting Channels**: Create easy and anonymous ways for employees to report security issues. This could be through a ticketing system, a designated security officer, or even an encrypted email address.
- **Encourage Transparency**: Make it clear that reporting a security concern is a **positive action**, not something that will lead to punishment. If an employee accidentally clicks on a phishing link, for example, they should feel safe reporting it without fear of retribution.
- **Act on Reports**: When employees report potential security threats or incidents, ensure that the issue is investigated and addressed promptly. This shows employees that their concerns are taken seriously.

Step 5: Integrate Cybersecurity into Your Business Processes

Cybersecurity should be embedded into your business's processes and procedures. Whether it's during **hiring**, **vendor selection**, or **data management**, cybersecurity should always be considered.

Practical Actions:

- **Secure the Onboarding Process**: Incorporate cybersecurity training into your onboarding process. New employees should understand the company's security policies and the importance of safeguarding business data right from the start.
- **Vendor Security Assessments**: Before partnering with a vendor, ensure they meet your cybersecurity standards. This is especially important when dealing with third-party vendors who have access to sensitive data.
- **Secure Data Practices**: Make sure employees understand the importance of **encrypting data, using secure file storage systems**, and **following best practices for handling customer data**.

Step 6: Reward Good Security Practices

Acknowledge and reward employees who follow best practices and contribute to the overall security of the business. This can help reinforce a security-first culture and motivate others to be more vigilant.

Practical Actions:

- **Create a Reward System**: Offer incentives for employees who actively participate in cybersecurity practices, such as spotting phishing attempts, adhering to password protocols, or suggesting new security improvements.
- **Public Recognition**: Recognize employees who make notable contributions to improving security. This could be in the form of a

shout-out in a company-wide meeting or a cybersecurity "champion" of the month award.

Case Study: A Small Business Builds a Culture of Cybersecurity

The Challenge:
A small marketing agency had recently experienced a phishing attack that compromised some client data. After the incident, the owner realized that their employees were **unaware** of the risks and **ill-equipped** to handle cyber threats. They needed to build a culture where security wasn't just the responsibility of the IT department but the whole company.

The Solution:
The agency took the following steps to build a culture of cybersecurity:

1. **Leadership Commitment**: The owner made cybersecurity a top priority in every meeting and allocated budget for proper training and tools.
2. **Employee Education**: They implemented a monthly cybersecurity training program for all staff, with interactive sessions, quizzes, and real-life phishing simulations.
3. **Open Reporting Culture**: Employees were encouraged to report security concerns via a dedicated reporting system without fear of punishment.
4. **Security Rewards Program**: The company introduced a "Cybersecurity Hero" award for employees who demonstrated strong security practices.

The Outcome:
Over the course of a year, the agency saw a **significant reduction in phishing attacks** and **improved employee engagement** with security practices. Employees felt empowered and responsible for protecting the business, and customer trust was restored.

Flowchart: Building a Culture of Cybersecurity

```
                        Start
                          |
                          V
            [Commitment from Leadership?]
                          |
                          V
         [Lead by Example, Allocate Resources]
                          |
                          V
               [Employee Education Plan]
                          |
                          V
        [Conduct Regular Training & Simulations]
                          |
                          V
             [Create Open Reporting Channels]
                          |
                          V
      [Incorporate Security into Business Processes]
                          |
                          V
             [Reward Good Security Practices]
                          |
                          V
            Culture of Cybersecurity Achieved!
```

Building a culture of cybersecurity is an ongoing process that requires dedication, leadership, and involvement from every member of your team. By prioritizing cybersecurity from the top down, educating employees, and creating an environment where security is everyone's responsibility, you can protect your business from cyber threats and ensure long-term success.

Chapter 4: Simple First Steps to Secure Your Business

When it comes to cybersecurity, securing your business doesn't have to be overwhelming or expensive. The first steps to protecting your digital assets are often the simplest yet most effective. While sophisticated security measures like firewalls, intrusion detection systems, and encryption tools are important, **the basics**—such as **password hygiene**, **regular software updates**, and **using free or low-cost tools**—can significantly reduce your business's vulnerability to cyberattacks.

In this chapter, we'll walk through three **simple first steps** you can take today to improve your security posture. These actions are easy to implement and cost little or nothing, but they can make a world of difference in protecting your business.

4.1: Password Hygiene and Authentication

In the digital age, where information is more valuable than ever, your business's security begins with one simple—but critical—element: **passwords**. Passwords are the gatekeepers to your sensitive data, financial accounts, and business systems. However, many businesses still use weak, easily guessable passwords, putting them at risk for **cyberattacks**.

In this chapter, we'll dive deep into the concept of **password hygiene**—a set of practices that ensure your passwords are strong, secure, and well-managed—and **authentication**, which adds an extra layer of protection to your accounts. We'll break down why password hygiene is so important, provide actionable steps you can take to improve it, and offer practical examples and tips for safeguarding your business's login credentials.

Why Password Hygiene Matters

Imagine leaving your office door wide open with a "Welcome" mat and a **key under the door** for anyone who wants to enter. That's essentially what weak or reused passwords are—easy for cybercriminals to guess or steal. In fact, a report from **Verizon's 2020 Data Breach Investigations Report** found that **80% of hacking-related breaches** involved **stolen or weak passwords**.

Here's why password hygiene is critical:

- **Weak passwords** are easily cracked by cybercriminals using automated tools. For example, "123456" or "password" are guesses that take mere seconds to break.
- **Password reuse** across multiple accounts increases the risk. If one account is compromised, it opens the door to other accounts.
- **Storing passwords insecurely** (like writing them down or storing them in an unencrypted document) is asking for trouble. If someone gains physical or digital access to that information, they have easy access to your business systems.

By practicing good password hygiene, you significantly reduce the chances of a **cyberattack** or **data breach**. Let's walk through how you can implement secure password practices.

What is Password Hygiene?

Password hygiene is essentially the practice of **managing and maintaining strong, secure passwords** in a way that minimizes risk. Good password hygiene includes choosing strong, unique passwords, using tools to store them securely, and following best practices for password management. It's one of the easiest and most effective ways to protect your business from cyber threats.

Here's a breakdown of good password hygiene practices:

---

1. Use Strong, Unique Passwords

What Makes a Strong Password?

A strong password is difficult for cybercriminals to guess or crack, making it a barrier to unauthorized access. The key elements of a strong password include:

- **Length**: At least **12-16 characters**.
- **Complexity**: A combination of uppercase and lowercase letters, numbers, and special characters.
- **Unpredictability**: Avoid using easily guessable information, like names, birthdates, or common words. For example, "Summer2021!" is better than "password123".

Tips for Strong Passwords:

- **Avoid Common Phrases**: Don't use names, dates, or easily guessed words. If you must use a phrase, choose a **passphrase** instead of a single word. For example, "TheQuickBrownFox!42" is stronger than "password".
- **Use Randomized Characters**: Consider using **randomly generated passwords**. A password manager can generate long, complex passwords for you, so you don't have to think of them yourself.

Practical Example:
If your business email's password is "abc123" or "admin", it's time to change it immediately. Use a password like "E9n!qZ_2r#7m1z" or a random combination to make it harder for attackers to crack.

---

2. Don't Reuse Passwords Across Accounts

The Danger of Reused Passwords:

Reusing passwords across multiple accounts is a huge vulnerability. If one of your accounts is breached (for example, if a hacker cracks a social media account password), the attacker can use the same password to access other accounts—email, banking, or even your business systems.

How to Prevent Password Reuse:

- **Use a unique password** for each account. This ensures that even if one password is compromised, other accounts remain safe.
- **Password Managers**: A password manager like **LastPass, 1Password**, or **Bitwarden** can help you store and generate unique passwords for each account. These tools can also help ensure you don't forget complex passwords.

Practical Example:
If your email password is "Summer2021!" and you use the same password for your business bank account, a breach in one account could expose both. A password manager helps you store **unique passwords** for each service, ensuring no overlap.

---

3. Store Passwords Securely

Why Storing Passwords Securely is Important:

Storing passwords on paper, in unsecured documents, or even in your browser's "save password" feature can expose you to serious risks. If someone gains access to your computer or paper notes, they can easily retrieve your passwords.

How to Store Passwords Securely:

- **Password Managers**: A password manager is the most secure way to store and retrieve passwords. These tools encrypt your password vault, ensuring that only you have access to them.
- **Avoid Storing Passwords in Unsecure Locations**: Don't write down passwords on sticky notes, in notebooks, or store them in plain text files on your computer.

Practical Example:
Instead of writing down your business's online banking password on a

sticky note, store it in a password manager. This ensures that it's encrypted and protected, even if your physical workspace is compromised.

---

4. Implement Multi-Factor Authentication (MFA)

What is MFA and Why is It Important?

Multi-factor authentication adds an extra layer of security to your accounts. Even if a hacker gets hold of your password, they still need to pass a second form of verification to gain access. This second factor could be:

- A **text message** with a one-time code.
- A **mobile app** like **Google Authenticator** or **Authy** that generates a time-sensitive code.
- **Biometric authentication**, like fingerprints or facial recognition.

How to Implement MFA:

- Enable MFA on **critical accounts**—email, banking, cloud storage, and any other services that store sensitive data.
- Choose an MFA method that best suits your business—SMS, mobile apps, or hardware tokens.

Practical Example:
Your business email and cloud storage should have MFA enabled. Even if your password is compromised, an attacker would still need the second factor—whether it's a code sent to your phone or an app like **Google Authenticator**—to access your accounts.

---

5. Regularly Update and Change Passwords

Why You Should Regularly Update Passwords:

Changing passwords periodically is a good security practice, especially if you suspect that your password has been exposed or compromised. For example, if you've used the same password for a while and it's part of a data breach, changing it regularly reduces the risk.

How to Update Passwords:

- Set a reminder to change **critical account passwords** (such as your business email and banking) every 3-6 months.
- **Avoid using the same old passwords**. When changing passwords, ensure that the new password is strong and unique.

Practical Tip:
You can use a password manager to help remind you to rotate passwords and help generate new ones that are complex and unique each time.

Flowchart: Best Practices for Password Hygiene

```
                        Start
                          |
                          V
    [Create Strong Passwords (12+ characters, mix of letters,
                  numbers, symbols)]
                          |
                          V
              [Use a Password Manager?]
                  | Yes |  No
                  V        V
    [Store All Passwords Securely] [Avoid Storing Passwords in
                  Unsecure Locations]
                          |
                          V
        [Enable Multi-Factor Authentication (MFA)]
                          |
                          V
        [Change Passwords Regularly (3-6 months)]
                          |
                          V
      [Use Unique Passwords for Different Accounts]
                          |
                          V
            Maintain Optimal Password Hygiene!
```

Case Study: A Small Business Transforms Its Security with Good Password Hygiene

The Challenge:
A small consulting business had been using the same weak password for its main business email account for several years. Despite numerous warnings about phishing and cyber threats, the owner didn't think to change the password or implement any security measures. One day, the email account was hacked, and sensitive client information was exposed, causing a **data breach** and **reputational damage**.

The Solution:
After the breach, the business owner realized the importance of **strong password hygiene** and implemented the following changes:

1. **Password Manager**: The business adopted **Bitwarden**, a free password manager, and started using strong, random passwords for each account.
2. **Multi-Factor Authentication**: The owner enabled MFA on all critical accounts, including email and cloud storage.
3. **Employee Training**: The business introduced regular security training, with a focus on password best practices and phishing awareness.
4. **Regular Password Changes**: The company established a routine for changing passwords every 3 months.

The Outcome:
With better password hygiene in place, the business significantly reduced the risk of further breaches. Employees were more vigilant about securing their accounts, and the company's overall cybersecurity posture improved.

Effective **password hygiene** is one of the simplest, most cost-effective ways to secure your business. By using strong passwords, implementing multi-factor authentication, storing passwords securely, and regularly updating them, you lay a solid foundation for a secure digital environment. It's an easy change that yields great results and dramatically reduces the chances of a cyberattack.

4.2: Regular Software Updates and Patches

In the world of cybersecurity, one of the most straightforward but critical tasks you can do to protect your business is **regular software updates**. Cybercriminals are always on the lookout for vulnerabilities in software, whether it's your operating system, applications, or even hardware firmware. Developers regularly release **patches** to fix these vulnerabilities. However, many businesses fail to install these patches on time, leaving their systems exposed to potential threats.

In this chapter, we will dive deep into **why regular software updates** and **patch management** are essential for your business, how to ensure you're applying them effectively, and what could happen if you don't.

Why Regular Software Updates and Patches Are Critical

Software updates and patches are one of the easiest ways to safeguard your systems, but many businesses overlook them. Keeping your systems and software up to date ensures that your defenses remain strong against evolving cyber threats.

The Importance of Software Updates:

1. **Fixing Vulnerabilities**:
   Every piece of software has potential vulnerabilities. Hackers exploit these weaknesses to gain unauthorized access to systems or steal data. Regular updates fix these vulnerabilities, making it much harder for attackers to exploit them.
2. **Improved Performance**:
   Besides security, updates often improve the overall performance and stability of your software. These updates can fix bugs, address compatibility issues, and add new features, making your systems run more efficiently.

3. **Compliance**:
   Many industries have compliance requirements that mandate businesses apply security patches. Failing to update software could result in non-compliance and expose your business to legal risks, especially if customer data is breached.
4. **Protecting Sensitive Information**:
   Cyberattacks often target data. If your systems are not updated, it becomes easier for attackers to gain access to sensitive information. For businesses that handle sensitive customer data, **keeping systems updated** is not just a best practice—it's a must.

How Cyberattacks Exploit Unpatched Software:

When software vendors release patches, they are usually responding to **zero-day vulnerabilities** (flaws that were previously unknown and unprotected). Cybercriminals who exploit these vulnerabilities are well aware that many businesses fail to install patches promptly.

For instance, the **WannaCry ransomware attack** in 2017 exploited a vulnerability in Microsoft Windows that had been patched **months** earlier. Organizations that had not applied the security update were compromised, leading to massive disruptions and financial losses.

How to Ensure Regular Software Updates and Patches

While applying software updates might seem like a simple task, it requires an organized approach to ensure that everything stays up-to-date, especially in larger organizations. Here are the steps you can follow to make patch management part of your regular routine.

Step 1: Automate Software Updates Where Possible

One of the easiest ways to ensure that your software stays updated is by automating the update process. Many modern software tools and operating systems come with **auto-update features**, which ensure that updates are downloaded and installed without requiring manual intervention.

Practical Actions:

- **Enable Automatic Updates**:
  - For **Windows**: Go to **Settings > Update & Security > Windows Update** and ensure **automatic updates** are enabled.
  - For **Mac OS**: Go to **System Preferences > Software Update** and check the box to **Automatically keep my Mac up to date**.
  - For **Mobile Devices**: Enable **auto-updates** for apps on both Android and iOS devices to ensure timely updates.
- **Schedule Updates for Non-Business Hours**:
  For businesses, updating during work hours can cause interruptions. Schedule updates to run during off-peak hours or overnight to minimize downtime.

Step 2: Regularly Check for Updates on Critical Software

Although automation can help, there are cases where manual intervention is required. Some business-critical software, particularly legacy systems or specialized applications, may not support automatic updates. In these cases, regular checks for new updates are necessary.

Practical Actions:

- **Set a Monthly Schedule for Updates**:
  Create a reminder to check for updates on systems, software, and applications at least once a month. Ensure that all critical software—like antivirus tools, accounting software, CRM tools, etc.—is up to date.
- **Use Update Management Tools**:
  For larger businesses, use **update management systems** like **Microsoft WSUS (Windows Server Update Services)** or **third-party patch management tools** to track and apply updates across all systems.

Step 3: Test Updates Before Deployment

While updates are important, sometimes they may interfere with your current operations, particularly if they're large updates or updates to core systems. Therefore, it's essential to test updates before deploying them across the entire organization.

Practical Actions:

- **Create a Staging Environment**:
  Set up a **testing environment** where you can apply and test updates on non-critical systems first. This ensures the update doesn't cause unexpected downtime or performance issues in your live environment.
- **Test Compatibility**:
  If you're updating a system that interacts with other software (like an ERP or accounting system), ensure that the update doesn't create compatibility issues with other programs.

Step 4: Keep Track of Patches and Updates

It's crucial to have a clear record of all patches and updates that are applied. This helps to ensure that no important updates are overlooked and allows you to track which systems are secure and which are still pending updates.

Practical Actions:

- **Maintain a Patch Management Log**:
  Keep a log of all applied updates and patches. This could be a simple spreadsheet or a more sophisticated system to track all security updates and patch statuses for every device and system in your organization.
- **Use Automated Patch Management Software**:
  Solutions like **Patch My PC** or **SolarWinds Patch Manager** can automate patching and keep track of which systems have received updates.

Step 5: Stay Informed About New Threats and Updates

Cybersecurity is constantly evolving, and staying informed about the latest threats and vulnerabilities is critical. As soon as a new patch is released to address a security vulnerability, you need to apply it as quickly as possible.

Practical Actions:

- **Subscribe to Security Bulletins**:
  Most software vendors publish security bulletins or advisories about vulnerabilities and patches. Subscribe to these bulletins to receive updates about critical patches.
  - For example, **Microsoft Security Bulletins** and **Apple Security Updates** provide detailed information on vulnerabilities and their patches.
- **Join Cybersecurity Forums and Communities**:
  Stay updated by joining industry forums, groups, or subscribing to cybersecurity newsletters. Communities like **Reddit's r/cybersecurity**, **KrebsOnSecurity**, and **US-CERT** (United States Computer Emergency Readiness Team) provide timely information on emerging threats.

Case Study: A Small Business Protects Itself with Regular Updates

The Challenge:
A small e-commerce business had experienced repeated hacking attempts, and customer data was exposed due to outdated software. They realized that despite having strong firewalls and antivirus software, the lack of regular updates on their servers and payment processing systems had left critical vulnerabilities exposed.

The Solution:
The business owner decided to implement a **comprehensive patch management strategy**:

1. **Automated Updates**: They set up **automatic updates** for all systems, including operating systems and applications, ensuring all security patches were applied in real time.
2. **Patch Testing**: They created a **staging environment** where updates were first tested for compatibility before being rolled out across their live systems.
3. **Security Bulletins**: They subscribed to relevant security bulletins and advisories to stay informed about newly discovered vulnerabilities.

The Outcome:
By implementing a regular update and patch management system, the business saw a **reduction in security breaches** and improved **website performance**. They also improved customer trust, as the website was now fully secured and up to date.

Flowchart: Managing Software Updates and Patches

```
                        Start
                          |
                          V
                [Enable Automatic Updates?]
                          |
                          V
              [Automate Updates for All Software]
                       | Yes | No
                       V       V
        [Set Manual Update Schedule]   [Test Updates in Staging
                                            Environment]
                    |                           |
                    V                           V
        [Deploy Updates Across Systems]   [Deploy Updates and
                          Monitor]
                          |
                          V
              [Maintain Patch Management Log]
                          |
                          V
        [Stay Informed About New Threats and Vulnerabilities]
                          |
                          V
              Secure Business with Up-to-Date Systems!
```

Regularly applying software updates and patches is one of the most basic, yet effective ways to keep your business secure. By ensuring that your systems are up to date with the latest security patches, you reduce the risk of cyberattacks that exploit known vulnerabilities. While it may seem like a simple task, the impact it has on your business's cybersecurity cannot be overstated.

4.3: Using Free or Low-Cost Tools for Basic Security

Cybersecurity might seem like an expensive, complex topic, especially for small businesses with limited budgets. But here's the truth: you don't need a **million-dollar** security solution to protect your business. There are many **free and low-cost tools** available that can provide excellent protection against cyber threats.

In this chapter, we'll explore how to leverage these tools to secure your business without breaking the bank. We'll dive into the essential security tools every small business should have, explain how they work, and show you how to use them effectively.

You'll see that building a solid security foundation doesn't need to be expensive or complicated. Let's explore these **accessible tools** to help you protect your business today.

Why Free and Low-Cost Tools Matter for Small Businesses

Small businesses often face unique challenges when it comes to cybersecurity. The **budget** is tight, the **IT team** is small or non-existent, and **cybersecurity threats** are constantly evolving. However, this doesn't mean that small businesses are immune to cyberattacks or that they can't implement a solid security strategy.

Free and low-cost tools can offer a practical, effective way to secure your business, especially when combined with sound security practices and a **security-first mindset**. These tools help you protect your business from basic threats like **viruses, malware, phishing attacks, and unsecured networks**.

Best of all, many of these tools are **easy to implement**, even for small businesses with no dedicated IT department.

Essential Free and Low-Cost Security Tools for Your Business

Now, let's look at the specific tools you can use to strengthen your cybersecurity without spending a fortune.

1. Antivirus Software: Protecting Against Malware

Malware is one of the most common threats that businesses face. It can infect systems, steal sensitive information, and cause widespread damage. **Antivirus software** is one of the first lines of defense against these types of attacks.

Free Antivirus Tools:

1. **Microsoft Defender** (Windows):
    This built-in security tool for Windows devices provides essential malware protection, firewall protection, and real-time monitoring. It's simple to use and automatically updates, offering decent protection without any extra cost.
2. **Avast Free Antivirus**:
    Avast offers free protection for both Windows and macOS, with features like real-time scanning, malware detection, and phishing protection.
3. **AVG AntiVirus Free**:
    Similar to Avast, AVG provides free virus and malware protection, including real-time updates and email scanning.

How to Use Antivirus Tools Effectively:

- **Schedule regular scans**: Set up weekly or daily automated scans to check your systems for malware.
- **Enable real-time protection**: Ensure that real-time protection is turned on to catch malicious files as they arrive.
- **Update regularly**: Even free tools need to be updated regularly to protect against the latest threats.

2. Firewalls: Blocking Unwanted Traffic

A **firewall** acts as a barrier between your internal network and the internet, blocking malicious traffic and preventing unauthorized access. Having a firewall is essential for any business, especially one with an internet-facing presence (like a website or cloud service).

Free and Low-Cost Firewall Options:

1. **Windows Firewall** (Built-in):
   Windows operating systems come with a built-in firewall that is simple to use and highly effective at blocking unwanted traffic. It's already enabled by default on Windows devices.
2. **ZoneAlarm Free Firewall**:
   ZoneAlarm offers a free firewall for Windows users that adds an extra layer of protection by monitoring inbound and outbound network traffic, blocking malicious attacks.
3. **Comodo Free Firewall**:
   Another good option for Windows users, Comodo provides both a personal firewall and security for your local network. It's easy to install and configure.

How to Use Firewalls Effectively:

- **Enable the firewall on all devices**: Don't leave any device unprotected, whether it's a laptop, desktop, or mobile.
- **Customize firewall settings**: Some advanced firewalls allow you to control specific inbound and outbound connections. Use this to block potentially harmful traffic or unknown sources.

- **Regularly check firewall logs**: Monitor your firewall's logs to spot any suspicious activity or blocked connections.

---

3. Virtual Private Networks (VPN): Secure Remote Access

With many businesses adopting remote work or accessing data from public networks, using a **VPN** has become an essential security practice. A VPN encrypts your internet connection, making it harder for hackers to intercept data when you're online.

Free and Low-Cost VPN Options:

1. **ProtonVPN**:
   ProtonVPN offers a free plan with no data limits and excellent privacy policies. The free version gives access to servers in three countries.
2. **Windscribe**:
   Windscribe's free VPN plan offers **10GB of data per month**, which is ideal for small businesses that need basic protection while browsing or working remotely.
3. **TunnelBear**:
   TunnelBear offers a free plan with a **500MB monthly limit**, but it's a great option for light users who need quick and easy security.

How to Use a VPN Effectively:

- **Use VPNs on public networks**: Always activate your VPN when using public Wi-Fi networks (like coffee shops or airports).
- **Encrypt sensitive data**: Use your VPN whenever you need to send sensitive information over the internet to ensure it's encrypted.
- **Limit data sharing**: Some free VPNs have data limitations, so avoid using them for large downloads or streaming.

---

4. Backup Solutions: Protecting Your Data

Backups are your last line of defense in case of data loss due to cyberattacks, system failures, or natural disasters. Regularly backing up your business data ensures that you can recover quickly from an incident.

Free and Low-Cost Backup Solutions:

1. **Google Drive (15GB Free)**:
   Google Drive offers 15GB of free storage, which is great for backing up documents and files. It integrates seamlessly with Google Workspace apps, such as Google Docs and Sheets.
2. **OneDrive (5GB Free)**:
   Microsoft's OneDrive provides free cloud storage and offers easy integration with Windows devices, which makes it a good backup option for businesses using Microsoft Office tools.
3. **Backblaze**:
   For a more comprehensive backup solution, **Backblaze** offers unlimited backup storage for a low cost (around $6/month). It automatically backs up files and is very user-friendly.

How to Back Up Effectively:

- **Automate backups**: Set up automatic backups on a daily or weekly schedule to ensure no important files are missed.
- **Use the 3-2-1 backup rule**: Keep **three copies** of your data, store **two copies locally** (e.g., on an external hard drive), and keep **one copy offsite** (in the cloud).
- **Regularly test your backups**: Ensure that your backups are functioning properly and can be restored if needed.

---

5. Email Security: Protecting Against Phishing

Phishing remains one of the most common and effective attack methods used by cybercriminals. To protect your business, it's crucial to implement email security tools to prevent phishing and other malicious email threats.

Free and Low-Cost Email Security Tools:

1. **SpamAssassin**:
   A free open-source tool that filters spam and phishing emails. It's highly customizable and can be integrated with many email servers.
2. **Mailwasher Free**:
   This free tool helps you screen and delete unwanted email messages before they even reach your inbox. It includes spam filters and phishing detection features.
3. **Barracuda Email Security Gateway**:
   For a low-cost, enterprise-grade email security solution, Barracuda offers spam filtering, phishing protection, and encryption.

How to Use Email Security Tools Effectively:

- **Activate spam filtering**: Always enable spam and phishing filters in your email service or client.
- **Educate employees on phishing**: Provide regular training on identifying suspicious emails. Encourage them to report any potential phishing attempts.
- **Use secure email protocols**: Ensure that your email system uses **SMTP with TLS** encryption to secure the communication channel.

Case Study: A Small Business Improves Security with Free Tools

The Challenge:
A small digital marketing agency was struggling with **cyberattacks**, including phishing emails and malware infections. With a limited budget for security, they needed to find cost-effective tools that could provide protection without breaking the bank.

The Solution:
The agency implemented the following free and low-cost tools:

1. **Avast Free Antivirus**: For real-time malware protection on all devices.

2. **ProtonVPN**: To ensure secure connections for remote employees accessing the company network.
3. **Google Drive**: To back up important client documents and project files.
4. **SpamAssassin**: To filter phishing and spam emails before they reached employees' inboxes.
5. **Password Manager**: The team adopted **Bitwarden** to securely store and manage passwords.

The Outcome:
After implementing these tools, the agency saw a **significant reduction in cyberattacks**. Employees were more vigilant against phishing emails, the VPN ensured secure remote work, and regular backups protected their data from potential loss. They were able to bolster their cybersecurity without exceeding their budget.

Flowchart: Using Free or Low-Cost Tools for Basic Security

```
                        Start
                          |
                          V
            [Identify Key Security Needs]
                          |
                          V
           [Choose Free Antivirus Solution]
                          |
                          V
         [Set Up Firewall (Free or Low-Cost)]
                          |
                          V
         [Enable VPN for Remote Work Security]
                          |
                          V
         [Set Up Backup System (Cloud or Local)]
                          |
                          V
      [Implement Email Security Tools (Spam Filters)]
                          |
                          V
        [Use Password Manager for Strong Passwords]
                          |
                          V
```

Building a strong security foundation for your small business doesn't have to be expensive. By leveraging **free and low-cost tools**, you can implement robust cybersecurity measures like antivirus protection, firewalls, VPNs, data backups, email security, and password management. These tools provide essential protection from common cyber threats and give you a solid starting point for securing your business against attacks.

Part 2: Protecting Digital Assets Using Accessible Tools (Intermediate Level)

Chapter 5: Securing Your Devices and Networks

In a world where technology is at the center of almost every business, securing your **devices** and **networks** is crucial. Whether it's a desktop computer in the office, a mobile phone, or your home router, each piece of technology you use is a potential gateway for cybercriminals. If compromised, these devices can lead to data breaches, financial loss, or a loss of customer trust.

In this chapter, we will guide you through securing your **devices** (computers, mobile, routers), configuring **firewalls** and **antivirus software**, and using **VPNs** and **endpoint protection**. These measures are essential to ensuring that your business remains safe from threats and vulnerabilities.

5.1: Protecting Devices (Computers, Mobile, Routers)

In the digital age, the devices we use—whether they're computers, smartphones, or even routers—are the gateways to all our information, transactions, and business operations. They are also prime targets for cybercriminals looking to exploit vulnerabilities and gain unauthorized access to sensitive data. As a small business, you rely on these devices to keep everything running smoothly, so it's critical to protect them.

This chapter explores how to **secure your computers**, **mobile devices**, and **routers**. We'll walk through best practices for each category, provide practical advice for implementation, and share case studies and flowcharts to guide you in securing your devices.

Why Device Security is Crucial

Imagine if your computer, phone, or router were compromised. Sensitive information like customer data, financial records, and confidential emails could be exposed. Even if you have top-notch security software in place, if your devices are improperly secured, they can be the entry point for hackers.

Each device represents a potential vulnerability in your overall cybersecurity strategy. Here's why protecting them is non-negotiable:

- **Computers and laptops** are where you store and access sensitive data.
- **Mobile devices** are used for both personal and professional tasks, and they can access business accounts and data.
- **Routers** are the gateway to your network and could expose your entire system to the outside world if left unsecured.

Securing all these devices is essential to prevent unauthorized access, data breaches, and potential financial losses.

---

1. Protecting Computers (Desktops and Laptops)

Why Secure Computers?

Computers are the most obvious and often the most vulnerable entry point for cybercriminals. They store sensitive information, including business plans, customer data, financial records, and much more. If a hacker gains access to a computer, they could easily access your network and cause significant damage.

Best Practices for Computer Protection:

1. **Install Antivirus and Anti-Malware Software**
   Antivirus software is your first line of defense against viruses, spyware, ransomware, and other malicious software. Choose reliable antivirus software that offers real-time protection and updates frequently to stay ahead of evolving threats.
   - Recommended tools: **Bitdefender, Norton, Kaspersky**.
2. **Enable Full Disk Encryption**
   If a computer is stolen or accessed without authorization, disk

encryption ensures that its data cannot be read. **BitLocker** (Windows) and **FileVault** (MacOS) provide full-disk encryption.

- o **Windows**: Go to **Control Panel > System and Security > BitLocker Drive Encryption** and enable it.
- o **MacOS**: Go to **System Preferences > Security & Privacy > FileVault** and turn it on.

3. **Regular Software and OS Updates**
   Make sure your operating system (OS) and all software applications are regularly updated. Updates often contain **security patches** to fix vulnerabilities that could be exploited by cybercriminals.
   - o Turn on **automatic updates** for both the OS and software whenever possible.

4. **Use Strong, Unique Passwords**
   Use long, complex passwords for your computers. Avoid common passwords like "123456" or "password". Tools like **1Password**, **LastPass**, or **Bitwarden** can help you generate and store strong passwords securely.

5. **Enable Multi-Factor Authentication (MFA)**
   Whenever possible, enable **MFA** for any critical accounts on your computer, including email, cloud storage, and banking. This adds an extra layer of protection in case a password is compromised.

Practical Tip:
Ensure that **autolock** is enabled on all computers. This means that after a set period of inactivity, the system will lock automatically, requiring a password to access it again.

---

2. Protecting Mobile Devices (Smartphones and Tablets)

Why Secure Mobile Devices?

Smartphones and tablets are often used for both personal and business tasks, making them a **high-risk target** for cybercriminals. Mobile devices have access to sensitive data like emails, business apps, and cloud storage. They also have physical portability, meaning they can be easily lost or stolen.

Best Practices for Mobile Protection:

1. **Install Security Apps**
    Use mobile security apps to detect and prevent malware, phishing, and other attacks. These apps can also help track lost devices.
    - Recommended tools: **Lookout Mobile Security**, **Avast Mobile Security**.
2. **Enable Device Encryption**
    Both **iPhones** and **Android phones** have built-in encryption features that ensure the data on your phone is protected.
    - **iPhone**: Device encryption is enabled by default when you set a passcode.
    - **Android**: Go to **Settings > Security > Encrypt Phone**.
3. **Use Strong Authentication Methods**
    Enable **biometric authentication** (e.g., Face ID, fingerprint) on your mobile devices. This ensures that only you can unlock the device and access sensitive information.
    - Use strong passcodes or PINs in combination with biometric options.
4. **Install Apps Only from Trusted Sources**
    Download apps only from the **Google Play Store** or **Apple App Store**. Be cautious of third-party app stores, as they may host malicious apps.
5. **Enable Remote Wipe**
    In case of theft or loss, ensure that you have the ability to remotely wipe all data from the device to prevent unauthorized access.
    - For iPhones: Use **Find My iPhone** to locate or remotely wipe your device.
    - For Android: Use **Find My Device** by Google to track and remotely wipe your phone.

Practical Tip:
Regularly review and manage the apps installed on your phone. Delete any unnecessary or suspicious apps to reduce potential vulnerabilities.

---

3. Protecting Your Router and Network

Why Secure Your Router?

Your router is the entry point to your network. If it's not secured, it could expose all the devices connected to it to external threats. Unsecured routers are especially vulnerable to attacks like **man-in-the-middle** attacks, where attackers intercept communication between devices on your network.

Best Practices for Router Protection:

1. **Change Default Router Passwords**
   Routers come with default login credentials (usually found on the back of the device), which are easily accessible to hackers. Change these credentials to something strong and unique immediately after setting up the router.
2. **Enable WPA3 Encryption**
   Use the **WPA3** encryption standard (the latest Wi-Fi encryption standard) for your wireless network. WPA3 is more secure than its predecessors and helps prevent unauthorized access.
   - Log into your router's settings via its IP address (usually **192.168.1.1**) and enable WPA3 or WPA2 if WPA3 is unavailable.
3. **Disable WPS (Wi-Fi Protected Setup)**
   WPS is a feature that allows easy device connection to a router, but it's vulnerable to hacking. It's best to disable this feature in your router's settings.
4. **Keep Router Firmware Updated**
   Router manufacturers regularly release updates to patch security vulnerabilities. Ensure that your router's firmware is always up-to-date to protect it from new threats.
5. **Use a Guest Network**
   If you allow visitors or clients to access your Wi-Fi, set up a **guest network**. This keeps your main network secure and limits access to your sensitive devices and data.

Practical Tip:
Set up an **administrator account** with a strong password for your router and disable remote administration features. This helps protect the router from external attempts to change settings.

Case Study: A Small Business Secures Its Devices and Network

The Challenge:
A small design agency had recently experienced a **phishing attack** that compromised one of its employee's computers. The breach wasn't extensive, but it exposed vulnerabilities in the agency's devices and network.

The Solution:
The business owner decided to implement a comprehensive security strategy:

1. **Computer Protection**:
    - They installed **Kaspersky Antivirus** and enabled **Windows BitLocker encryption** on all business computers.
    - **MFA** was enabled on business email accounts to secure access.
2. **Mobile Protection**:
    - Employees were encouraged to use **Lookout Mobile Security** and enable **biometric authentication** on their smartphones.
3. **Router Protection**:
    - The default **router password** was changed to something strong and unique.
    - **WPA3 encryption** was enabled, and the **WPS feature** was disabled.
4. **Regular Backups**:
    - **Cloud backups** were set up for all critical data, ensuring that any future cyberattack or data loss wouldn't cripple the business.

The Outcome:
The design agency significantly reduced its vulnerability to further attacks. Employees were more aware of security best practices, and the business owner felt confident that the devices and network were secure.

Flowchart: Protecting Devices and Networks

```
                        Start
                          |
                          V
              [Identify Devices to Secure]
                          |
                          V
        [Protect Computers (Antivirus, Encryption)]
                          |
                          V
         [Secure Mobile Devices (Encryption, Apps)]
                          |
                          V
          [Secure Router (Change Password, WPA3)]
                          |
                          V
          [Enable WPA3 and Disable WPS on Router]
                          |
                          V
         [Keep Router Firmware Updated Regularly]
                          |
                          V
            [Use Strong Passwords for All Devices]
                          |
                          V
           [Enable Remote Wipe for Mobile Devices]
                          |
                          V
            Secure Your Devices and Network!
```

Securing your devices and networks is a fundamental part of any strong cybersecurity strategy. By following the best practices outlined in this chapter—securing your computers, mobile devices, and routers—you lay the foundation for a more secure business environment. With the right tools, encryption, and practices, you can protect your business from cyber threats and ensure that sensitive information stays safe.

5.2: Configuring Firewalls and Antivirus Software

In cybersecurity, **firewalls** and **antivirus software** act as the first line of defense against the most common types of cyberattacks. Think of them as digital **security guards** for your devices and networks. Firewalls monitor and filter traffic between your network and the internet, while antivirus software scans your devices for malware and other threats.

Without these tools in place, your business is vulnerable to a wide range of cyberattacks, from malware and viruses to unauthorized access by hackers. Fortunately, **configuring** and **optimizing** these tools is simpler than it might seem. In this chapter, we'll break down how to effectively configure **firewalls** and **antivirus software** to ensure your business is well-protected.

Why Firewalls and Antivirus Software Matter

1. Firewalls: The First Line of Defense

A **firewall** is a barrier between your internal network (your computers, servers, devices) and the external world (the internet). It controls the flow of data, either allowing or blocking traffic based on predetermined security rules. Firewalls are essential for protecting your business from unauthorized access, preventing hackers from gaining access to your internal network.

Firewalls are crucial for:

- **Blocking unwanted traffic**: Prevents hackers from exploiting vulnerabilities.
- **Monitoring network traffic**: Detects and blocks suspicious connections.
- **Defining security rules**: Allows only authorized traffic based on your security policies.

2. Antivirus Software: Detecting and Removing Malware

Antivirus software is designed to detect and remove malicious software (malware) like viruses, ransomware, spyware, and trojans. It regularly scans files and applications for known patterns of malicious code and provides real-time protection against potential threats.

Antivirus software is essential for:

- **Preventing malware infections**: Detects and stops malicious programs before they can damage your devices.
- **Scanning for hidden threats**: Identifies malware that may be running in the background without the user's knowledge.
- **Providing ongoing protection**: Continually monitors your devices to ensure they are safe from new threats.

Together, **firewalls** and **antivirus software** create a strong defense against external attacks and internal threats. Now, let's dive into how to configure them for maximum effectiveness.

Configuring Firewalls

What Is a Firewall and How Does It Work?

Firewalls monitor the flow of traffic between your network and external networks (the internet). They act based on a set of predefined security rules, determining which incoming and outgoing traffic is allowed. There are two main types of firewalls:

- **Hardware Firewalls**: These are physical devices placed between your network and the internet. They provide robust protection for all devices on your network.
- **Software Firewalls**: These are installed on individual devices (like a computer or server). They are essential for protecting devices even when connected to unsecured networks.

While software firewalls are common on personal computers and small office setups, a **hardware firewall** is typically used in larger businesses to protect multiple devices at once.

Best Practices for Configuring Firewalls:

1. **Enable the Built-In Firewall**
   Both **Windows** and **MacOS** come with built-in firewalls that should be enabled by default.

- Windows: Go to **Control Panel > System and Security > Windows Defender Firewall** and ensure it's turned on.
- MacOS: Go to **System Preferences > Security & Privacy > Firewall** and turn it on.

2. **Create Custom Rules**
   Customize your firewall settings based on the needs of your business. For example, if your business requires specific services or software, allow traffic from these services and block everything else.
   - **Windows Firewall**: You can define rules for specific apps or ports by navigating to **Windows Defender Firewall > Advanced Settings**.
   - **MacOS Firewall**: Go to **Firewall Options** to configure app-specific rules.

3. **Block Inbound and Outbound Traffic**
   By default, firewalls block incoming traffic unless you explicitly allow it. This is useful for blocking hackers from entering your network. However, you should also ensure **outbound traffic** is controlled to prevent malware from sending data out of your network.

4. **Enable Logging and Monitoring**
   Set up your firewall to log all activity and monitor it regularly. Reviewing these logs can help detect unusual activity, such as unauthorized login attempts or unexpected data transfers.

5. **Use the Latest Security Rules**
   Ensure your firewall is using the latest security rules and updates. Many modern firewalls update automatically, but it's always a good practice to check for the latest definitions and patches regularly.

Practical Tip:
Regularly review and adjust your firewall settings as needed. If your business adopts new software or services, make sure to update your firewall to allow traffic from trusted sources.

Configuring Antivirus Software

What Is Antivirus Software and How Does It Work?

Antivirus software protects your devices from malware by scanning files and programs for signatures of malicious code. The software constantly updates its database of known malware signatures, so it can detect new threats.

Best Practices for Configuring Antivirus Software:

1. **Install Reliable Antivirus Software**
   Choose a reputable antivirus software solution that fits your business needs. Free versions like **Avast Free Antivirus** or **Windows Defender** are a good starting point, but for more comprehensive protection, consider paid options like **Norton**, **Kaspersky**, or **Bitdefender**.
2. **Enable Real-Time Protection**
   Real-time protection is a critical feature of antivirus software that actively scans files and processes as they run, preventing malware from executing. Make sure this feature is enabled in your software settings.
   - o **Windows Defender**: This feature is enabled by default, but ensure it's turned on under **Settings > Update & Security > Windows Security > Virus & Threat Protection**.
3. **Schedule Regular Scans**
   Set up automatic scans to run on a regular basis. This ensures that even if new malware sneaks past real-time protection, it will be caught during the scan.
   - o **Full Scan**: Set the software to run a full scan weekly or bi-weekly, depending on your business activity.
   - o **Quick Scan**: A quick scan can be run daily to check the most common areas of infection, such as running processes and active memory.
4. **Keep Virus Definitions Updated**
   Antivirus software relies on up-to-date virus definitions to detect new threats. Ensure your software updates these definitions automatically to stay protected from the latest malware.
5. **Avoid False Positives**
   Sometimes antivirus software can flag legitimate programs as threats, which can cause issues with your business software. If you are confident in the safety of a program, **whitelist** it to prevent it from being flagged in future scans.

Practical Tip:
Regularly update your antivirus software and make sure it's running in the background. Even if you're not actively using the device, it should be monitoring for potential threats.

Case Study: Small Business Secures Its Network with Firewalls and Antivirus Software

The Challenge:
A small accounting firm was experiencing frequent slowdowns and odd behavior on their computers. After an investigation, they discovered that malware had infected several devices on their network. This was due to outdated antivirus software and improperly configured firewalls.

The Solution:
The business took the following steps to secure their devices:

1. **Installed Kaspersky Antivirus** on all workstations and enabled real-time protection.
2. **Updated the built-in Windows Defender Firewall** and added custom rules to block unneeded ports and applications.
3. **Enabled automatic updates** for both antivirus software and the Windows firewall.
4. **Ran full system scans** to remove any existing malware and ensure the network was clean.

The Outcome:
After implementing these measures, the business reported fewer security-related issues. They also established a monthly review of firewall and antivirus configurations to ensure their protection stayed up to date.

Flowchart: Configuring Firewalls and Antivirus Software

```
Start
  |
  V
```

```
          [Install Antivirus Software]
                      |
                      V
          [Enable Real-Time Protection]
                      |
                      V
        [Schedule Regular Scans (Full & Quick)]
                      |
                      V
     [Keep Antivirus Definitions and Firewall Updated]
                      |
                      V
       [Configure Firewall (Set Rules, Enable Logs)]
                      |
                      V
        [Enable Inbound and Outbound Protection]
                      |
                      V
      [Monitor Firewall and Antivirus Logs Regularly]
                      |
                      V
           Secure Your Devices and Network!
```

Configuring **firewalls** and **antivirus software** is crucial for maintaining a secure business environment. These tools protect your devices from external threats like hackers and internal risks like malware. By enabling real-time protection, keeping software up-to-date, and monitoring logs regularly, you ensure that your business stays safe from evolving threats.

5.3: Using VPNs and Endpoint Protection

In today's increasingly connected world, protecting your devices and data from cyber threats requires more than just firewalls and antivirus software. **Virtual Private Networks (VPNs)** and **Endpoint Protection** offer additional layers of security that are critical for businesses, particularly those with remote workers or teams that access sensitive data across different devices.

In this chapter, we'll explore the importance of **VPNs** and **endpoint protection**, explain how they work, and show you how to effectively configure and use these tools to enhance your security strategy. Whether you're working from the office or remotely, these tools will ensure your data is protected as it travels across the internet and your devices are secure from potential threats.

What Are VPNs and Endpoint Protection?

1. Virtual Private Networks (VPNs)

A **VPN** is a tool that **encrypts your internet connection**, ensuring that data sent over the internet remains private and secure. It creates a **secure, encrypted tunnel** between your device and the internet, preventing unauthorized access and protecting sensitive data, especially when using **public networks** like Wi-Fi in coffee shops, airports, or other shared spaces.

Why VPNs Matter:

- **Secure Remote Work**: As businesses transition to remote or hybrid work environments, VPNs ensure that employees accessing the company network from home or on the go do so securely.
- **Protection on Public Networks**: Public Wi-Fi networks are often insecure and easy targets for hackers. A VPN protects your data from eavesdropping and man-in-the-middle attacks when connected to these networks.
- **Bypass Geo-Restrictions**: VPNs can help employees access company resources that may be restricted based on geographic location, ensuring seamless work from anywhere.

2. Endpoint Protection

Endpoint protection refers to the security measures taken to protect **devices** (also called **endpoints**) that connect to your network. These devices include **computers, smartphones, tablets**, and even **Internet of Things (IoT) devices**. Endpoint protection involves a combination of software and practices that secure these devices from attacks, data breaches, and other malicious activities.

Why Endpoint Protection Matters:

- **Increased Risk from Remote Devices**: As more employees use personal devices (BYOD – Bring Your Own Device) for work, the risk of introducing malware or unsecured devices into the company network increases. Endpoint protection ensures that all devices accessing your network are secure.
- **Protecting Data on the Device**: Endpoint protection software often includes **data encryption**, **firewall settings**, and **anti-malware protection** to keep data secure even if the device is lost or stolen.

Now, let's take a closer look at how to configure and use these tools effectively.

Configuring and Using VPNs

How VPNs Work:

When you use a VPN, it works by:

1. **Encrypting your data**: Your internet traffic is encrypted, meaning that anyone trying to intercept your data will see only unreadable gibberish.
2. **Hiding your IP address**: Your real IP address is replaced with an IP address from the VPN provider. This makes your online actions harder to trace back to you, increasing privacy.
3. **Routing traffic through secure servers**: Your data travels through secure servers provided by the VPN service before reaching the internet, which masks your real location and secures your communication.

Best Practices for VPN Configuration:

1. **Choose a Reliable VPN Service**:
   Select a VPN provider with a strong reputation for security, privacy, and speed. Some trusted VPN providers include **ExpressVPN**, **NordVPN**, and **ProtonVPN**. Be sure to review their **no-logs policy**, which ensures that your browsing activity isn't recorded.

2. **Enable Kill Switch Feature**:
   Most premium VPNs offer a **kill switch** feature, which automatically disconnects your internet connection if the VPN connection drops. This ensures your sensitive data doesn't get exposed if the VPN fails.
3. **Choose the Right VPN Protocol**:
   VPN protocols define how data is encrypted and transmitted. The most secure protocols are **OpenVPN**, **WireGuard**, and **IKEv2/IPSec**. Choose the protocol that offers both high security and good speed.
4. **Configure for All Devices**:
   Install the VPN on **all devices** your employees use to access company data—whether it's a laptop, smartphone, or tablet. Many VPN providers offer apps for **Windows, Mac, Android**, and **iOS**, making installation seamless.
5. **Set Up Split Tunneling (Optional)**:
   Split tunneling allows you to choose which applications or websites go through the VPN connection and which can access the internet directly. This is useful for optimizing speed without compromising security for certain tasks.

Practical Tip:
Ensure that **remote employees** or workers on the go are **required to use the VPN** whenever they are accessing company resources. This should be enforced by internal policy and monitored with automated systems.

Configuring and Using Endpoint Protection

How Endpoint Protection Works:

Endpoint protection is a comprehensive security solution that includes:

- **Antivirus**: Protects against viruses, trojans, and other malware.
- **Firewall**: Monitors and controls incoming and outgoing network traffic based on security rules.
- **Data Encryption**: Ensures that sensitive data stored on the device is protected, even if the device is lost or stolen.
- **Intrusion Detection**: Monitors for suspicious behavior or unauthorized access attempts.

- **Patch Management**: Automatically updates devices with the latest security patches to fix vulnerabilities.

Best Practices for Endpoint Protection:

1. **Install a Comprehensive Endpoint Protection Solution**:
   Choose an endpoint protection solution that combines antivirus, firewall, and real-time threat detection. Popular options include **CrowdStrike**, **Sophos**, and **McAfee Endpoint Security**.
2. **Ensure Automatic Updates and Patches**:
   Ensure that the endpoint protection software automatically updates with the latest virus definitions and patches. Most endpoint protection tools provide **automatic updates** by default, but double-check to confirm.
3. **Enable Device Encryption**:
   Enable **full disk encryption** on all devices (laptops, desktops, mobile devices) to protect sensitive data. This is especially important for employees who work remotely or travel with their devices.
   - **Windows**: Enable **BitLocker** for full disk encryption.
   - **MacOS**: Enable **FileVault** for full disk encryption.
   - **Mobile Devices**: Ensure **device encryption** is enabled through the settings.
4. **Monitor Endpoint Activity Regularly**:
   Use an endpoint protection platform that provides **centralized monitoring** so you can review all endpoints in your organization from a single dashboard. This enables you to track suspicious activity across all devices.
5. **Integrate with a Centralized Management System**:
   For businesses with many employees or devices, consider using **endpoint management software** to streamline updates, monitor compliance, and address any potential vulnerabilities.
6. **Use Device Control Policies**:
   Set up policies to control which devices can connect to your network. This helps prevent unauthorized devices from gaining access and reduces the risk of infections.

Practical Tip:
Always require endpoint protection on devices that access sensitive business data, and **periodically audit** the effectiveness of your endpoint security solutions.

Case Study: A Growing Startup Secures Remote Workforce with VPNs and Endpoint Protection

The Challenge:
A fast-growing tech startup had recently transitioned to a **remote-first model**. As employees began working from various locations, the company's leadership realized that protecting sensitive data on laptops, mobile devices, and over public Wi-Fi networks was becoming increasingly important.

The company had experienced a **phishing attack** that led to a data breach on one of its employee's laptops. This exposed vulnerabilities in their security practices.

The Solution:
The startup took the following steps to secure its remote workforce:

1. **Implemented a Company-Wide VPN**:
   They chose **NordVPN** for its high security and ability to offer connections across multiple devices. Every remote employee was required to connect to the company network via the VPN, ensuring encrypted traffic.
2. **Installed Endpoint Protection on All Devices**:
   Endpoint protection software was deployed across all employee devices, including mobile phones and laptops. This software provided real-time threat detection, antivirus protection, and device encryption.
3. **Encrypted All Devices**:
   Every device was encrypted to protect sensitive information in case it was lost or stolen.
4. **Educated Employees on Safe Remote Work Practices**:
   Employees were trained on how to use the VPN, recognize phishing attempts, and keep their devices secure. The company also implemented a **device management policy** that required employees to install the company's endpoint protection software.

The Outcome:
After implementing these security measures, the company saw a significant reduction in security breaches. Employees felt more confident

using their devices securely, and the company could ensure that data remained encrypted and protected, regardless of location.

Flowchart: Configuring VPNs and Endpoint Protection

```
                    Start
                      |
                      V
         [Choose Reliable VPN Provider]
                      |
                      V
          [Install VPN on All Devices]
                      |
                      V
    [Enable Kill Switch & Use Strong VPN Protocol]
                      |
                      V
        [Monitor VPN Connections Regularly]
                      |
                      V
        [Choose Endpoint Protection Solution]
                      |
                      V
       [Install Endpoint Protection on Devices]
                      |
                      V
         [Enable Device Encryption & Updates]
                      |
                      V
            [Monitor Endpoint Activity]
                      |
                      V
Secure Remote Workforce with VPN & Endpoint Protection!
```

VPNs and endpoint protection are essential for securing your business's remote workforce and protecting devices from cyber threats. By implementing these tools, you create a secure environment for your team to access sensitive data, work remotely, and keep your network safe from external attacks.

Chapter 6: Safeguarding Your Business Data

In the digital age, **data** is a business's most valuable asset. Whether it's **client records**, **financial data**, or **intellectual property**, protecting this information is not just about compliance or good practice; it's essential for maintaining your business's reputation, trust, and operational continuity. Cyberattacks are becoming more frequent, and the risks of data breaches have never been higher.

This chapter will guide you through the critical steps needed to safeguard your business data. From **data encryption** and **secure backups** to protecting sensitive customer information and leveraging **cloud solutions** for enhanced security, we'll cover the tools and strategies every small business should implement to ensure its data remains secure.

6.1: Data Encryption and Secure Backups

In today's interconnected digital world, **data** is the lifeblood of any business, from **customer records** to **financial documents** and **intellectual property**. As cyber threats evolve, businesses must adopt proactive strategies to protect their most valuable asset—data. **Data encryption** and **secure backups** are two of the most critical components of a comprehensive cybersecurity strategy. These tools not only protect your data from theft but also ensure business continuity in case of a disaster.

In this chapter, we will dive deep into the concepts of **data encryption** and **secure backups**, explain how they work, why they are essential, and provide practical steps to implement these measures effectively.

What is Data Encryption?

Data encryption is the process of transforming readable data into an unreadable format using a cipher, making it inaccessible to unauthorized individuals. Only those with the decryption key can return the encrypted data to its original, readable form.

Why is Data Encryption Important?

1. **Protects Sensitive Information**:
   If your data is intercepted by cybercriminals, encryption ensures that it remains useless without the decryption key. This is especially critical for personal, financial, or proprietary business information.
2. **Mitigates Data Breach Risks**:
   Encrypting sensitive business data, such as customer information and business strategies, ensures that even if a breach occurs, the compromised data remains protected.
3. **Compliance with Regulations**:
   Many data protection regulations, like the **General Data Protection Regulation (GDPR)** and the **Health Insurance Portability and Accountability Act (HIPAA)**, require businesses to use encryption as part of their data security practices.
4. **Secures Data in Transit and at Rest**:
   Encryption is essential for protecting data not just when it's stored on your devices (data at rest) but also when it's being transmitted over networks (data in transit).

Types of Data Encryption:

- **At Rest Encryption**:
  This protects data that is stored on a device, server, or cloud system. It ensures that sensitive data is unreadable if unauthorized access occurs. Examples include **BitLocker** for Windows and **FileVault** for macOS.
- **In Transit Encryption**:
  This protects data when it is being transferred between devices, servers, or over the internet. **SSL/TLS encryption** is commonly used for websites and email communications to secure data during transmission.

Best Practices for Data Encryption:

1. **Encrypt All Sensitive Data**:
   Anything that could cause harm if exposed—**customer records**, **financial information**, and **intellectual property**—should be encrypted. This is particularly important when transferring data over the internet.
2. **Use Strong Encryption Standards**:
   AES-256 is currently one of the most robust encryption algorithms available. Ensure that your encryption software uses strong, industry-standard encryption protocols.
3. **Protect Encryption Keys**:
   The security of your encryption is only as strong as the protection of your encryption keys. Use a **key management system** to store and rotate encryption keys regularly, ensuring they are kept secure.
4. **Encrypt Cloud Data**:
   Many cloud providers offer encryption as part of their service, but consider encrypting your data **before** uploading it to ensure it is protected at all stages of its lifecycle.

What Are Secure Backups?

Backups refer to the process of creating copies of your important data, so you can restore it if something happens to the original. Regular backups ensure that if your business experiences a data loss event (due to malware, human error, or physical damage), your data can be recovered quickly.

Why Secure Backups Are Crucial?

1. **Protection Against Data Loss**:
   Whether from **hardware failure**, **accidental deletion**, **ransomware**, or **natural disasters**, backups are your insurance against losing critical data.
2. **Business Continuity**:
   With a solid backup strategy, your business can **continue operations** with minimal disruption, even if data is lost or corrupted. This is especially important for industries that rely on **client data** and **financial records**.

3. **Cyberattack Recovery**:
   Ransomware attacks are becoming more common, where cybercriminals encrypt your files and demand a ransom for their release. Secure backups allow businesses to **restore data without paying the ransom**.

Best Practices for Secure Backups:

1. **Follow the 3-2-1 Backup Rule**:
   This rule ensures redundancy in your backup strategy:
   - **3 copies** of your data (1 original + 2 backups).
   - **2 different media** types (e.g., external hard drives, cloud storage).
   - **1 offsite copy** (in case of physical disasters like fires or floods).
2. **Automate Backups**:
   Set your backup solution to run automatically on a scheduled basis—daily, weekly, or monthly—so you never have to worry about manually backing up data.
3. **Test Backups Regularly**:
   Perform regular tests to ensure that your backups are functioning correctly and can be restored without data corruption.
4. **Use Cloud Backups**:
   Cloud storage is a secure, scalable option for backups. Make sure that the cloud provider uses **end-to-end encryption** and complies with relevant regulations (like **GDPR**).
5. **Encrypt Your Backups**:
   As with your primary data, ensure that your backup copies are encrypted. This is especially important for sensitive information stored on **external drives** or in **cloud services**.

Implementing Data Encryption and Secure Backups

Step-by-Step Guide to Implementing Data Encryption:

1. **Identify Sensitive Data**:
   - Identify all types of sensitive data within your business, including customer information, employee records, financial data, and intellectual property.

2. **Choose the Right Encryption Solution**:
   - o For **computers**: Enable **BitLocker** (Windows) or **FileVault** (macOS).
   - o For **files**: Use encryption software like **VeraCrypt** for file-level encryption.
   - o For **cloud storage**: Ensure your provider supports encryption or use a service like **Tresorit** that offers end-to-end encryption.
3. **Encrypt Data at Rest and in Transit**:
   - o Ensure that both your stored data and the data you send across the internet (emails, file transfers) are encrypted using appropriate tools (e.g., **SSL/TLS** for web data, **AES** for file storage).
4. **Set Up Key Management**:
   - o Store encryption keys securely using a **key management system**. Ensure that keys are rotated regularly and that access to them is limited to authorized personnel.
5. **Educate Your Team**:
   - o Train your team on the importance of encryption and how they can securely handle encrypted data.

Step-by-Step Guide to Implementing Secure Backups:

1. **Select a Backup Solution**:
   - o Choose a **cloud backup service** like **Backblaze** or **Google Drive** for easy, automatic backups.
   - o Consider **external hard drives** or **network-attached storage (NAS)** for local backups.
2. **Set Backup Schedule**:
   - o Set your system to back up critical data daily, with a **weekly full backup** and **incremental backups** in between.
3. **Follow the 3-2-1 Rule**:
   - o Ensure you have three copies of your data—one original copy and two backup copies. Store these backups on **two different media** types, and keep at least one copy **offsite** (e.g., on cloud storage).
4. **Encrypt Your Backups**:
   - o Encrypt backup files to ensure they remain secure. Use **AES-256** encryption for maximum security.
5. **Test Backup Restoration**:

- Regularly test your backups by restoring them to ensure data is intact and the backup process works as expected.

Case Study: A Local Retail Store Secures Its Data

The Challenge:
A small retail store, which processes customer transactions and stores sensitive information, was recently **hit by a ransomware attack**. The attackers encrypted the store's data, and the business was forced to pay the ransom. However, they were still uncertain about the recovery process, as they didn't have secure, encrypted backups.

The Solution:
After the attack, the store implemented a robust **data encryption** and **backup** strategy:

1. **Data Encryption**:
   They encrypted all customer and transaction data using **AES-256** encryption and implemented full-disk encryption on all computers and mobile devices with **BitLocker** and **FileVault**.
2. **Backup Solution**:
   They set up an **automated cloud backup** solution that adhered to the **3-2-1 rule**. They kept encrypted backups in both the **cloud** and on **external hard drives**.
3. **Staff Training**:
   They trained all employees on the importance of securing sensitive data, identifying phishing attempts, and following security protocols.

The Outcome:
After implementing these measures, the store has been able to recover data quickly and securely in case of any future incidents. They no longer face the constant fear of data loss or ransomware attacks, and customer trust has been restored.

Flowchart: Data Encryption and Secure Backups

```
                         Start
                           |
                           V
            [Identify Sensitive Business Data]
                           |
                           V
          [Choose the Right Encryption Solution]
                           |
                           V
          [Encrypt Data at Rest and in Transit]
                           |
                           V
       [Set Up Key Management System for Encryption]
                           |
                           V
     [Select Cloud or Local Backup Solution for Critical Data]
                           |
                           V
       [Encrypt Backup Data and Automate Backup Schedule]
                           |
                           V
             [Follow the 3-2-1 Backup Rule]
                           |
                           V
           [Test Backup Restoration Regularly]
                           |
                           V
        Secure Your Data with Encryption and Backups!
```

In today's digital landscape, ensuring the security of your data is not a choice—it's a necessity. Implementing **data encryption** and **secure backups** provides the foundation of a robust data protection strategy. Encryption ensures that even if your data is stolen or accessed illegally, it remains unreadable, while secure backups ensure you can restore lost or corrupted data quickly.

6.2: Protecting Sensitive Customer Information

Sensitive customer information is the cornerstone of most businesses today. From **credit card details** to **personal identifiers**, **addresses**, and

transaction history, this data is highly valuable—not just to your business, but also to cybercriminals. A breach involving customer data can lead to **financial losses, reputational damage**, and **legal consequences**. In fact, data breaches have become so common that they are now a major concern for businesses of all sizes.

In this chapter, we will discuss **best practices** for protecting **sensitive customer information**. We'll go through the practical steps your business can take to ensure that your customers' data is secured, and that your business complies with relevant data protection regulations.

Why Protect Customer Information?

Before we dive into the methods of securing sensitive data, it's important to understand why it's crucial to protect this information:

1. **Compliance with Regulations**:
   Data protection regulations, such as **GDPR** (General Data Protection Regulation), **CCPA** (California Consumer Privacy Act), and **HIPAA** (Health Insurance Portability and Accountability Act), impose stringent requirements on how businesses must handle and protect customer data. Failing to comply can lead to significant penalties.
2. **Customer Trust**:
   Customers expect businesses to protect their personal and financial information. If your business suffers a data breach, trust can be permanently damaged, and customers may choose to take their business elsewhere.
3. **Financial Security**:
   Protecting customer data not only prevents financial losses from fraud or breach-related fines, but also helps maintain the financial security of your business by preventing malicious actors from stealing money or manipulating transactions.
4. **Prevention of Fraud and Identity Theft**:
   Sensitive customer information, like social security numbers or credit card details, is a prime target for cybercriminals. If this data is exposed, it can lead to **identity theft** or **financial fraud**, impacting both the customer and your business.

By implementing the right data protection strategies, your business can prevent breaches, comply with legal requirements, and retain customer trust.

Best Practices for Protecting Sensitive Customer Information

1. Data Minimization

Data minimization means only collecting the **bare minimum** amount of customer information necessary to provide a service. The less data you collect, the less risk you face in case of a breach.

How to Implement Data Minimization:

- Only ask for the information you need. For example, if your business doesn't need a customer's birth date, don't collect it.
- Use **optional fields** on forms to allow customers to provide only what is necessary.
- Regularly review your data collection practices to ensure you're not collecting excessive or outdated information.

2. Data Encryption

Encryption is one of the most effective ways to protect sensitive data. Encryption ensures that even if data is intercepted, it remains unreadable to unauthorized users.

How to Encrypt Customer Information:

- **At Rest**: Use encryption to protect data stored in databases, servers, or on devices.
  - **AES-256** is currently the gold standard for encrypting sensitive data.
  - For businesses using **cloud services**, ensure that the cloud provider uses encryption for data at rest and allows you to manage your encryption keys.

- **In Transit**: Encrypt data during transmission, especially when customers interact with your business online.
  - ○ **SSL/TLS** (Secure Sockets Layer/Transport Layer Security) encrypts the communication between the customer's browser and your website, ensuring that sensitive information (like credit card numbers) remains protected.
  - ○ Ensure your website uses **HTTPS**, not just HTTP, to provide a secure connection.

Practical Tip:
Enable **auto-encryption** for emails that contain sensitive customer data. Use services like **ProtonMail** or **Gmail's S/MIME** encryption to ensure that customer communications remain private.

---

3. Access Control and Role-Based Permissions

Controlling access to customer data within your organization is critical. Not every employee needs access to all customer data, so **access control** systems can help limit exposure and reduce the risk of unauthorized access.

How to Implement Access Control:

- **Role-Based Access Control (RBAC)**: Limit access to sensitive customer data based on an employee's role within the organization. For example, only the finance team may need access to payment details, while customer service reps may only need access to contact information.
- **Multi-Factor Authentication (MFA)**: Require **MFA** for employees accessing customer data. This adds an additional layer of security by requiring users to provide more than just a password—such as a one-time code sent to their mobile device.

Practical Tip:
Regularly audit your employee access logs to ensure that only authorized individuals are accessing sensitive customer information. Make sure to **revoke access** promptly when an employee leaves the company.

---

4. Secure Payment Systems

If your business processes payments, **PCI compliance** (Payment Card Industry Data Security Standard) is essential. PCI DSS outlines a set of standards that ensure payment card information is handled securely.

Best Practices for Securing Payment Information:

- Use a **third-party payment processor**: If you're not a financial institution, avoid storing sensitive payment card details on your servers. Instead, use trusted payment processors (like **Stripe**, **PayPal**, or **Square**) that comply with PCI DSS standards and handle payment data securely.
- **Tokenization**: Tokenization replaces sensitive payment data (like credit card numbers) with a unique identifier or **token**, reducing the risk of exposure.
- Implement **strong encryption** for all stored payment data and ensure that access is tightly controlled.

Practical Tip:
Never store **credit card details** or **CVV numbers** on your system. Only store the minimum required information, such as the last four digits of the card number, if absolutely necessary.

---

5. Regular Data Backups

Secure backups are critical for ensuring that customer data is recoverable in case of a disaster, data corruption, or cyberattack (like ransomware). If your backup files are not secured, they can be a target for malicious actors.

How to Back Up Customer Data Securely:

- **Encrypt Backup Files**: Ensure that your backup systems use encryption to protect sensitive data.
- **Follow the 3-2-1 Backup Rule**: Keep three copies of your data— two on different types of media (e.g., external drives, cloud storage), and one offsite (such as in the cloud).
- **Test Backups Regularly**: Periodically test the backup system to ensure that data can be restored quickly and accurately.

Practical Tip:
Store backups in **multiple locations**: have both **on-premise backups** (external hard drives or NAS devices) and **cloud-based backups** to ensure redundancy and protection.

---

6. Regular Security Audits and Vulnerability Scanning

To ensure your systems are secure, it's essential to conduct regular security audits and vulnerability scans. These audits help you identify weaknesses in your systems before they are exploited.

How to Implement Security Audits:

- **Penetration Testing**: Hire ethical hackers to test your systems for vulnerabilities. Pen tests simulate real-world attacks, helping identify weaknesses in your network.
- **Automated Vulnerability Scanners**: Use automated tools like **Qualys** or **Nessus** to scan your systems for vulnerabilities and patch any issues before they can be exploited.

Practical Tip:
Schedule **quarterly security audits** to ensure your systems remain up to date and that new vulnerabilities are addressed promptly.

Case Study: A Retail Business Secures Customer Information

The Challenge:
A local retail business experienced a data breach when customer credit card information was compromised by a hacker who gained unauthorized access to their payment system. The breach was traced back to weak security measures in their payment processing system.

The Solution:
The business took the following steps to secure their customer information:

1. **PCI Compliance**:
   They switched to a **third-party payment processor** (Stripe) and stopped storing sensitive credit card data on their systems.
2. **Data Encryption**:
   They implemented **AES-256 encryption** to secure all customer information stored on their servers and encrypted all data in transit using **SSL/TLS**.
3. **Role-Based Access Control**:
   Only authorized personnel from the **finance team** were allowed access to payment data, and they required **multi-factor authentication (MFA)** to access sensitive customer records.
4. **Regular Security Audits**:
   They began performing **quarterly security audits** to identify vulnerabilities and address them before they could be exploited.

The Outcome:
After implementing these changes, the business significantly improved its security posture, reducing the risk of data breaches. Customers regained confidence in the business, and the company's reputation was restored.

Flowchart: Protecting Sensitive Customer Information

```
                    Start
                      |
                      V
        [Identify Sensitive Customer Data]
                      |
                      V
           [Minimize Data Collection]
                      |
                      V
        [Encrypt Data at Rest and in Transit]
                      |
                      V
        [Implement Role-Based Access Control]
                      |
                      V
          [Secure Payment Systems (PCI DSS)]
                      |
                      V
         [Backup Data Regularly and Securely]
                      |
                      V
```

```
        [Conduct Regular Security Audits]
                      |
                      V
        Protect Customer Information Effectively!
```

Protecting sensitive customer information is a vital part of any business's cybersecurity strategy. By implementing **data minimization**, **encryption**, **role-based access control**, and **regular security audits**, you can mitigate risks and ensure that your customer data remains secure. Adopting these best practices not only protects your business from legal and financial repercussions but also builds customer trust and confidence.

6.3: Using Cloud Solutions for Enhanced Security

As businesses continue to embrace digital transformation, the **cloud** has become an essential component of modern operations. The cloud offers flexibility, scalability, and **cost-efficiency**, but it also introduces new security challenges. Despite these challenges, cloud solutions can enhance your business's overall **security posture** if implemented correctly. By leveraging **cloud security features**, businesses can secure sensitive data, improve accessibility, and safeguard against common cyber threats.

In this chapter, we will explore how **cloud solutions** can be used to improve your security infrastructure. We'll cover the **benefits of cloud security**, how to choose the right provider, and best practices for safeguarding your data in the cloud.

Why Use Cloud Solutions for Enhanced Security?

Before we delve into the specific strategies for securing your business in the cloud, let's understand why cloud solutions offer such strong security benefits:

1. **Advanced Security Features**:
   Cloud providers invest heavily in **security infrastructure**. They provide enterprise-grade features like **encryption, multi-factor authentication (MFA)**, and **automated patch management**, which may be expensive or complex for small businesses to implement on their own.
2. **Scalability and Flexibility**:
   As your business grows, so does the need for scalable security. Cloud services offer flexible plans that allow businesses to scale their security solutions without the need for significant upfront investments.
3. **Disaster Recovery**:
   The cloud offers reliable **backup** and **disaster recovery** options. In the event of a hardware failure, natural disaster, or cyberattack, your data can be quickly restored from cloud backups, ensuring **business continuity**.
4. **Reduced Costs**:
   By moving to the cloud, businesses can reduce the costs of maintaining on-premise security systems and infrastructure. Cloud providers offer **pay-as-you-go models**, so you only pay for what you use.
5. **Compliance with Regulations**:
   Many cloud providers offer tools and services designed to help businesses comply with industry regulations such as **GDPR, HIPAA**, and **PCI DSS**. This can help ease the burden of managing compliance requirements.

Choosing the Right Cloud Provider for Security

Not all cloud providers are created equal. When selecting a cloud provider, it's crucial to consider their **security offerings** to ensure they meet your needs. Here's a step-by-step guide on what to look for when choosing a cloud provider:

1. Assess Security Certifications

Leading cloud providers should have relevant certifications and compliance standards in place to ensure their security practices meet industry norms.

Key Certifications to look for:

- **ISO 27001**: A global standard for managing information security.
- **SOC 2**: Ensures that the cloud provider follows strict protocols for safeguarding customer data.
- **PCI DSS**: Ensures compliance with **payment card industry** data security standards.
- **GDPR Compliance**: For businesses operating in the European Union, GDPR compliance is essential to ensure data privacy and protection.

2. Evaluate Data Encryption

Ensure that your cloud provider supports **encryption** for both **data at rest** (stored data) and **data in transit** (data moving between your device and the cloud).

- **Encryption at Rest**: Protects data stored in cloud storage or databases. This prevents unauthorized access to your sensitive information even if an attacker gains access to your cloud storage.
- **Encryption in Transit**: Secures data during transfer. **SSL/TLS** protocols ensure that data remains secure when sent over the internet.

3. Look for Multi-Factor Authentication (MFA)

Cloud solutions that support **multi-factor authentication (MFA)** provide an additional layer of security to prevent unauthorized access to your data. With MFA, users must provide two or more verification methods before gaining access to the system (e.g., password and SMS code).

- **Implement MFA for all cloud accounts**: Ensure that your employees and administrators use MFA for their cloud accounts, especially for critical systems like cloud email, data storage, and finance.

4. Review Access Control and Role-Based Permissions

A good cloud provider should allow you to set detailed access controls and **role-based permissions (RBAC)** for employees. This ensures that users only have access to the data necessary for their roles, reducing the risk of data exposure.

- **Access Control Lists (ACLs)**: Define which users or systems have access to specific data or resources within the cloud system.
- **Audit Logs**: Look for providers that offer detailed **audit logs** so you can track who is accessing your data and when.

5. Backup and Disaster Recovery Capabilities

A strong cloud provider should offer **automated backups** and a robust disaster recovery system. This ensures that your data is consistently backed up and can be recovered quickly if something goes wrong.

- **Set up automated backups**: Schedule regular backups of critical business data to ensure you don't lose anything important.
- **Test your disaster recovery**: Periodically simulate data loss scenarios to make sure your recovery process works smoothly.

Best Practices for Securing Data in the Cloud

Once you've chosen the right cloud provider, it's important to implement best practices to enhance your cloud security. Here are some practical steps to take:

1. Enable Encryption Everywhere

As mentioned, encryption is crucial for protecting sensitive information. Ensure that:

- **Data at rest** is encrypted using industry-standard algorithms like **AES-256**.
- **Data in transit** is encrypted using **SSL/TLS** or similar protocols.
- Use **end-to-end encryption** for highly sensitive data, especially when transferring it between internal and cloud-based systems.

2. Regularly Monitor Cloud Access and Activity

Monitor access logs and activity to ensure that only authorized users are accessing your cloud systems. Many cloud providers offer **security information and event management (SIEM)** tools that can provide real-time alerts and analysis.

- **Implement user behavior analytics (UBA)**: Use tools that track users' activities in the cloud. This helps identify suspicious behavior patterns, such as multiple failed login attempts or unusual data access requests.

3. Perform Regular Vulnerability Scanning

Conduct vulnerability scans on cloud systems to ensure they are free of weaknesses. Many cloud providers offer built-in tools for vulnerability assessment.

- **Automated scanning**: Use automated scanning tools to check for vulnerabilities in your cloud infrastructure and applications.
- **Third-party assessments**: Conduct regular **penetration testing** or hire ethical hackers to test the security of your cloud-based systems.

4. Educate Employees on Cloud Security Best Practices

Since many data breaches are the result of human error, it's essential to **educate** your team on how to use the cloud securely. Here are some key areas to focus on:

- **Password management**: Encourage strong, unique passwords and use of **password managers**.
- **Recognizing phishing attempts**: Teach employees how to identify phishing emails and other social engineering attacks that target cloud services.
- **Secure file sharing**: Ensure employees use secure file-sharing practices, especially when working with external partners or clients.

Case Study: A Small Business Secures Its Data Using Cloud Solutions

The Challenge:
A small marketing agency was struggling to manage and protect its growing volume of client data. The team was working remotely, and many employees were using personal devices to access business files. Despite using traditional security tools, the agency experienced several near-misses with data breaches and lacked a reliable backup system.

The Solution:
To improve security, the agency decided to transition to cloud-based solutions with robust security features:

1. **Selected a Cloud Provider**.
   The agency chose **Google Cloud** for its security certifications (ISO 27001, GDPR compliance), strong encryption practices, and **easy integration** with their existing tools.
2. **Enabled Multi-Factor Authentication**:
   The agency required all employees to use **MFA** to access Google Cloud services, ensuring an additional layer of protection beyond passwords.
3. **Automated Backups and Disaster Recovery**:
   The agency configured **automated backups** of all critical files and set up a disaster recovery plan within the cloud, which could be accessed in the event of a system failure.
4. **Educated the Team on Cloud Security**:
   The business conducted training sessions on how to securely access cloud systems, use strong passwords, and recognize phishing attempts.

The Outcome:
After adopting these cloud-based security measures, the agency experienced fewer security incidents and was able to recover from a previous data loss incident in minutes. Clients felt more confident in the agency's ability to safeguard their data, which led to stronger business relationships.

Flowchart: Securing Data in the Cloud

```
                        Start
                          |
                          V
      [Choose a Cloud Provider with Strong Security Features]
                          |
                          V
          [Enable Data Encryption for All Data Types]
                          |
                          V
          [Set Up Multi-Factor Authentication (MFA)]
                          |
                          V
          [Define Role-Based Access Control for Users]
                          |
                          V
        [Automate Backups and Set Up Disaster Recovery]
                          |
                          V
          [Regularly Monitor Cloud Activity Logs]
                          |
                          V
      [Educate Employees on Cloud Security Best Practices]
                          |
                          V
        Secure Your Business Data with Cloud Solutions!
```

Cloud solutions offer significant advantages in terms of scalability, flexibility, and cost-effectiveness. However, they also require careful planning and implementation to ensure that your business data is properly protected. By choosing a reputable cloud provider, enabling strong security measures like **data encryption**, **multi-factor authentication**, and **automated backups**, you can leverage the cloud to improve your overall security posture.

Chapter 7: Protecting Your Website and Online Presence

In today's business landscape, your **website** and **online presence** are critical to your company's success. They're often the first point of contact between your business and potential customers. As such, securing your website is essential to maintain customer trust, prevent data breaches, and protect your reputation. The internet is full of potential threats, from malicious hackers to data-stealing bots, and without proper security measures, your website can become an easy target.

In this chapter, we'll explore how to protect your website and online presence. We'll cover the importance of **SSL certificates**, securing **Content Management Systems (CMS)**, ensuring your **e-commerce and payment systems** are safe, and monitoring for **hacking attempts and suspicious activity**. Each of these steps is vital for ensuring that your website remains secure, your customers' data stays protected, and your business continues to thrive online.

7.1: Securing Your Website (SSL, CMS Security)

Your website is more than just an online presence; it's the face of your business. Whether you're running a **simple blog**, an **e-commerce store**, or a **corporate site**, your website handles interactions with customers, clients, and even partners. Securing this gateway is paramount. Without proper security measures, your website is vulnerable to a wide range of attacks, from data breaches to malware injections.

In this chapter, we'll break down the steps for securing your website, focusing on two crucial areas: **SSL (Secure Sockets Layer)** and **CMS (Content Management System) security**. We'll guide you through understanding why these are essential, how to implement them effectively, and the tools you can use to ensure your website stays safe and trustworthy.

What is SSL, and Why Is It Essential for Website Security?

Understanding SSL (Secure Sockets Layer)

SSL (now replaced by **TLS – Transport Layer Security**) is a cryptographic protocol that provides **secure communication** over a computer network. In simpler terms, SSL ensures that the data transferred between a user's browser and your website is encrypted and secure, protecting it from eavesdropping and tampering.

When SSL is enabled on a website, the URL in the browser's address bar changes from **HTTP** to **HTTPS**, with the "S" standing for **Secure**. The browser also displays a **padlock icon**, indicating that the connection is encrypted.

Why SSL is Important:

1. **Data Protection**: SSL protects sensitive data such as login credentials, payment information, and personal details from being intercepted by malicious third parties.
2. **SEO Benefits**: Google gives preference to secure websites (those using HTTPS) in search rankings. Having SSL is a ranking factor, making it vital for SEO.
3. **Customer Trust**: Consumers are more likely to trust a website that uses SSL encryption. A lack of SSL may cause customers to abandon their purchases or even avoid your website entirely.
4. **Compliance**: For businesses that handle **credit card information** or other personal data, SSL is a requirement for complying with **PCI DSS (Payment Card Industry Data Security Standard)**.

How to Secure Your Website with SSL:

1. **Purchase an SSL Certificate**:
   SSL certificates are issued by **Certificate Authorities (CAs)** like

DigiCert, **Comodo**, **GeoTrust**, and **Let's Encrypt** (a free, widely trusted provider). Choose a certificate that matches your website's needs:

- o **Single Domain**: For a single website.
- o **Wildcard**: For multiple subdomains under one domain.
- o **Multi-domain (SAN)**: For several domains.

2. **Install the SSL Certificate**:
   After purchasing the certificate, follow your hosting provider's instructions to install it on your server. Most web hosts provide a straightforward installation process for SSL certificates.

3. **Force HTTPS**:
   Once SSL is installed, make sure that all traffic is directed to the secure version of your website (HTTPS). You can do this by:
   - o Redirecting HTTP traffic to HTTPS using a **301 redirect**.
   - o Updating your **.htaccess** file (for Apache servers) to force HTTPS.
   - o Enabling **HTTP Strict Transport Security (HSTS)** to enforce HTTPS and reduce the chances of SSL stripping attacks.

4. **Test SSL Installation**:
   After installation, use an online tool like **SSL Labs' SSL Test** to verify your SSL certificate is correctly installed and providing strong encryption.

Securing Your CMS (Content Management System)

What is a CMS?

A **Content Management System (CMS)** like **WordPress**, **Joomla**, or **Drupal** is the platform that powers your website. It provides an interface for managing and creating digital content without needing extensive coding knowledge. However, CMS platforms are a frequent target for hackers due to their widespread use.

Securing your CMS is critical to protecting your website from attacks, such as **SQL injections**, **cross-site scripting (XSS)**, and **brute force login attempts**.

Best Practices for Securing Your CMS:

1. **Keep Your CMS Updated**:
   - **Why It Matters**: Security patches and bug fixes are regularly released by CMS developers to patch vulnerabilities. Failing to update your CMS can leave it open to exploits.
   - **How to Implement**:
     - Regularly check for updates and install them immediately. Most CMS platforms offer **automatic updates** for minor patches, so enable this feature.
     - Don't delay **major updates**, as these often contain critical security patches.
2. **Secure Your Admin Panel**:
   - **Why It Matters**: The admin panel gives full access to your website's backend. If compromised, hackers can gain control over your entire website.
   - **How to Implement**:
     - **Use Strong Passwords**: Ensure that your admin account uses a **strong, unique password**. Avoid easily guessable passwords like "admin123".
     - **Limit Login Attempts**: Implement a plugin or tool that limits failed login attempts. This will protect your site from **brute-force attacks**, where hackers try many combinations of usernames and passwords.
     - **Enable Multi-Factor Authentication (MFA)**: MFA adds an extra layer of security by requiring an additional verification step (such as an SMS code or an authenticator app).
3. **Install Security Plugins**:
   - **Why It Matters**: Many CMS platforms have security plugins designed to protect against common attacks.
   - **How to Implement**:
     - **WordPress**: Use plugins like **Wordfence** or **iThemes Security** to monitor and protect your website from threats.
     - **Joomla/Drupal**: Use **Akeeba Backup** (for backups) and **Joomla Security Suite** for added security.

- o **What These Plugins Do**: These plugins scan for malware, block suspicious IPs, and provide real-time alerts about potential security breaches.
4. **Backup Your Website Regularly**:
   - o **Why It Matters**: Regular backups ensure that your website can be restored in case of an attack or data loss.
   - o **How to Implement**:
     - Use a CMS-specific backup plugin or third-party service (like **UpdraftPlus** for WordPress) to automate backups.
     - Store backups both locally (on a hard drive) and remotely (in cloud storage, like **Google Drive** or **Dropbox**).
5. **Secure File Permissions**:
   - o **Why It Matters**: Incorrect file permissions can allow unauthorized users to modify or access sensitive parts of your website.
   - o **How to Implement**:
     - Check your file permissions regularly and make sure that only authorized users have access to critical files (like **wp-config.php** for WordPress).
     - Set file permissions to **644** for files and **755** for directories.

Case Study: A Small E-commerce Business Secures Its Website

The Challenge:
An online store selling fashion products was frequently facing hacking attempts on its WordPress site. The attackers tried brute-force login attempts, and there were occasional reports of customers receiving suspicious emails asking for login credentials. The store owner was concerned about a potential data breach and losing customer trust.

The Solution:
The business owner took several steps to secure their website:

1. **SSL Installation**:
   They purchased an SSL certificate from **Let's Encrypt** and forced

HTTPS across the entire site using a **301 redirect** in the `.htaccess` file.

2. **CMS Security**:
   o The store's **WordPress** platform was regularly updated to the latest version.
   o They installed **Wordfence** to monitor security and limit login attempts. This prevented brute-force attacks by locking out any user after five failed attempts.
   o They set up **two-factor authentication (2FA)** using the **Google Authenticator** plugin to ensure that only authorized users could access the backend.

3. **Backup and Disaster Recovery**:
   The store started using **UpdraftPlus** for automated daily backups, which were stored both in the cloud and on an external hard drive.

The Outcome:
After these security improvements, the store noticed a significant reduction in attempted attacks and an increase in customer trust. The store owner also felt confident that, should an attack occur in the future, they could quickly restore their website from a secure backup.

Flowchart: Securing Your Website (SSL & CMS Security)

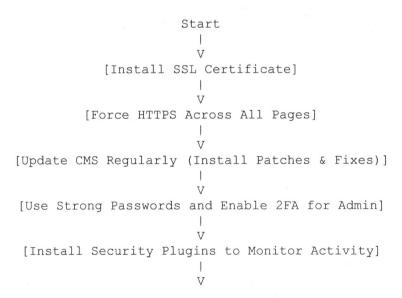

```
                        Start
                          |
                          V
                [Install SSL Certificate]
                          |
                          V
            [Force HTTPS Across All Pages]
                          |
                          V
    [Update CMS Regularly (Install Patches & Fixes)]
                          |
                          V
      [Use Strong Passwords and Enable 2FA for Admin]
                          |
                          V
      [Install Security Plugins to Monitor Activity]
                          |
                          V
```

```
            [Backup Website Regularly and Securely]
                            |
                            V
           [Monitor File Permissions and Restrict Access]
                            |
                            V
              Secure Your Website and Online Presence!
```

Securing your website is a vital part of protecting your business and
customer data. By implementing **SSL encryption**, ensuring the security of
your **Content Management System (CMS)**, and using best practices like
strong passwords, **MFA**, and **backup solutions**, you can build a robust
security posture for your website. These steps will help you prevent
attacks, build trust with your customers, and maintain a secure online
environment for your business.

7.2: Protecting E-commerce and Payment Systems

In the world of **e-commerce**, the ability to handle transactions securely is
paramount. Your online store is not just a showcase of your products or
services—it's also a platform where **sensitive customer data** is
exchanged, including **payment details**. Securing your e-commerce
platform is crucial to prevent fraud, protect your customers, and maintain
trust in your business.

In this chapter, we will discuss how to **protect e-commerce and payment
systems** from threats like **data breaches**, **fraudulent transactions**, and
payment fraud. We'll explore the importance of **PCI DSS compliance**,
secure payment gateways, **tokenization**, **SSL/TLS encryption**, and
fraud prevention techniques. Additionally, we'll provide practical steps
you can take to safeguard your customers' sensitive payment data.

Why E-commerce Security Matters

E-commerce security isn't just about protecting your website—it's about ensuring that your customers' sensitive information, especially **payment details**, is safe from theft or compromise. A **data breach** or **fraudulent transaction** can have devastating effects on your business, including:

1. **Loss of Customer Trust**: Customers are less likely to purchase from a store that has experienced a security breach.
2. **Legal Penalties**: Failure to comply with **data protection regulations** such as **PCI DSS** or **GDPR** can result in hefty fines.
3. **Financial Losses**: Fraudulent transactions can lead to chargebacks, legal fees, and loss of revenue.
4. **Reputation Damage**: Word of a security breach can spread quickly, causing long-lasting damage to your brand reputation.

Given these risks, investing in securing your e-commerce platform is not just a good practice—it's an absolute necessity.

Securing Payment Systems: Best Practices

1. Use a Secure Payment Gateway

The **payment gateway** is the technology that securely transmits customer payment information from your e-commerce store to the payment processor. A **secure payment gateway** ensures that sensitive payment details like **credit card numbers** are handled safely.

Why It's Important:
A payment gateway that doesn't implement proper security measures can leave your website vulnerable to **data interception, fraudulent transactions**, and **data breaches**.

Best Practices for Secure Payment Gateways:

- **Use Reputable Payment Providers**: Only use trusted payment gateways like **PayPal, Stripe, Square**, or **Authorize.Net**. These services are PCI DSS-compliant and offer built-in fraud protection features.
- **Avoid Storing Credit Card Information**: Never store sensitive payment details on your website unless absolutely necessary.

Payment processors like **Stripe** and **PayPal** handle this for you, ensuring compliance and security.

- **Enable 3D Secure (3DS)**: 3D Secure is an added security layer that requires cardholders to authenticate transactions. Popular systems like **Verified by Visa** and **MasterCard SecureCode** use 3DS to reduce fraud.

2. Ensure PCI DSS Compliance

PCI DSS (Payment Card Industry Data Security Standard) is a set of security standards designed to protect card information during and after financial transactions. **E-commerce businesses** are required to comply with PCI DSS if they handle **credit card payments**.

Why It's Important:
Compliance with PCI DSS ensures that your payment system meets the necessary security requirements to prevent fraud, protect cardholder data, and secure sensitive information.

Best Practices for PCI DSS Compliance:

- **Encrypt Cardholder Data**: Encrypt payment information both in transit (SSL/TLS) and at rest (AES encryption).
- **Use Strong Access Control Measures**: Limit access to sensitive payment information to only authorized personnel and use role-based access control (RBAC).
- **Implement Monitoring and Logging**: Continuously monitor and log all access to payment data, including administrative activities.

3. Implement Tokenization

Tokenization is the process of replacing sensitive payment data, such as a credit card number, with a **unique token** that has no real value. Tokenization helps minimize the risk of exposure because the token can't be used outside the context of your payment system.

Why It's Important:
Even if a hacker gains access to your payment system, they will only see **tokens**, not the actual payment data. This significantly reduces the risk of data theft.

Best Practices for Tokenization:

- **Implement Tokenization for Payment Transactions**: Most payment processors, like **Stripe** or **Square**, offer tokenization as part of their service. Use it for every transaction that involves sensitive cardholder data.
- **Store Tokens Securely**: Ensure that tokens are stored in an encrypted database with limited access.

4. Use SSL/TLS Encryption

SSL/TLS (Secure Sockets Layer / Transport Layer Security) are cryptographic protocols that ensure the data transmitted between your website and your customers is encrypted. This protects sensitive payment information from being intercepted during transmission.

Why It's Important:
Without SSL/TLS encryption, your customers' payment details can be intercepted by malicious third parties during the payment process, leading to fraud and data breaches.

Best Practices for SSL/TLS Encryption:

- **Use HTTPS on All Pages**: Ensure that SSL is implemented across all pages of your website, particularly those where payment information is entered (e.g., checkout pages).
- **Use Strong SSL/TLS Certificates**: Purchase an SSL certificate from a reputable provider, and make sure it supports the latest encryption standards (e.g., **AES-256**).
- **Update SSL/TLS Protocols Regularly**: SSL and TLS protocols evolve, so it's important to update to the latest versions to protect against known vulnerabilities.

Fraud Prevention Techniques

1. Implement Anti-Fraud Tools

There are several tools available to help detect and prevent fraudulent transactions. These tools use machine learning and other techniques to spot patterns of fraud, such as unusual spending behavior or multiple transactions from the same IP address.

Why It's Important:
Fraudulent transactions can lead to chargebacks, which not only hurt your revenue but can also damage your reputation with payment processors.

Best Practices for Fraud Prevention:

- **Use Fraud Detection Software**: Tools like **Kount**, **Signifyd**, and **Riskified** use AI to detect fraudulent activities in real-time, preventing transactions before they are completed.
- **Set Up Fraudulent Transaction Filters**: Most payment processors offer filters that block suspicious transactions based on certain parameters like IP address, geolocation, and device fingerprinting.

2. Implement Behavioral Analysis

Behavioral analysis tools monitor **customer behavior** on your website, such as browsing patterns, cart abandonment, and time spent on different pages. These tools use machine learning to detect abnormal behavior, which could indicate fraudulent activities or bots attempting to access your site.

Why It's Important:
Proactive monitoring and analysis can help you detect fraud before it impacts your business.

Best Practices for Behavioral Analysis:

- **Set Up Real-Time Alerts**: Use software that provides real-time alerts for suspicious activities, such as login attempts from different countries or failed payment transactions.
- **Track IP Addresses and Device Fingerprinting**: Track user behavior across devices and IP addresses. Unusual patterns, like logging in from different locations in short periods, can indicate fraud.

Case Study: E-commerce Business Secures Payment System

The Challenge:
An e-commerce store selling electronics had been facing an increasing number of fraudulent transactions. Customers' payment information was compromised, and the store received numerous chargebacks, resulting in significant financial losses and a damaged reputation.

The Solution:
The store took several measures to improve its payment system security:

1. **Integrated a Secure Payment Gateway**:
   The store switched to **Stripe**, a trusted payment provider that uses **tokenization** and is PCI DSS-compliant. They no longer stored sensitive payment information on their website.
2. **Implemented 3D Secure**:
   To reduce fraud, they implemented **3D Secure** for all transactions. This added an extra step during the payment process, requiring customers to verify their identity using an additional layer of authentication.
3. **SSL Encryption**:
   The store installed an **SSL certificate** on their website, ensuring that all customer data (including payment information) was encrypted during transmission.
4. **Fraud Detection Software**:
   They integrated **Signifyd**, a fraud detection tool, to monitor and prevent fraudulent transactions in real-time. The tool flagged suspicious orders, and the store could review them before processing.
5. **Behavioral Analysis**:
   The store used **Kount** to analyze user behavior and detect irregularities in browsing patterns. This helped flag potential fraudulent activities early on.

The Outcome:
After implementing these security measures, the store saw a significant reduction in fraud, chargebacks, and customer complaints. Their payment processing became more secure, and customer confidence was restored. The store's revenue and customer trust grew as a result.

Flowchart: Protecting E-commerce and Payment Systems

```
                        Start
                          |
                          V
            [Choose a Secure Payment Gateway]
                          |
                          V
       [Ensure PCI DSS Compliance for Payment Systems]
                          |
                          V
          [Implement Tokenization for Payment Data]
                          |
                          V
         [Use SSL/TLS Encryption for All Transactions]
                          |
                          V
          [Implement Anti-Fraud Tools and Detection]
                          |
                          V
      [Track Behavior and Implement Fraudulent Transaction
                         Filters]
                          |
                          V
         Secure Your E-commerce and Payment Systems!
```

Securing your e-commerce and payment systems is crucial to protecting both your business and your customers. By following the best practices outlined in this chapter—such as using secure payment gateways, ensuring PCI DSS compliance, enabling tokenization, and using SSL/TLS encryption—you can safeguard sensitive payment data and reduce the risk of fraud. Fraud detection and behavioral analysis add an additional layer of protection, allowing you to catch potential issues before they escalate.

7.3: Monitoring for Hacking Attempts and Suspicious Activity

In today's digital world, cyberattacks are becoming increasingly sophisticated. While securing your website and payment systems is essential, maintaining a **continuous watch** for hacking attempts and suspicious activity is just as crucial. Hackers are constantly evolving their tactics, so proactive **monitoring** of your website and systems is key to identifying threats before they cause significant harm.

This chapter focuses on how to **monitor for hacking attempts**, detect **suspicious activity**, and respond swiftly to potential threats. We'll explore the best practices, tools, and techniques for monitoring your website, including **intrusion detection systems (IDS)**, **real-time alerts**, and **log management**. By the end of this chapter, you'll be equipped with the knowledge to stay one step ahead of cybercriminals and protect your business from potential breaches.

Why Monitoring for Suspicious Activity is Essential

1. Early Detection of Cyberattacks:
The sooner you detect an intrusion or hacking attempt, the quicker you can mitigate the damage. Cyberattacks often leave traces, and catching those traces early can prevent major security breaches.

2. Prevent Financial Losses:
Many attacks, such as **fraudulent transactions** or **data breaches**, can result in significant financial losses. Early monitoring helps prevent these types of attacks from causing harm to your bottom line.

3. Ensure Customer Trust and Compliance:
If a data breach occurs, it can damage your reputation and lead to legal consequences. Regular monitoring ensures that you stay compliant with **data protection regulations** like **GDPR** and **PCI DSS**, helping you avoid costly fines and retain customer trust.

4. Minimize the Risk of Advanced Threats:
Many advanced threats, such as **zero-day attacks** (exploiting previously unknown vulnerabilities), may go undetected for months. Continuous monitoring is essential to catch these threats early, before they can do real damage.

Best Practices for Monitoring for Hacking Attempts and Suspicious Activity

1. Set Up Intrusion Detection Systems (IDS)

An **Intrusion Detection System (IDS)** monitors network traffic and system activity to detect malicious activity or policy violations. IDS systems can help identify potential threats, such as unauthorized login attempts, malware activity, or attempted data exfiltration.

Why It's Important:
IDS systems can alert you in real-time when malicious activity is detected, enabling you to respond quickly and prevent further harm.

Best Practices for IDS Implementation:

- **Choose the Right IDS Type**:
  There are two main types of IDS:
  - **Network-Based IDS (NIDS)**: Monitors network traffic for suspicious activity, such as unusual traffic spikes or unauthorized data access.
  - **Host-Based IDS (HIDS)**: Focuses on monitoring individual systems or servers, detecting any unauthorized changes or suspicious behavior on those machines.
- **Configure Alerts and Notifications**:
  Set up real-time alerts to be notified immediately when a potential threat is detected. Alerts can be sent via email, SMS, or through your security monitoring system.
- **Regularly Update Signatures**:
  IDS systems rely on **signatures** (known patterns of malicious behavior). Ensure your IDS system is regularly updated with the latest signatures to detect new types of threats.

Example Tools:

- **Snort**: An open-source IDS used for real-time traffic analysis.
- **Suricata**: Another open-source IDS that is fast and scalable.

2. Log Management and Monitoring

Log management involves collecting and storing log data from various sources (e.g., web servers, payment systems, and application servers) and analyzing it for signs of suspicious activity.

Why It's Important:
Logs provide a detailed record of actions taken on your website and systems. Reviewing these logs helps identify potential threats, such as **failed login attempts**, **unauthorized file access**, or **unusual system errors**.

Best Practices for Log Management:

- **Centralized Log Storage**:
  Store all logs in a centralized location (using tools like **ELK Stack** or **Splunk**). This makes it easier to manage and analyze logs from multiple sources.
- **Set Log Retention Policies**:
  Determine how long logs should be retained. Store logs for a period of time that is compliant with regulations like **GDPR** or **PCI DSS** (typically 1–2 years).
- **Analyze Logs for Patterns**:
  Regularly analyze logs for signs of suspicious activity, such as:
    - **Multiple failed login attempts**: Indicates potential **brute-force attacks**.
    - **Unusual data transfers**: Could indicate **data exfiltration**.
    - **Abnormal traffic patterns**: Indicates possible **DDoS attacks** or **bot activity**.

Example Tools:

- **Splunk**: A powerful tool for searching, monitoring, and analyzing machine data.
- **ELK Stack**: A combination of **Elasticsearch, Logstash**, and **Kibana**, which can aggregate and visualize log data for easier monitoring.

3. Implement Real-Time Alerts for Suspicious Activity

Real-time alerts help detect threats as they happen, allowing you to respond immediately. These alerts should be configured to notify you about the most common types of suspicious activities, such as unauthorized logins, failed login attempts, and abnormal traffic patterns.

Why It's Important:
If an attacker gains access to your system, you want to know about it as soon as possible. Real-time alerts provide instant notification, enabling rapid action to mitigate damage.

Best Practices for Real-Time Alerts:

- **Configure Alert Thresholds:**
  Set thresholds for certain actions, such as **5 failed login attempts** within a 5-minute window, and trigger an alert when these thresholds are exceeded.
- **Use Security Information and Event Management (SIEM) Tools:**
  SIEM tools aggregate data from multiple sources and trigger alerts based on pre-defined rules. These tools provide real-time monitoring and a centralized view of security events.

Example Tools:

- **PagerDuty**: An incident management tool that can notify your team in real-time.
- **Zabbix**: A monitoring tool that offers real-time alerts for a wide range of events.

---

4. Monitor for Suspicious IP Addresses and Geolocations

Monitoring for suspicious IP addresses and geolocations can help detect **bot traffic** or **hacking attempts**. By analyzing the origin of traffic, you can identify if certain IP addresses are known for **cyberattacks** or **fraudulent activities**.

Why It's Important:
Hackers often use **IP spoofing** to hide their true location. By monitoring IP addresses and geolocations, you can spot anomalies, such as logins from unexpected countries or high-risk regions, and take immediate action.

Best Practices for IP and Geolocation Monitoring:

- **Use IP Blacklists**:
  Maintain a list of known malicious IP addresses that can be blocked from accessing your site. You can find regularly updated blacklists on **abuse.ch** or **Spamhaus**.
- **Analyze Traffic Patterns**:
  If traffic is coming from an unusual geographic location or IP address, it could be a sign of suspicious behavior. Set up alerts to notify you of such traffic.
- **Geolocation Restrictions**:
  If your business only serves certain regions or countries, you can restrict access to your website from other regions to prevent attacks from outside your business's area of operation.

---

5. Use Web Application Firewalls (WAFs)

A **Web Application Firewall (WAF)** is designed to protect web applications from various threats, including **SQL injection**, **cross-site scripting (XSS)**, and **bot traffic**. WAFs sit between your website and the internet, inspecting incoming traffic and blocking malicious requests.

Why It's Important:
A WAF helps prevent common attacks, providing an extra layer of defense in addition to traditional firewalls.

Best Practices for WAFs:

- **Deploy a WAF to Block Malicious Traffic**:
  WAFs can be configured to block specific attack vectors, such as SQL injection attempts or **XSS attacks**.

- **Use WAFs with Real-Time Protection**:
  Choose a WAF solution that offers **real-time threat intelligence**, ensuring it stays up to date with emerging attack methods.
- **Customize WAF Rules**:
  Tailor your WAF rules to your specific business needs and common attack patterns.

Example Tools:

- **Cloudflare**: Offers a WAF with **DDoS protection** and real-time threat intelligence.
- **Sucuri**: Provides cloud-based WAF and performance optimization.

Case Study: E-commerce Store Monitors for Suspicious Activity

The Challenge:
An online clothing retailer noticed an uptick in fraudulent orders. The fraudsters were using stolen credit card information to make large purchases, and the store was facing multiple chargebacks, resulting in financial losses.

The Solution:
The store implemented several monitoring and security measures:

1. **Installed a WAF**:
   They used **Cloudflare's WAF** to protect against common attacks like SQL injection and cross-site scripting.
2. **Set Up Real-Time Alerts**:
   The store configured **real-time alerts** using **Splunk**, notifying them when there were multiple failed login attempts or orders from high-risk regions.
3. **Monitored IP Geolocation**:
   They used **MaxMind** to monitor traffic and identify **unusual geolocations**. If a customer was logging in from a high-risk country, their order was flagged for manual review.
4. **Implemented Fraud Detection**:
   The store integrated **Signifyd**, a fraud detection tool, to analyze

transactions in real-time. If the system detected a suspicious order, it was flagged for further verification.

The Outcome:
After implementing these monitoring measures, the store saw a **30% reduction in fraud** and **chargebacks**. Customers' payment data was better protected, and the store could more effectively track suspicious behavior and prevent fraudulent orders.

Flowchart: Monitoring for Hacking Attempts and Suspicious Activity

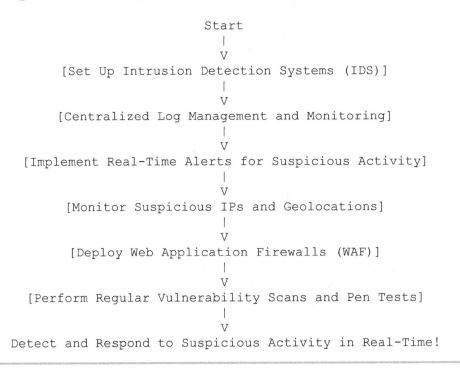

```
                         Start
                          |
                          V
        [Set Up Intrusion Detection Systems (IDS)]
                          |
                          V
        [Centralized Log Management and Monitoring]
                          |
                          V
    [Implement Real-Time Alerts for Suspicious Activity]
                          |
                          V
        [Monitor Suspicious IPs and Geolocations]
                          |
                          V
         [Deploy Web Application Firewalls (WAF)]
                          |
                          V
      [Perform Regular Vulnerability Scans and Pen Tests]
                          |
                          V
    Detect and Respond to Suspicious Activity in Real-Time!
```

Monitoring for hacking attempts and suspicious activity is a vital part of any strong cybersecurity strategy. By using **IDS**, setting up **real-time alerts**, and **monitoring IP addresses** and **geolocations**, you can identify and stop potential threats before they cause significant damage. Combining these techniques with **WAFs** and continuous monitoring ensures that your website remains safe from cybercriminals.

Chapter 8: Basic Compliance and Legal Requirements

As cyber threats continue to grow in sophistication, governments and regulatory bodies have introduced laws and standards designed to protect personal data and ensure businesses handle it responsibly. Compliance with these regulations is not only critical for maintaining trust with customers but also for avoiding hefty penalties, legal consequences, and reputational damage.

In this chapter, we will explore key **cybersecurity regulations** that every business should be aware of—such as **GDPR**, **CCPA**, and **PCI-DSS**—and provide a step-by-step guide on how to achieve and maintain compliance. Whether you're a small business owner or an enterprise leader, understanding these requirements and implementing necessary measures is essential for protecting your business and customers.

8.1: Overview of Key Cybersecurity Regulations

In the ever-changing landscape of cybersecurity, businesses must stay on top of the legal and regulatory requirements surrounding data protection. With more and more personal information being shared online, both consumers and regulators have become increasingly concerned about how businesses handle sensitive data. Various **cybersecurity regulations** have emerged in response, aiming to protect individuals' privacy and ensure businesses take the necessary steps to prevent data breaches.

In this section, we'll take a deep dive into the key cybersecurity regulations that businesses must be aware of, including **GDPR**, **CCPA**, and **PCI-DSS**. Understanding these regulations is essential for **compliance**, reducing the risk of **legal consequences**, and building **customer trust**. Let's explore the **fundamentals** of these regulations, their impact, and the steps businesses need to take to stay compliant.

1. General Data Protection Regulation (GDPR)

The **General Data Protection Regulation (GDPR)** is one of the most significant and far-reaching data protection regulations to date. It came into effect on **May 25, 2018**, and applies to businesses worldwide that process the personal data of **EU residents**, regardless of where the business itself is located.

Key Features of GDPR:

1. **Personal Data**:
   GDPR defines personal data as any information related to an identified or identifiable individual, such as **names, email addresses, IP addresses**, and even **location data**. It applies not only to data collected directly but also to information inferred from other data points.
2. **Data Subject Rights**:
   Under GDPR, individuals (referred to as **data subjects**) have specific rights regarding their personal data, including:
   - **Right to Access**: Individuals can request to know what data a business holds about them.
   - **Right to Rectification**: Individuals can request corrections to inaccurate data.
   - **Right to Erasure**: Also known as the **Right to be Forgotten**, individuals can request the deletion of their data.
   - **Right to Portability**: Individuals can request their data in a structured, commonly used format and transfer it to another service.
   - **Right to Object**: Individuals can object to the processing of their data in certain situations, such as direct marketing.
3. **Consent**:
   Businesses must obtain **explicit consent** from individuals before processing their personal data. Consent must be informed, specific, and freely given.
4. **Data Breach Notification**:
   GDPR mandates that businesses must notify both the relevant **supervisory authority** and affected individuals within **72 hours** of

discovering a data breach, if the breach poses a risk to individuals' rights and freedoms.

5. **Data Protection Officer (DPO)**:
   Certain businesses, particularly those involved in large-scale processing of sensitive data, are required to appoint a **DPO** to oversee compliance.

6. **Penalties for Non-Compliance**:
   Non-compliance with GDPR can result in fines of up to **€20 million** or **4% of global annual revenue**, whichever is greater.

Why GDPR Matters:

The GDPR represents a shift in how businesses are required to manage data. It puts the control of personal data back into the hands of individuals and imposes strict obligations on businesses to protect that data. Given the potential for significant financial penalties and reputational damage, compliance is critical for any business interacting with EU customers.

Practical Steps for GDPR Compliance:

- **Review Data Collection Practices**: Ensure that your business only collects the necessary data and obtains explicit consent.
- **Update Privacy Policies**: Your privacy policies should clearly explain how you collect, process, and protect personal data.
- **Implement Data Protection Measures**: Secure data using encryption, access controls, and other protective measures.
- **Appoint a DPO**: If necessary, designate a Data Protection Officer to oversee GDPR compliance.

---

2. California Consumer Privacy Act (CCPA)

The **California Consumer Privacy Act (CCPA)**, which came into effect on **January 1, 2020**, is a state-level privacy law designed to protect the personal information of **California residents**. While it shares many similarities with GDPR, it is specifically tailored to the needs of businesses operating in California.

Key Features of CCPA:

1. **Personal Information**:
   CCPA defines personal information as data that can be used to identify, relate to, or describe a consumer, such as **names**, **email addresses**, **social security numbers**, and **purchase history**.
2. **Consumer Rights**:
   Under CCPA, California residents have the right to:
   - **Know**: The right to know what personal information is being collected and to request access to it.
   - **Delete**: The right to request the deletion of personal information collected by businesses.
   - **Opt-Out**: The right to opt-out of the sale of personal data to third parties.
   - **Non-Discrimination**: Businesses cannot discriminate against consumers who choose to exercise their rights under CCPA.
3. **Business Requirements**:
   Businesses that meet certain criteria (such as having **annual gross revenues** over **$25 million**) are required to:
   - Provide a **clear opt-out mechanism** for data sales.
   - Respond to consumer requests regarding data access, deletion, and opt-out within **45 days**.
4. **Penalties for Non-Compliance**:
   Violations of CCPA can result in penalties of up to **$7,500** per intentional violation, with potential for **private lawsuits** if consumer rights are violated.

Why CCPA Matters:

For businesses that collect personal information from California residents, CCPA provides consumers with more transparency and control over how their data is handled. It's crucial for businesses, particularly in the digital economy, to stay compliant with CCPA to avoid significant penalties and lawsuits.

Practical Steps for CCPA Compliance:

- **Update Privacy Policies**: Ensure your privacy policies reflect the rights and information required by CCPA.

- **Allow Data Access and Deletion Requests**: Implement processes to facilitate consumer requests to access or delete their personal data.
- **Opt-Out Mechanisms**: Provide users with a clear way to opt-out of the sale of their data.
- **Train Employees**: Ensure that your staff understands consumer rights under CCPA and knows how to handle requests accordingly.

---

3. Payment Card Industry Data Security Standard (PCI-DSS)

PCI-DSS is a set of security standards designed to ensure that businesses processing **credit card transactions** maintain a secure environment. The PCI-DSS standards apply to any business that processes, stores, or transmits **credit card information**, regardless of its size.

Key Features of PCI-DSS:

1. **Protect Cardholder Data**:
   PCI-DSS requires businesses to protect cardholder data through encryption and secure storage.
2. **Maintain Secure Networks**:
   Businesses must regularly test their networks, apply firewalls, and secure systems to protect against unauthorized access.
3. **Access Control**:
   Only authorized individuals should have access to payment card information. Businesses must implement **role-based access control (RBAC)** and **multi-factor authentication (MFA)** for employees who access sensitive data.
4. **Regular Testing**:
   Businesses must conduct regular vulnerability scans and penetration tests to identify potential security weaknesses.
5. **Logging and Monitoring**:
   Businesses must log and monitor all access to payment card information and regularly review logs for suspicious activity.

Why PCI-DSS Matters:

Non-compliance with PCI-DSS can result in fines, loss of the ability to process credit card payments, and data breaches. PCI-DSS compliance is essential for any business involved in handling **payment card transactions**.

Practical Steps for PCI-DSS Compliance:

- **Encrypt Payment Data**: Ensure that sensitive payment card information is encrypted both during transmission (SSL/TLS) and at rest (AES encryption).
- **Install Strong Firewalls**: Protect your network with robust firewalls and implement intrusion detection systems (IDS).
- **Implement Multi-Factor Authentication**: Enforce multi-factor authentication (MFA) for employees accessing sensitive payment data.
- **Regular Audits and Vulnerability Scans**: Perform regular audits and vulnerability scans to ensure that your systems remain secure.

Why Compliance with Cybersecurity Regulations Matters

Compliance with **GDPR**, **CCPA**, and **PCI-DSS** is more than just a legal obligation—it's a critical part of building trust with your customers and maintaining a secure business environment. Here's why staying compliant matters:

1. **Avoid Legal Penalties**: Non-compliance can result in severe financial penalties, including fines and lawsuits.
2. **Protect Your Customers**: By securing sensitive data and respecting customers' privacy rights, you demonstrate that you take their security seriously.
3. **Maintain Customer Trust**: A secure and transparent business practices help you build long-lasting relationships with customers, which can result in **brand loyalty** and **higher conversion rates**.

Case Study: E-Commerce Business Navigates Compliance with GDPR and PCI-DSS

The Challenge:
An e-commerce website specializing in outdoor gear had been expanding its customer base internationally. The company realized that they needed to ensure compliance with **GDPR** to continue selling to **EU customers** while also ensuring their payment system was PCI-DSS compliant.

The Solution:

1. **GDPR Compliance**:
   o The company updated their **privacy policy** to reflect GDPR's requirements, including the **right to access** and **right to erasure**.
   o They implemented a system for users to easily **opt-in** to data collection and a **cookie consent tool** to ensure transparency.
2. **PCI-DSS Compliance**:
   o The e-commerce site switched to a **PCI-compliant payment gateway** (like **Stripe**) to handle all customer payments securely.
   o The company encrypted all **payment card data** and restricted access to sensitive information to authorized personnel only.

The Outcome:
The company successfully achieved **GDPR and PCI-DSS compliance**, avoiding penalties and securing customer trust. They were able to expand their market to the EU without legal concerns, and their reputation as a secure business grew.

Flowchart: Steps for Achieving Compliance

```
                        Start
                          |
                          V
    [Identify Relevant Regulations (GDPR, CCPA, PCI-DSS)]
                          |
```

```
                        V
        [Conduct Data Protection Audit]
                        |
                        V
    [Implement Required Security Measures]
                        |
                        V
    [Update Privacy Policies and Terms of Service
```

In this chapter, we've explored the key cybersecurity regulations that affect businesses worldwide, including **GDPR**, **CCPA**, and **PCI-DSS**. Compliance with these regulations is not just a legal requirement; it's a foundational element of your business's cybersecurity strategy, safeguarding sensitive data and building trust with customers.

8.2: Steps for Achieving Compliance

Achieving compliance with **cybersecurity regulations** is more than just a legal requirement—it's a crucial step towards protecting sensitive data, building customer trust, and safeguarding your business from costly penalties and reputational damage. With various regulations like **GDPR**, **CCPA**, and **PCI-DSS** covering different aspects of data privacy and security, it can seem like a daunting task for businesses to navigate. However, breaking down the process into manageable steps can simplify the journey.

This guide will walk you through a **step-by-step approach** to achieving **compliance** with key cybersecurity regulations. The steps are designed to be practical, actionable, and adaptable to businesses of all sizes. Whether you're a **small business owner** or part of a larger organization, this approach will help you understand how to align your practices with **GDPR, CCPA, PCI-DSS**, and other regulations.

Step 1: Understand the Regulations and Their Applicability

Key Regulations to Consider:

1. **GDPR (General Data Protection Regulation)**:
   Enforced by the **European Union (EU)**, GDPR governs how businesses must protect **personal data** of EU citizens. It applies to any business, anywhere in the world, that processes or stores data of EU residents.
2. **CCPA (California Consumer Privacy Act)**:
   CCPA is a privacy law for California residents. It applies to businesses that meet certain criteria, such as **annual revenue** above **$25 million**, or those that collect data from **50,000 or more consumers**.
3. **PCI-DSS (Payment Card Industry Data Security Standard)**:
   PCI-DSS applies to businesses that handle **payment card information**. It sets security standards to ensure that cardholder data is securely handled during transactions.

Why It's Important:

You must first determine which regulations apply to your business based on your **data handling practices** and **geographical presence**. This helps you focus your efforts on the right regulations and avoid unnecessary steps for non-applicable laws.

How to Implement This Step:

- **Identify the Types of Data You Handle**:
  Review whether you handle personal data (for GDPR), consumer data (for CCPA), or payment card information (for PCI-DSS).
- **Evaluate the Regions You Operate In**:
  If you have customers in **California**, you'll need to comply with CCPA. If your business deals with the EU market, GDPR applies. If you process payments, PCI-DSS compliance is mandatory.

Step 2: Conduct a Data Audit

The **data audit** is the foundation of your compliance efforts. It allows you to understand where your data is coming from, how it's being processed, and where it's stored. By conducting a thorough audit, you can identify potential compliance gaps and mitigate risks before they turn into legal or security problems.

What to Include in Your Data Audit:

1. **Data Mapping**:
   o Identify **all data sources**—where does your personal data come from? Does it come from customer sign-ups, third-party vendors, or payment systems?
   o **Track data flow** through your organization to understand how it's used, processed, stored, and shared.
2. **Assess Third-Party Relationships**:
   o Review any third-party vendors or services that handle personal or payment data on your behalf (e.g., payment processors, email marketing tools, cloud providers).
   o Ensure they also comply with relevant regulations and have proper security measures in place.
3. **Data Retention and Deletion**:
   o How long do you store customer data? Under **GDPR**, data should only be stored as long as necessary for business purposes.
   o Create a data retention and deletion policy that aligns with **regulations** and reduces unnecessary risk.
4. **Access Control**:
   o Identify who has access to sensitive data and ensure that only authorized personnel can access it.
   o Ensure your data access is aligned with the principle of **least privilege**, ensuring individuals only have access to the data required for their roles.

Why It's Important:

A data audit helps you understand your business's current practices and provides a foundation for **data security improvements**. It ensures that you can track where and how personal data is handled across your organization, and helps you comply with **transparency** and **accountability** requirements.

Step 3: Implement Security Measures

Once you understand your data handling practices, you need to implement the security measures necessary to comply with relevant regulations. Protecting sensitive data is critical to maintaining compliance with **GDPR**, **CCPA**, and **PCI-DSS**. Security measures must focus on encryption, access controls, and regular vulnerability testing.

Key Security Measures to Implement:

1. **Data Encryption**:
   - Encrypt **personal data** at rest (stored data) and in transit (data being transferred between systems).
   - **SSL/TLS encryption** ensures that customer data is protected when transferred over the web. **AES encryption** is recommended for data at rest.
2. **Access Controls**:
   - Implement **role-based access control (RBAC)** to limit who can access sensitive data. Ensure that employees only have access to data necessary for their roles.
   - **Multi-factor authentication (MFA)** should be used for systems that access sensitive or regulated data.
3. **Regular Penetration Testing**:
   - Conduct **penetration testing** to identify and address vulnerabilities in your systems. It's a proactive way to identify weaknesses before attackers do.
   - Use vulnerability scanners and monitoring tools to regularly check for flaws.
4. **Third-Party Security Measures**:
   - Ensure that any third-party vendors who process or store your data also comply with the required regulations. This might involve reviewing their **security certifications** (e.g., **SOC 2, ISO 27001**).
5. **Backup and Recovery Plans**:
   - Implement a secure **backup strategy** to ensure that your data can be restored in case of a disaster, such as a cyberattack or hardware failure.
   - Regularly test your **disaster recovery** plan to ensure data integrity.

Implementing robust security measures ensures that your business is protecting data as required by **GDPR, CCPA**, and **PCI-DSS**. This not only reduces the risk of breaches but also ensures you are following **best practices** in data protection.

Step 4: Update Privacy Policies and Procedures

Your **privacy policies** and **terms of service** are key documents that outline how your business collects, processes, and protects data. These documents must be updated regularly to reflect **compliance requirements** and ensure transparency with customers about how their data is handled.

What to Include in Your Privacy Policies:

1. **Data Collection and Use**:
   - Clearly explain what data you collect, why you collect it, and how you use it. Make sure this aligns with **GDPR's transparency** requirements.
2. **User Rights**:
   - Include how users can exercise their **data rights**, including their ability to **access, delete**, or **opt-out** of data collection (required by **GDPR** and **CCPA**).
3. **Cookies and Tracking**:
   - If you use cookies or other tracking technologies, disclose this and explain how users can manage their cookie preferences (a key aspect of **GDPR** and **CCPA**).
4. **Data Sharing and Third-Party Vendors**:
   - Be transparent about how and when you share data with third parties and ensure that your partners are compliant with **data protection laws**.
5. **Breach Notification**:
   - Outline the steps your business will take in the event of a data breach and how you will notify affected individuals, as required by **GDPR**.

Why It's Important:

Having clear, transparent policies not only keeps your customers informed but also helps your business comply with **legal obligations**. Up-to-date policies build trust with your customers and demonstrate your commitment to privacy.

Step 5: Train Employees on Compliance Practices

Achieving compliance is not just about technology; it's about creating a **culture of security** within your business. Your employees must understand how to handle data securely, recognize potential security threats, and understand their role in maintaining compliance.

Key Topics for Employee Training:

1. **Data Handling Procedures**:
   o Train employees on how to handle sensitive data securely, including how to store, transmit, and dispose of data properly.
2. **Phishing and Social Engineering**:
   o Teach employees how to identify phishing emails and social engineering tactics that could compromise data security.
3. **Incident Reporting**:
   o Ensure employees understand the importance of reporting suspicious activity, including potential breaches or security incidents.
4. **GDPR and CCPA Rights**:
   o Employees should be familiar with the data rights of customers and how to handle requests for data access, correction, or deletion.

Why It's Important:

Educating your employees ensures they are not the weak link in your security chain. Proper training empowers them to act in compliance with the regulations and helps prevent inadvertent mistakes that could lead to breaches.

Step 6: Regularly Monitor and Audit Compliance

Compliance is an ongoing effort, not a one-time event. You must continually monitor your systems, policies, and data handling practices to ensure that they remain aligned with **GDPR**, **CCPA**, and **PCI-DSS**.

Key Monitoring Activities:

1. **Regular Audits**:
    - Conduct periodic **data security audits** to evaluate your compliance. These audits should assess access controls, encryption practices, and data storage methods.
2. **Vulnerability Scanning**:
    - Implement automated vulnerability scanning tools to identify any weaknesses in your systems that could expose data.
3. **Compliance Reports**:
    - Generate compliance reports for internal purposes and external audits. This ensures transparency and helps identify areas where improvements are needed.
4. **Continuous Risk Assessment**:
    - Assess new risks as your business grows and changes. For example, new third-party integrations may require adjustments to your compliance measures.

Why It's Important:

Regular monitoring and auditing allow you to stay ahead of evolving threats, regulatory changes, and potential vulnerabilities. It also helps ensure your compliance practices remain up to date.

Case Study: Small E-commerce Store Achieves CCPA and PCI-DSS Compliance

The Challenge:

An e-commerce store that sold products to California residents faced the challenge of becoming compliant with both **CCPA** and **PCI-DSS**. The store processed payments and collected personal information but had not previously implemented structured compliance processes.

The Solution:

1. **CCPA Compliance**:
   - The store updated its **privacy policy** to include consumer rights under **CCPA**, such as the right to access, delete, and opt-out of data sales.
   - They integrated a **clear opt-out mechanism** on their website for customers who wanted to stop their data from being sold.
2. **PCI-DSS Compliance**:
   - The store partnered with **Stripe** for secure payment processing, ensuring that all credit card data was handled according to PCI-DSS standards.
   - They implemented **SSL encryption** on the checkout pages to protect payment information during transmission.
3. **Employee Training**:
   - The store provided training to employees on how to handle customer data securely and recognize potential phishing attempts.

The Outcome:

The store successfully achieved both **CCPA** and **PCI-DSS** compliance, avoiding potential fines and building customer trust. Customers felt confident knowing their data was protected, and the business was able to continue operating in California without legal concerns.

Flowchart: Steps for Achieving Compliance

```
                    Start
                      |
                      V
          [Identify Relevant Regulations]
                      |
                      V
```

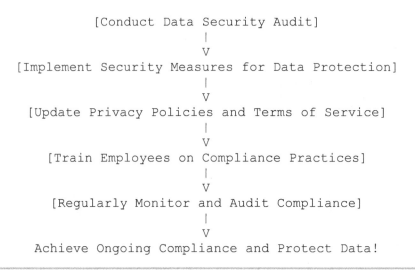

```
        [Conduct Data Security Audit]
                     |
                     V
   [Implement Security Measures for Data Protection]
                     |
                     V
     [Update Privacy Policies and Terms of Service]
                     |
                     V
       [Train Employees on Compliance Practices]
                     |
                     V
        [Regularly Monitor and Audit Compliance]
                     |
                     V
      Achieve Ongoing Compliance and Protect Data!
```

Achieving compliance with **cybersecurity regulations** like **GDPR**, **CCPA**, and **PCI-DSS** is a structured, ongoing process that requires careful planning, continuous monitoring, and employee engagement. By following these steps—understanding which regulations apply to your business, conducting data audits, implementing security measures, and training your employees—you'll be well-equipped to ensure your business is compliant and secure.

8.3: Avoiding Penalties and Legal Consequences

In today's data-driven world, businesses face mounting pressure to protect sensitive data and adhere to various regulatory standards. **Failure to comply** with laws such as **GDPR, CCPA**, and **PCI-DSS** can result in significant **penalties**, **reputational damage**, and **legal consequences**. The stakes are high, and it is crucial for businesses to not only understand these regulations but also to implement effective strategies to avoid violations.

In this chapter, we will explore the steps that businesses can take to avoid penalties and legal repercussions. We'll cover practical strategies for ensuring compliance, implementing risk mitigation measures, and responding effectively to any violations. Through actionable advice and case studies, this guide will help you understand how to protect your business from unnecessary legal issues.

Why Penalties and Legal Consequences Matter

Compliance with data protection regulations is not optional. The penalties for non-compliance can be severe, ranging from financial fines to legal action from customers, business partners, or regulatory authorities. Understanding the potential consequences is essential for motivating proactive efforts to ensure compliance.

Types of Legal Consequences Businesses Face:

1. **Financial Penalties**:
   Many regulations impose hefty fines for non-compliance. For example:
   - **GDPR**: Fines can be up to **€20 million** or **4% of global annual revenue**, whichever is greater.
   - **CCPA**: Fines for non-compliance can range from **$2,500** per violation to **$7,500** for intentional violations.
   - **PCI-DSS**: Businesses may face **fines** and **loss of payment processing privileges** if they fail to comply.
2. **Reputation Damage**:
   A data breach or failure to comply with regulations can severely damage your brand's reputation. Loss of customer trust can result in lost business, especially in industries where privacy is paramount.
3. **Legal Action from Consumers**:
   In some cases, consumers may have the right to sue businesses for violating their privacy rights. **CCPA** and **GDPR** allow for private lawsuits if consumer rights are not respected.
4. **Loss of Business**:
   Regulatory bodies can restrict or revoke your ability to process payments (in the case of **PCI-DSS**), or even shut down your business if compliance is not achieved. Regulatory penalties often carry long-lasting effects.

Understanding these consequences underscores the urgency of compliance. It's not just about avoiding fines—it's about protecting your customers, business partners, and brand from long-term harm.

Step 1: Stay Up-to-Date with Regulatory Changes

Cybersecurity regulations are constantly evolving as new threats emerge and privacy concerns grow. To avoid penalties, businesses must stay informed about changes to relevant laws and adapt their compliance efforts accordingly.

How to Implement This Step:

1. **Regularly Review Regulations**:
   - **Subscribe to newsletters** from regulatory bodies (e.g., **EU GDPR** updates, **CCPA amendments**).
   - Monitor the **official websites** of relevant regulatory authorities, such as the **European Commission** for GDPR or the **California Attorney General's Office** for CCPA.
2. **Engage Legal Experts**:
   - Work with **legal advisors** specializing in data privacy laws to keep up with regulatory changes and ensure your policies and practices remain compliant.
3. **Use Compliance Tools**:
   - Leverage **regulatory technology (RegTech)** solutions that track compliance changes and help you stay ahead of new requirements.

Why It's Important:

Staying up to date ensures your business adapts quickly to new requirements, avoiding **retroactive fines** and **penalties** that could arise from outdated policies.

Step 2: Implement Strong Data Protection Practices

Implementing effective data protection measures is the core of regulatory compliance. Not only does it reduce the risk of data breaches, but it also strengthens your defense against potential legal actions or penalties.

Key Data Protection Practices:

1. **Data Encryption**:
   - **Encrypt** sensitive data at both **rest** and **in transit**. This is required by **GDPR** and **PCI-DSS**, and it mitigates the risks associated with data breaches.
   - Use **AES-256** encryption for data at rest and **SSL/TLS** for data in transit to protect consumer and payment data.
2. **Access Control**:
   - Implement **role-based access control (RBAC)** to ensure that only authorized employees can access sensitive data. This reduces the risk of internal data breaches.
   - Enforce **multi-factor authentication (MFA)** for access to systems containing personal or payment data.
3. **Data Minimization**:
   - Follow the principle of **data minimization**, which means collecting only the **data you need** to perform your business functions.
   - Regularly review your data collection practices to ensure compliance with **GDPR's data minimization requirements**.
4. **Backup and Recovery Plans**:
   - Ensure your business has a solid **data backup and recovery plan** in place. In case of a breach, the ability to restore data quickly reduces the potential damage.
5. **Vulnerability Scanning and Penetration Testing**:
   - Regularly scan your systems for vulnerabilities and conduct **penetration tests** to identify potential weaknesses in your data protection measures.

How to Implement This Step:

- **Establish Data Protection Policies**: Draft clear policies on how sensitive data is handled and ensure that all employees are trained to follow them.

- **Use Automated Tools**: Implement automated monitoring and scanning tools that can detect and alert you about potential security issues in real time.

Why It's Important:

Effective data protection not only minimizes the risk of breaches but also demonstrates your business's commitment to **security** and **compliance**. If your data protection practices align with regulatory standards, you're less likely to face penalties.

Step 3: Educate Employees and Contractors

Employee error is one of the leading causes of data breaches and non-compliance violations. Training your staff on compliance requirements and data protection best practices is essential for avoiding penalties.

Key Areas for Employee Training:

1. **Data Privacy Laws and Regulations**:
   - Ensure employees understand the implications of **GDPR**, **CCPA**, and **PCI-DSS** and the rights of consumers regarding their data.
2. **Phishing Awareness**:
   - Educate employees on how to recognize phishing attempts and avoid inadvertently exposing sensitive data to malicious actors.
3. **Handling Data Securely**:
   - Train employees on the proper methods of storing, transferring, and accessing sensitive data. Ensure they understand the importance of following **company policies** on data protection.
4. **Incident Reporting**:
   - Implement procedures for reporting suspected breaches or security incidents and ensure employees know how to act quickly if an incident occurs.

How to Implement This Step:

- **Regular Training**: Provide quarterly or biannual compliance training sessions to keep employees updated on the latest security and compliance best practices.
- **Simulated Phishing Tests**: Conduct simulated phishing attacks to test your employees' ability to spot and avoid fraudulent attempts.

Why It's Important:

Informed employees are your first line of defense against cyber threats and compliance violations. By ensuring everyone understands the importance of data protection, you reduce the risk of human error leading to penalties or breaches.

Step 4: Develop an Incident Response Plan

In the event of a **data breach**, how your business responds is crucial. Having an effective **incident response plan (IRP)** can help mitigate the damage and demonstrate to regulators that your business takes data protection seriously.

Key Elements of an Incident Response Plan:

1. **Immediate Action**:
   - Identify the breach and contain it. This might involve disconnecting affected systems from the network, patching vulnerabilities, or freezing compromised accounts.
2. **Breach Notification**:
   - Notify affected individuals promptly. Under **GDPR**, businesses must report breaches to the relevant authority within **72 hours**.
   - For **CCPA**, you must notify California residents if their data is exposed.
3. **Investigation and Documentation**:
   - Document the breach thoroughly and investigate how it occurred. This helps with reporting and provides a clear record for future audits.

4. **Corrective Action**:
   o Identify the cause of the breach and take corrective actions to prevent it from happening again. This might include updating security protocols or providing additional employee training.

How to Implement This Step:

- **Create a Cross-Departmental Response Team**: Establish a team of key stakeholders (IT, legal, communications, etc.) responsible for managing a breach.
- **Simulate Breach Scenarios**: Conduct mock data breach exercises to ensure that everyone knows how to react quickly and effectively in case of a real breach.

Why It's Important:

Having an effective IRP not only minimizes the damage of a breach but also demonstrates compliance with regulations that require timely breach notification. Prompt and organized responses reduce potential fines and legal consequences.

Step 5: Engage Legal and Compliance Experts

If your business handles significant amounts of sensitive data or operates in multiple regions, engaging with **legal experts** and **compliance consultants** can provide essential guidance in navigating complex regulations.

Why It's Important:

Legal experts and consultants have specialized knowledge of the regulatory landscape and can help ensure your business is always compliant. They can also assist in defending against legal action in case of a breach or non-compliance issue.

How to Implement This Step:

- **Consult with Privacy Attorneys**: Work with lawyers who specialize in data privacy and cybersecurity laws to ensure your business is fully compliant.
- **Engage Compliance Consultants**: Hire consultants with expertise in **GDPR**, **CCPA**, and **PCI-DSS** to guide your compliance efforts and perform audits.

Case Study: E-commerce Platform Avoids GDPR Penalties

The Challenge:
An e-commerce platform selling digital products globally faced a potential penalty for non-compliance with **GDPR**. They had collected customer data but hadn't updated their **privacy policy** or implemented the necessary data protection measures required by GDPR.

The Solution:

1. **Conducted a Data Audit**:
   The business mapped out all personal data collection processes, identified third-party data processors, and ensured data was only retained as necessary.
2. **Implemented Data Protection Practices**:
   They encrypted all **payment card data** and **personal customer information**, and implemented **access controls** with **multi-factor authentication (MFA)**.
3. **Updated Privacy Policies**:
   The company updated their privacy policy to include GDPR-required elements, such as **data subject rights** and **cookie consent**.
4. **Trained Employees**:
   They conducted GDPR training for all employees, focusing on handling **data subject access requests** and preventing data mishandling.

5. **Incident Response Plan**:
    The company developed and tested an incident response plan to ensure fast and compliant handling of any future data breaches.

The Outcome:
By implementing these practices, the e-commerce platform successfully avoided a GDPR penalty, maintained customer trust, and continued to operate in the EU without legal issues.

Flowchart: Steps to Avoid Penalties and Legal Consequences

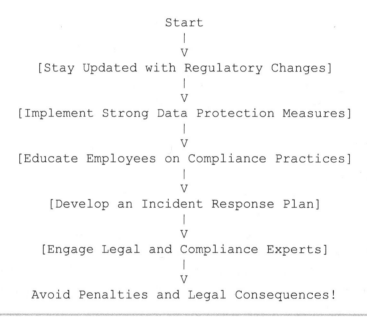

```
                        Start
                          |
                          V
         [Stay Updated with Regulatory Changes]
                          |
                          V
       [Implement Strong Data Protection Measures]
                          |
                          V
        [Educate Employees on Compliance Practices]
                          |
                          V
          [Develop an Incident Response Plan]
                          |
                          V
          [Engage Legal and Compliance Experts]
                          |
                          V
        Avoid Penalties and Legal Consequences!
```

Achieving compliance with data protection regulations and avoiding legal penalties requires a comprehensive approach. By staying informed, implementing strong security practices, educating employees, and preparing for potential incidents, your business can reduce the risk of facing penalties. The steps outlined in this chapter provide a roadmap for ensuring compliance, protecting your customers, and safeguarding your business's future.

Part 3: Creating Cybersecurity Policies and Emergency Plans (Advanced Level)

Chapter 9: Developing Cybersecurity Policies for Your Business

As cyber threats evolve, it is essential for businesses to establish clear and effective **cybersecurity policies**. These policies serve as the foundation for how a business protects its sensitive data, systems, and infrastructure. Without well-defined cybersecurity policies, even the most advanced security measures can be ineffective. Policies create a roadmap for protecting assets, establishing protocols for handling data securely, and providing a framework for employees to follow.

In this chapter, we will explore how to develop **cybersecurity policies tailored to your business**, the **key areas to address**, and how to **enforce** these policies to ensure a secure work environment. Whether you're a small business or a larger organization, establishing strong cybersecurity policies is essential for safeguarding your business from cyber risks.

9.1: Writing Cybersecurity Policies Tailored to Your Business

In the digital age, every business—regardless of size—needs a **cybersecurity policy** to protect its data, systems, and operations from threats. Cybersecurity policies are more than just technical measures; they are comprehensive guidelines that help employees understand their role in safeguarding company assets. However, one of the most common mistakes businesses make is adopting generic cybersecurity policies that don't align with their unique operational needs or risks.

In this section, we'll walk you through the process of writing cybersecurity policies **tailored to your business**. This approach will ensure that the policies are practical, relevant, and easy to implement.

Whether you're a small startup or a large corporation, crafting tailored policies is crucial for achieving strong security and compliance.

Step 1: Understand Your Business Needs and Risks

The first step in writing a tailored cybersecurity policy is understanding **your business's unique needs** and **security risks**. Every business operates in different environments, handles different types of data, and faces distinct threats. Writing a generic policy without considering these factors can result in ineffective or irrelevant guidelines.

Key Considerations When Assessing Your Business:

1. **What Type of Data Do You Handle?**
   - Personal data (names, addresses, email, etc.)
   - Payment information (credit card numbers, bank account details)
   - Intellectual property (trade secrets, designs, software code)
   - Health-related information (for healthcare businesses)
2. **Who Has Access to Data?**
   - Do you have a small team with limited access to sensitive data, or a large team with a variety of permissions and roles?
   - Are employees working remotely or on-site? The risks associated with **remote access** will differ from those in an office setting.
3. **What Are the Legal and Regulatory Requirements?**
   - **GDPR, CCPA**, and **PCI-DSS** may apply to your business if you process personal data, interact with California residents, or handle credit card information, respectively. Regulatory requirements will influence your policies and procedures.
4. **What Are the Common Security Threats in Your Industry?**
   - Businesses in **e-commerce** are particularly vulnerable to **payment fraud** and **phishing** attacks.
   - **Healthcare providers** need to protect patient data under **HIPAA** regulations and avoid **ransomware** attacks.
   - **Financial services** firms must secure **confidential financial data** and comply with **SOX** or **GDPR** standards.

Example: Tailoring for an E-Commerce Business

For an e-commerce business, your cybersecurity policy must prioritize the security of payment data, user accounts, and product inventory systems. You must also address vulnerabilities related to **online payment gateways** and **customer data protection** under **PCI-DSS**.

Step 2: Define Clear Objectives for Your Policy

Once you understand the specific risks your business faces, you can begin defining the **objectives** of your cybersecurity policy. Your policy should clearly outline the specific goals you want to achieve, which might include:

1. **Protecting Sensitive Data**: Safeguard **personal data**, **customer payment information**, and **intellectual property** from unauthorized access or breaches.
2. **Establishing Secure Access Control**: Ensure only authorized individuals have access to sensitive data and systems by defining access rights and permissions.
3. **Ensuring Business Continuity**: Mitigate the risk of **data loss** or **downtime** through regular backups, disaster recovery, and incident response plans.
4. **Promoting Security Awareness**: Educate employees about **safe computing practices**, including how to recognize phishing attempts, use strong passwords, and report suspicious activity.
5. **Compliance with Laws and Regulations**: Ensure your business meets the requirements of relevant data protection laws like **GDPR**, **CCPA**, and **PCI-DSS**.

Step 3: Develop the Key Sections of the Cybersecurity Policy

Cybersecurity policies should be comprehensive but easy to follow. Below are the key sections you should include in your tailored policy, along with practical guidance on how to implement each one:

1. Data Protection and Privacy

This section outlines how personal and sensitive data should be handled, stored, and protected.

- **Data Classification**: Define the types of data (e.g., personal, financial, confidential) and specify how each category should be handled.
- **Data Encryption**: Mandate **encryption** for all sensitive data, both in transit and at rest. This is especially important for **payment information** and **customer details**.
- **Data Access and Handling**: Establish guidelines for who can access sensitive data and the procedures they must follow. Implement **role-based access control (RBAC)**.

Practical Implementation:

- Use **full-disk encryption** for devices storing sensitive data.
- Implement **two-factor authentication (2FA)** for systems where sensitive data is accessed.

2. Password Management

Password policies are essential for protecting accounts and systems from unauthorized access.

- **Strong Password Guidelines**: Require complex passwords (e.g., minimum of 12 characters with a mix of uppercase, lowercase, numbers, and special characters).
- **Password Storage**: Implement **password managers** for secure password storage, and prohibit storing passwords in plaintext or unencrypted files.
- **Password Expiry and Reset**: Enforce **periodic password changes** and ensure a clear process for resetting compromised passwords.

Practical Implementation:

- Use a password manager like **LastPass** or **1Password** to store and generate secure passwords.
- Require password changes every 90 days for critical systems.

3. Remote Work and Access

With the rise of remote work, it's critical to define how employees should access company systems when working outside the office.

- **VPN Access**: Require all remote workers to use a **Virtual Private Network (VPN)** to encrypt their internet traffic.
- **Device Security**: Specify security measures for **personal devices** (BYOD policies), including encryption, antivirus software, and password protection.
- **Remote Work Protocols**: Define rules for handling **company data** remotely, including file-sharing guidelines and how to securely access company systems.

Practical Implementation:

- Use **VPN solutions** like **NordVPN** or **Cisco AnyConnect** to secure remote connections.
- Require the use of **Mobile Device Management (MDM)** tools to enforce security on remote devices.

4. Incident Response and Reporting

Having a clear plan for handling cybersecurity incidents is vital for minimizing damage.

- **Incident Reporting**: Establish a process for reporting security incidents, including data breaches, unauthorized access, and suspicious activity.
- **Incident Response Plan**: Create an actionable plan for containing, investigating, and recovering from security incidents. This should include clear communication protocols and roles.
- **Root Cause Analysis**: After an incident, conduct a thorough investigation to identify the root cause and take steps to prevent future occurrences.

Practical Implementation:

- Implement an automated **incident response tool** like **PagerDuty** to monitor for security incidents.

- Conduct quarterly **tabletop exercises** to simulate security breaches and practice response procedures.

5. *Employee Training and Awareness*

Security policies are only effective if employees understand and follow them. This section outlines how to train employees to adhere to the cybersecurity policies.

- **Security Awareness Training**: Regularly provide training on topics like **password hygiene**, **phishing detection**, and **data handling procedures**.
- **Simulated Phishing Tests**: Run periodic **phishing simulations** to test employees' ability to recognize malicious emails.
- **Ongoing Education**: Keep employees updated on emerging cybersecurity threats and best practices through regular newsletters or meetings.

Practical Implementation:

- Use platforms like **KnowBe4** or **Cofense** to conduct phishing simulations and security training.
- Hold **quarterly security refresher courses** to reinforce good security habits.

Step 4: Create Clear Enforcement Procedures

Your cybersecurity policy must have clear enforcement mechanisms to ensure compliance. Without enforcement, policies will be ineffective.

How to Enforce Your Cybersecurity Policies:

1. **Monitor Compliance**: Use monitoring tools to track adherence to policies, such as password strength, VPN usage, and encryption practices.
2. **Audit and Review**: Conduct regular audits to ensure that policies are being followed and that systems remain secure.

3. **Disciplinary Actions**: Clearly outline consequences for non-compliance, including formal warnings, retraining, or termination in severe cases.

Practical Implementation:

- Implement **security monitoring tools** like **Splunk** or **Darktrace** to track user activity and detect violations.
- Review and update policies annually to account for new technologies or emerging threats.

Case Study: E-Commerce Business Writes Tailored Cybersecurity Policies

The Challenge:
An e-commerce business processing credit card transactions and handling customer data was struggling with unclear cybersecurity policies. Employees were not adhering to data protection best practices, and there were gaps in their incident response protocols.

The Solution:

1. **Conducted a Business Risk Assessment**:
   The company assessed its specific risks, including potential **data breaches** and **payment fraud**, and tailored its policy to address these concerns.
2. **Updated Data Protection Measures**:
   They implemented encryption for both **customer payment data** and **personal information**, ensuring compliance with **PCI-DSS** and **GDPR**.
3. **Defined Password Management Procedures**:
   The business required strong passwords, enforced **multi-factor authentication (MFA)** for all employee accounts, and set up a password manager to store credentials securely.
4. **Developed Remote Work Policies**:
   The company established a policy for remote work that included **VPN usage**, **device encryption**, and guidelines for handling customer data from home.

5. **Ongoing Employee Training**:
   The company set up regular **security training** sessions for all employees, including simulated phishing exercises and a mandatory annual review of their cybersecurity policies.

The Outcome:
After implementing these tailored policies, the

business saw a **reduction in data security incidents**, improved **employee adherence to security protocols**, and achieved better overall **compliance with PCI-DSS** and **GDPR**.

Flowchart: Steps for Writing Tailored Cybersecurity Policies

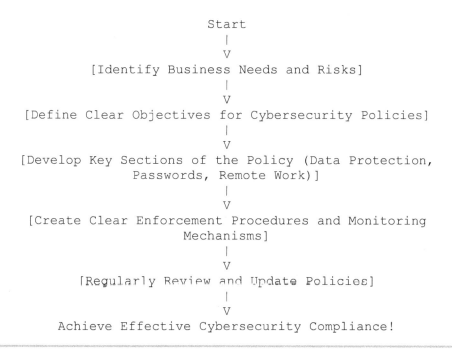

```
                        Start
                          |
                          V
            [Identify Business Needs and Risks]
                          |
                          V
        [Define Clear Objectives for Cybersecurity Policies]
                          |
                          V
        [Develop Key Sections of the Policy (Data Protection,
                  Passwords, Remote Work)]
                          |
                          V
        [Create Clear Enforcement Procedures and Monitoring
                       Mechanisms]
                          |
                          V
            [Regularly Review and Update Policies]
                          |
                          V
        Achieve Effective Cybersecurity Compliance!
```

Writing a tailored cybersecurity policy is essential for protecting your business from cyber threats, ensuring compliance with relevant regulations, and fostering a culture of security within your organization. By understanding your unique risks, defining clear objectives, and implementing enforceable practices, you can create a policy that not only protects your assets but also empowers your employees to work securely.

9.2: Key Areas for Policy Development (Password Management, Remote Work)

When creating a comprehensive **cybersecurity policy**, two areas demand particular attention: **Password Management** and **Remote Work**. These are not just technical requirements; they are foundational components that ensure the security of your business. A poor approach to managing passwords or remote access can lead to security breaches, making it critical for businesses to have clear, enforceable policies in place.

In this section, we will dive deep into **password management** and **remote work** policies, offering detailed guidance, practical implementations, and real-world insights. This will help you craft policies that not only protect your organization but are also clear, actionable, and easy for employees to follow.

Password Management Policies:

Passwords are the most common entry point for cybercriminals. They act as the first line of defense against unauthorized access to your systems and data. Strong password management is a cornerstone of any cybersecurity policy, yet many businesses neglect this aspect or set weak, ineffective guidelines.

Why Password Management is Critical:

1. **Weak Passwords Are Easy Targets**:
   Simple passwords or default credentials (e.g., "password123") are easily cracked through **brute force** or **dictionary attacks**. Cybercriminals often exploit weak passwords to gain access to company systems.

2. **Reusing Passwords Increases Risk**:
   Employees who reuse passwords across multiple systems increase the risk of a breach. Once a hacker gains access to one account, they can often use the same password to access others.
3. **Multi-Factor Authentication (MFA) Is a Necessity**:
   Passwords alone aren't enough to secure sensitive data. Adding a second layer of security, like **MFA**, helps to ensure that even if a password is compromised, the attacker cannot easily gain access.

Key Components of a Password Management Policy:

1. **Password Creation Rules**:
   o Require passwords to meet **complexity requirements**. A good password should include at least:
     ▪ 12 characters
     ▪ A mix of **uppercase and lowercase letters, numbers**, and **special characters**
     ▪ Avoiding easily guessed words, such as company names, personal names, or common phrases.
   o Example: **"S7!jKm@9X2*H"** instead of **"password123"**.
2. **Password Storage Guidelines**:
   o **Prohibit storing passwords in plain text** (e.g., in documents or on sticky notes).
   o Use **password managers** (like **LastPass**, **1Password**, or **Dashlane**) to store passwords securely and generate strong passwords for each account.
3. **Password Expiry and Rotation**:
   o Enforce **periodic password changes**, such as every **90 days**, especially for accounts with access to sensitive data.
   o However, avoid overly frequent changes that encourage weak, easily memorable passwords. Allow password changes only when necessary, such as after a security incident.
4. **Multi-Factor Authentication (MFA)**:
   o Require **MFA** for all **critical accounts**, including email, internal systems, and cloud platforms. MFA adds an additional layer of security beyond passwords, such as:
     ▪ SMS codes
     ▪ Authenticator apps (e.g., **Google Authenticator**)
     ▪ Biometrics (e.g., fingerprints or facial recognition)
5. **Access Control and Password Sharing**:

- Prohibit **password sharing**. Employees should never share passwords with coworkers, even if they are on the same team. If collaboration requires shared access, use secure tools like **shared password managers**.
- Implement **role-based access control (RBAC)** to ensure employees can only access systems and data that are necessary for their roles.

6. **Employee Training and Awareness**:
   - Regularly **educate employees** on the importance of password security, including how to identify phishing attempts that may compromise login credentials.
   - Include password management as part of your **cybersecurity training** for new hires and during ongoing employee education.

Practical Implementation Example:

A small business that handles financial data implemented the following:

- They required **12-character passwords** with a mix of letters, numbers, and symbols.
- They deployed **LastPass** as the company-wide password manager to store all login credentials securely.
- All employees were **enrolled in MFA** for accessing internal systems.
- A company-wide training session was conducted to reinforce password policies and educate staff on recognizing phishing attacks.

Outcome:
After implementing the new password management policy, the business experienced **fewer incidents of phishing attacks** and **stronger protection** for its financial data. Employees were more confident in their security practices, and the company reduced its risk of data breaches.

Remote Work Policies:

The rise of remote work has introduced new security challenges for businesses. Employees working outside the office often use **personal** devices, **public Wi-Fi**, and **unsecured home networks**, which increase the likelihood of security breaches. Having a clear and structured **remote work policy** is essential to protect both company data and employees.

Why Remote Work Policies Are Essential:

1. **Increased Exposure to Cyber Threats**:
   Remote workers frequently access business systems over **unsecured Wi-Fi networks**. Cybercriminals can exploit these networks to intercept data or launch attacks on company systems.
2. **Device Security Challenges**:
   Employees working remotely may use personal devices, such as laptops or smartphones, that do not have the same level of security controls as company-issued devices.
3. **Data Protection and Compliance**:
   When employees access sensitive data from outside the office, there is a greater risk of data exposure or loss, especially if data is being stored locally on devices.

Key Components of a Remote Work Policy:

1. **VPN Requirement**:
   - Require employees to use a **Virtual Private Network (VPN)** when accessing company systems remotely. VPNs encrypt internet traffic, protecting data from being intercepted on public or unsecured networks.
   - Consider providing employees with a **company-approved VPN solution**, such as **NordVPN** or **Cisco AnyConnect**.
2. **Device Security**:
   - If employees use personal devices (BYOD—Bring Your Own Device), establish clear guidelines on how these devices should be secured. This includes **password protection, antivirus software**, and **device encryption**.
   - If possible, issue **company-approved devices** that are pre-configured with necessary security measures, such as **firewalls, antivirus**, and **disk encryption**.
3. **Access Control**:
   - Use **role-based access control (RBAC)** to limit access to sensitive data based on the employee's role. Ensure that employees can only access the data they need to do their job.

- o Require **multi-factor authentication (MFA)** for remote access to ensure that only authorized employees can access company systems.
4. **Data Encryption**:
   - o Require that all data stored on remote devices be **encrypted**, especially for sensitive information like customer data, financial records, and intellectual property.
   - o Use **cloud-based storage** solutions with built-in encryption (e.g., **Google Drive**, **Microsoft OneDrive**) for document sharing and collaboration.
5. **Security Awareness Training**:
   - o Remote workers should undergo **cybersecurity training** to recognize common threats like **phishing emails**, **malware**, and **social engineering** attacks.
   - o Encourage employees to regularly update software on their devices and use strong, unique passwords for every application or service.
6. **Incident Reporting**:
   - o Establish clear **incident reporting protocols** for remote workers. Ensure that employees know what to do in the event of a suspected security breach or lost/stolen device.
   - o Set up a dedicated team or service desk for **24/7 support** to help remote workers address potential security incidents.

Practical Implementation Example:

A medium-sized software development company with a remote workforce implemented the following:

- All remote workers were **required to use a company-approved VPN** (with **Cisco AnyConnect**) for secure internet access.
- Employees working from home had to **use company-issued laptops** with **encrypted hard drives** and **anti-malware software** installed.
- They implemented **RBAC** for access to their development platforms, ensuring that only developers working on specific projects could access related files and repositories.
- They established a **clear reporting mechanism** for any cybersecurity incidents, with a response team available for emergencies.

Outcome:
The company saw a **reduction in security breaches** and **improved compliance** with data protection regulations like **GDPR**. Remote workers were able to collaborate securely, and the company's data remained protected, even when employees worked from different locations.

Case Study: Protecting a Law Firm with Password Management and Remote Work Policies

The Challenge:
A small law firm experienced difficulty protecting sensitive client information due to inconsistent password practices and unsecured remote access. Lawyers and administrative staff were frequently accessing client files from home or cafes, often using personal devices without adequate security measures.

The Solution:

1. **Password Management Policies**:
   - The firm implemented a **strong password policy** requiring all employees to use complex passwords and **multi-factor authentication (MFA)** for all cloud-based systems.
   - Employees were provided with a **password manager** to store and generate unique passwords for each application.
2. **Remote Work Security**:
   - The firm mandated the use of a **VPN** for all remote work, ensuring that all communications with clients and internal systems were encrypted.
   - They issued **company-approved devices** with **encryption, antivirus protection**, and **firewall settings** for remote workers.
3. **Employee Training**:
   - The firm conducted regular **cybersecurity training** sessions to educate employees on safe practices when working remotely, including **how to spot phishing emails** and **secure personal devices**.

The Outcome:
The law firm significantly reduced its risk of a data breach, and clients

became more confident in the firm's ability to protect their sensitive information. The firm's cybersecurity posture improved, leading to **greater client trust** and **compliance** with legal data protection standards.

Flowchart: Key Areas for Policy Development

```
                            Start
                              |
                              V
        [Identify Key Areas for Cybersecurity Policies]
                              |
                              V
            [Develop Password Management Policy]
                              |
                              V
            [Develop Remote Work Security Policy]
                              |
                              V
            [Implement Access Control Measures]
                              |
                              V
        [Enforce Multi-Factor Authentication (MFA)]
                              |
                              V
          [Regularly Update and Monitor Policies]
                              |
                              V
            Achieve Strong Cybersecurity Posture!
```

Developing effective **password management** and **remote work** policies is essential to securing your business and its data. By addressing the specific needs and risks associated with **passwords** and **remote work**, you can significantly reduce the chances of security breaches. With the right policies in place, you ensure that both employees and business data are protected, leading to a more resilient and secure organization.

9.3: Enforcing Cybersecurity Policies in Your Business

Developing effective **cybersecurity policies** is essential, but they are only as effective as their enforcement. Without proper enforcement, even the most robust policies can be ignored, leading to potential vulnerabilities and risks for your business. Cybersecurity policies must be clear, actionable, and, most importantly, **enforceable** to ensure they achieve the desired outcome—protecting your business's data, assets, and reputation.

This section will walk you through the key steps for **enforcing cybersecurity policies** in your business. From creating a **culture of security** to implementing **monitoring systems** and enforcing consequences for non-compliance, you'll gain the knowledge necessary to ensure your policies are followed and your business remains secure.

Why Enforcing Cybersecurity Policies Is Crucial

Cybersecurity threats are constantly evolving, and it's not enough to simply have policies in place. Employees and contractors must understand the **importance of these policies** and follow them diligently. Inconsistent enforcement leads to **gaps in security** and **non-compliance**, leaving your business vulnerable to attacks and regulatory penalties.

Key Reasons for Enforcement:

1. **Consistency**: Enforcing policies ensures that **all employees** follow the same standards and procedures, reducing the risk of security breaches.
2. **Compliance**: Many businesses are required by law to follow certain cybersecurity protocols (e.g., **GDPR, CCPA, PCI-DSS**). Non-compliance can lead to penalties or legal consequences.
3. **Employee Accountability**: Clear enforcement communicates that **cybersecurity is a shared responsibility**—not just the IT department's responsibility. Everyone has a role in maintaining security.

Step 1: Create a Culture of Security in Your Organization

The first step in enforcing cybersecurity policies is to establish a **culture of security** within your business. Policies are more likely to be adhered to if employees understand their importance and feel a sense of responsibility toward them.

How to Create a Culture of Security:

1. **Leadership Commitment**:
   - **Set the tone** at the top. Leadership must **demonstrate a commitment to cybersecurity** by following policies themselves. When senior leaders follow security protocols, it encourages employees to do the same.
2. **Clear Communication**:
   - Communicate the purpose of the cybersecurity policies clearly to employees. Ensure they understand **why** these policies exist, **how** they protect the business, and **what** their responsibilities are.
   - Use simple, **plain language** to describe the policies so that everyone—from technical staff to non-technical employees—can understand them.
3. **Employee Involvement**:
   - Involve employees in the creation and review of cybersecurity policies. When employees have a voice in the development of the policies, they are more likely to feel a sense of ownership and follow them.
4. **Promote Cybersecurity Awareness**:
   - Provide regular **training and workshops** on security best practices, emerging threats, and the importance of data protection.
   - Use **real-world examples** of cyber incidents to demonstrate the consequences of poor security practices.
5. **Reward Compliance**:
   - Recognize and reward employees who consistently follow security protocols. **Positive reinforcement** can go a long way in maintaining a security-conscious culture.

Practical Implementation Example:

A small marketing firm noticed that employees were frequently bypassing security protocols (e.g., skipping **password changes** or using weak passwords). The company's leadership took the following actions:

- **Held monthly security meetings** with all employees to explain the importance of secure practices.
- **Implemented a reward system** for employees who adhered to the company's **password management** policies, offering small incentives like gift cards.

Outcome:
The firm saw an increase in **password strength** and **employee engagement** with the company's cybersecurity protocols, leading to a noticeable reduction in security incidents.

Step 2: Implement Monitoring and Auditing Systems

Monitoring and auditing systems allow you to track whether employees are following security policies and identify any weaknesses or breaches early. These tools help enforce policies by providing insight into employee activities, security incidents, and policy adherence.

How to Implement Monitoring and Auditing:

1. **Set Up Security Monitoring Tools**:
    o Use **intrusion detection systems (IDS), firewalls**, and **endpoint protection software** to monitor systems and network traffic for unauthorized access or suspicious activities.
    o For example, if your business uses cloud-based tools, consider using **Cloud Access Security Brokers (CASBs)** to monitor user activity across cloud applications.
2. **Track Policy Compliance**:
    o Implement tools that can track compliance with specific cybersecurity policies, such as **password changes, device encryption**, and **use of multi-factor authentication (MFA)**.
    o Use **security information and event management (SIEM)** systems to aggregate logs from different sources, analyze them in real-time, and generate alerts for non-compliance.
3. **Regular Audits**:

- o Conduct **regular internal audits** of your systems and policies. This ensures that employees are consistently following protocols and that the policies remain relevant to emerging threats.
- o For example, you might audit access logs to ensure that employees aren't accessing sensitive data outside of business hours or without the proper authentication.
4. **Incident Detection and Response**:
   - o Set up automated alerts for suspicious activity (e.g., **multiple failed login attempts, unusual access patterns**). This helps you detect incidents early and respond quickly before they escalate.

Practical Implementation Example:

A tech company implemented **automated security monitoring** using a combination of **SIEM** and **endpoint protection software**. The system alerted them whenever:

- Employees failed to follow MFA login protocols.
- Suspicious behavior was detected on the company network, such as unusual file transfers.

Outcome:
The monitoring system helped the company detect a potential data exfiltration attempt before it became a major incident, preventing data loss and securing sensitive client information.

Step 3: Enforce Consequences for Non-Compliance

While creating a positive security culture is crucial, it's also necessary to have clear and enforceable consequences for non-compliance. Employees must understand that failing to follow security protocols has real consequences, not just for the individual but for the entire organization.

How to Enforce Consequences:

1. **Define Clear Consequences**:

- Clearly outline the consequences for non-compliance with cybersecurity policies. This could range from informal warnings to more serious actions like **suspension, termination**, or **legal action**.
- Be specific: For example, failure to use MFA on sensitive systems might result in a **formal warning**, while repeated violations could lead to **termination**.

2. **Communicate the Consequences**:
    - Ensure all employees are aware of the consequences of non-compliance from day one. This can be done during the **onboarding process** and reinforced through regular training.
    - Make sure that employees understand that these policies are in place to protect both the business and its employees.

3. **Consistent Enforcement**:
    - Enforce the policies consistently. If an employee violates a policy, the consequence should apply regardless of their position in the company. **Inconsistent enforcement** can undermine the credibility of the policies.

4. **Appeal Process**:
    - Provide employees with the opportunity to appeal decisions if they feel they were unfairly penalized. Having a transparent process fosters trust and allows employees to feel that the enforcement measures are not arbitrary.

Practical Implementation Example:

A manufacturing company faced challenges in ensuring that employees adhered to the company's **device encryption policy**. They implemented the following:

- **Clear penalties** for non-compliance, such as a **warning for the first violation** and **termination** for repeated offenses.
- Employees were required to sign an acknowledgment form during their **onboarding** to confirm that they understood the device encryption policy and the penalties for not following it.

Outcome:
Compliance with the encryption policy increased, and the company saw a marked reduction in lost or stolen devices containing unprotected company data.

Step 4: Continuous Improvement and Policy Updates

Cybersecurity is an evolving field. New threats, technologies, and regulations emerge regularly, so your policies must be adaptable and updated frequently.

How to Maintain and Improve Enforcement:

1. **Regular Policy Reviews**:
   - Review your policies at least annually, or more frequently if major security incidents or changes in the business environment occur. Ensure that the policies are up-to-date with the latest regulations and best practices.
2. **Employee Feedback**:
   - Encourage employees to provide feedback on the policies. They may have insights into challenges they face in following the policies, or they may highlight areas where the policies can be improved.
3. **Track Effectiveness**:
   - Monitor the effectiveness of your enforcement mechanisms. If employees repeatedly violate certain policies, it may indicate that the policy is too complicated or unclear. In such cases, revise the policy to make it more practical.

Practical Implementation Example:

A financial services firm reviews its **cybersecurity training** materials every 6 months to incorporate new phishing trends or emerging threats. They also gather employee feedback on training sessions and adjust content based on that feedback, ensuring the training remains relevant.

Outcome:
The firm found that the updates helped employees recognize more advanced **phishing attempts**, reducing incidents of social engineering attacks.

Flowchart: Enforcing Cybersecurity Policies

```
                        Start
                          |
                          V
              [Create a Culture of Security]
                          |
                          V
      [Implement Monitoring and Auditing Systems]
                          |
                          V
        [Enforce Consequences for Non-Compliance]
                          |
                          V
          [Review and Improve Policies Regularly]
                          |
                          V
      [Achieve a Secure and Compliant Business]
```

Enforcing cybersecurity policies is crucial to maintaining the security of your business. By creating a **culture of security**, implementing **monitoring and auditing systems**, and enforcing **clear consequences** for non-compliance, you set the stage for consistent adherence to cybersecurity protocols. Additionally, continuous improvement ensures that your policies remain relevant and effective in the face of evolving threats.

Chapter 10: Incident Response Planning

In an ideal world, cybersecurity threats would be entirely preventable. However, no system is foolproof, and the reality is that every organization is at risk of a cyberattack. Whether it's a **phishing attempt**, **ransomware**, or a **data breach**, your business needs to be prepared to respond effectively. A well-structured **incident response plan (IRP)** can make all the difference between a brief disruption and a **major data breach** that damages your reputation, costs you money, and puts customer trust at risk.

This chapter will guide you through the steps of creating a robust **incident response plan**, the actions to take when a cyberattack occurs, and how to effectively communicate with stakeholders post-attack. By the end of this chapter, you'll have the tools to respond confidently to cybersecurity incidents and minimize their impact on your organization.

10.1: How to Create an Incident Response Plan

A **Cybersecurity Incident Response Plan (IRP)** is a crucial document for any business, outlining the steps to take when a cyberattack occurs. Whether it's a **data breach**, **ransomware attack**, or **phishing attempt**, having a clear, well-defined response plan ensures your business can act swiftly to minimize damage and recover quickly. But a good IRP isn't just about reacting—it's about preparation. The more detailed your plan, the better equipped your organization will be to handle an attack effectively.

In this section, we'll walk through the essential steps to create an **Incident Response Plan** tailored to your business. From **preparation** to **recovery**, we'll ensure you have the tools and knowledge to safeguard your systems and data from attacks.

Step 1: Establish Your Incident Response Team

The first key element in creating an IRP is forming an **incident response team (IRT)**. This team will be responsible for executing the plan during a security incident. The team should include individuals with expertise in various areas of the business, ensuring all aspects of the response are covered.

Who Should Be on the Incident Response Team?

1. **Incident Response Leader**:
   This person oversees the entire incident response process. They are responsible for coordinating the team's actions and ensuring the incident is handled according to the plan. Typically, this is a **CISO** (Chief Information Security Officer) or **IT manager**.

2. **IT Security Experts**:
   These are the technical specialists who will work to identify, contain, and neutralize the threat. They'll focus on system analysis, network monitoring, and ensuring that security vulnerabilities are patched.

3. **Legal and Compliance Officers**:
   They will ensure the company remains compliant with any regulations that may apply (e.g., **GDPR**, **CCPA**). In the event of a breach involving sensitive customer data, they'll guide the legal aspects, including regulatory reporting.

4. **Communications Team**:
   A **communications lead** will be responsible for internal and external communication. Clear and timely communication is crucial, both for keeping employees informed and for addressing any external stakeholders such as customers, the press, and regulators.

5. **Human Resources (HR)**:
   HR can help in managing internal issues and ensure the appropriate steps are taken with employees if the breach involves insider threats or employee negligence.

6. **Other Relevant Departments**:
   Depending on the nature of the business, other departments such as **finance, operations**, or **customer support** may be involved. These teams may help manage the financial implications of the attack or communicate with clients who may be impacted.

Practical Implementation Example:

A **tech company** set up a dedicated **incident response team** with clear roles:

- The **CISO** acted as the team leader.
- **Network engineers** focused on identifying and isolating infected systems.
- The **PR manager** worked with legal advisors to communicate with affected customers and regulatory authorities.

Outcome:
When the company faced a **phishing attack** that targeted employee credentials, the team's swift coordination helped them identify the threat, contain the breach, and notify impacted customers within hours.

Step 2: Define What Constitutes an Incident

Before jumping into actions and tools, it's important to establish **what constitutes a security incident** for your business. Not all security events need the same level of response. Defining what qualifies as an "incident" helps your team prioritize actions and resources.

Types of Incidents to Consider:

1. **Data Breach**:
   Unauthorized access or disclosure of sensitive data, such as **personal** or **financial information**.
2. **Malware Attack**:
   When systems are infected by viruses, worms, or ransomware that affect business operations.
3. **Denial of Service (DoS) Attack**:
   When systems or networks are overwhelmed with traffic to cause them to crash or become unavailable.
4. **Phishing**:
   Fraudulent attempts to obtain sensitive information (like login credentials) through fake emails or websites.

5. **Insider Threats**:
   When an employee or contractor intentionally or unintentionally causes harm to the organization's systems or data.
6. **Unauthorized Access**:
   When someone gains access to systems or data without proper authorization.

How to Define Severity:

You should also establish a way to assess the **severity** of each incident. For example:

- **Critical**: A **data breach** affecting customer payment data or proprietary information.
- **High**: A **malware infection** that spreads to critical systems
- **Medium**: A **phishing attack** that results in compromised internal credentials.
- **Low**: A **non-critical vulnerability** identified during routine security scans.

Practical Implementation Example:

A **law firm** categorized cybersecurity events as follows:

- **Critical**: Breach of client data (attorneys' documents, personal details).
- **High**: Malware infection on internal networks.
- **Medium**: Employee credentials compromised via phishing.
- **Low**: Failed login attempts that are not indicative of an attack.

Outcome:
This categorization helped the firm allocate the right resources to each incident. For example, critical incidents triggered an immediate call to the incident response team, while medium or low events were reviewed and addressed in routine audits.

Step 3: Document Incident Response Procedures

Once your team is in place and you've defined what constitutes an incident, it's time to map out your **incident response procedures**. The procedures should be step-by-step guides that explain exactly what to do at each stage of an incident.

Key Phases of Incident Response:

1. **Preparation**:
   - Train staff on how to recognize and report incidents. Ensure that all employees know who to contact if they detect a potential security incident.
   - Set up the necessary tools, such as **firewalls, intrusion detection systems**, and **encryption**.
   - Establish an **incident response communication channel** to avoid confusion during an attack.
2. **Identification**:
   - Detail how incidents will be detected. Include which monitoring systems and tools will be used to identify unusual network activity, unauthorized access, or malware.
   - Define a **triage process** to prioritize incidents based on severity and potential impact.
3. **Containment**:
   - Outline steps for containing the incident, such as isolating affected systems, cutting off network access, or disabling compromised accounts.
   - Establish **short-term containment** actions (immediate response) and **long-term containment** measures (to stop the attack from spreading).
4. **Eradication**:
   - Define how the root cause of the incident will be removed from systems. This could include removing malware, deleting compromised files, or disabling affected services.
5. **Recovery**:
   - Set procedures for recovering from the incident, including restoring data from backups, rebuilding systems, or reinstalling software.
   - Monitor the systems post-recovery to ensure that the incident does not resurface.
6. **Lessons Learned**:
   - After the incident, conduct a **post-mortem** review to identify what went wrong, what went right, and how to

improve future responses. Update the incident response plan based on lessons learned.

Practical Implementation Example:

A **manufacturing company** created detailed **step-by-step procedures** for each phase:

- **Identification**: Use **SIEM tools** to detect unauthorized access.
- **Containment**: Disconnect affected systems from the network and block external IP addresses.
- **Eradication**: Run antivirus and malware removal tools to remove any threats.
- **Recovery**: Restore affected systems from **backup servers** and monitor for any residual vulnerabilities.

Outcome:
When the company faced a **ransomware attack**, their predefined procedures allowed the response team to act quickly, containing the ransomware spread and recovering encrypted files from backups with minimal downtime.

Step 4: Test and Refine Your Plan

A great incident response plan is one that is **tested** and **refined** over time. An IRP is a living document—it should be reviewed and updated regularly based on feedback, emerging threats, and lessons learned from previous incidents.

How to Test Your Incident Response Plan:

1. **Conduct Tabletop Exercises**:
   o Organize **tabletop exercises** with your response team. These are simulated attack scenarios where the team discusses how to handle a hypothetical incident in a controlled environment.
   o For example, simulate a **ransomware attack** and have the team walk through containment, recovery, and communication protocols.

2. **Perform Full-Scale Drills**:
   - **Conduct simulated full-scale attacks** where the response team practices identifying, containing, and recovering from an actual incident.
   - Include the communications team to practice internal and external communications during an attack.
3. **Post-Exercise Debrief**:
   - After testing, hold a **debrief** session to discuss what went well and what needs improvement. Update your plan accordingly.

Practical Implementation Example:

A **cybersecurity firm** tested its **incident response plan** by running **phishing drills** across different departments. Employees were sent simulated phishing emails, and the IRP team monitored how quickly employees identified and reported them.

Outcome:
The exercise revealed that the firm's communication protocols needed improvement, and they updated the **reporting process** for phishing attempts, resulting in quicker responses in future incidents.

Flowchart: Steps for Creating an Incident Response Plan

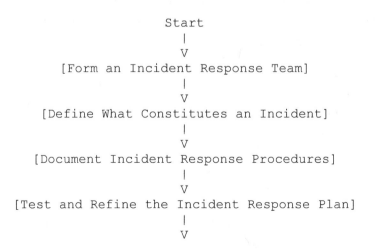

```
                        Start
                          |
                          V
              [Form an Incident Response Team]
                          |
                          V
            [Define What Constitutes an Incident]
                          |
                          V
          [Document Incident Response Procedures]
                          |
                          V
        [Test and Refine the Incident Response Plan]
                          |
                          V
```

Creating a detailed **incident response plan** (IRP) is a key part of any business's cybersecurity strategy. It ensures that when a cyberattack occurs, your team is ready to respond quickly and effectively. By preparing your team, defining incident types, documenting clear procedures, and testing your plan, you can dramatically reduce the potential impact of any security incident.

10.2: Steps to Take During a Cyberattack (Containment, Investigation, Recovery)

When a cyberattack occurs, every second counts. The difference between a successful and devastating response can often be traced to how quickly and effectively your team follows a **clear and structured** process. A solid incident response plan is crucial, but **real-time decision-making** during an attack makes all the difference.

This guide will walk you through the **critical steps** to take during a cyberattack, focusing on **containment**, **investigation**, and **recovery**. These three stages are essential in reducing damage, maintaining business continuity, and ensuring that future attacks are less likely to succeed.

By the end of this section, you will understand how to act decisively when a cyberattack occurs and how to manage the situation to minimize risk to your organization.

1. Containment: Prevent the Threat from Spreading

Containment is the first and most crucial step in managing a cyberattack. It involves stopping the attack from spreading further and mitigating its impact. This phase requires quick action and is about limiting the damage in the short term so that you can focus on investigating and recovering later.

Key Actions for Containment:

1. **Disconnect Affected Systems:**
   - **Isolate infected systems** to prevent the attack from spreading to other parts of your network. For example, in the case of **ransomware**, immediately disconnecting infected machines from the network can help stop the malware from encrypting other files or spreading to shared drives.
2. **Block Malicious Traffic:**
   - Use your firewall or intrusion detection systems (IDS) to **block malicious IP addresses** or domains associated with the attack. This will stop external communication between your network and the attackers' systems.
   - **Network segmentation** can also help limit the spread of the attack. If feasible, segmenting your network into smaller, isolated areas can reduce the scope of the attack.
3. **Disable Compromised Accounts:**
   - If the attack involves **compromised user credentials** (e.g., in a **phishing** or **password attack**), disable the affected user accounts and force password resets across all systems.
   - Use **multi-factor authentication (MFA)** to protect sensitive systems while you assess the extent of the breach.
4. **Activate Incident Response Systems:**
   - Activate any relevant **incident response tools** and alert your **response team**. This may include monitoring tools, backup systems, or software that helps with containment.

Practical Example:

A **global retail company** was hit with a **ransomware attack**. The response team took the following steps:

- **Immediately isolated the affected servers** to stop the ransomware from encrypting more files.
- Blocked **malicious IPs** that the ransomware was trying to communicate with to exfiltrate data.
- **Disabled** compromised user accounts that had been used to distribute the malware.

Outcome:
By isolating affected systems and blocking malicious communication early, the company minimized the ransomware's spread to other systems and limited damage to critical data.

---

2. Investigation: Understand the Scope and Source of the Attack

Once the immediate threat is contained, the next step is **investigation**. This stage focuses on understanding **how** the attack happened, **what systems** were affected, and **what data** might have been compromised. The goal is to identify the attack vector, assess the full scope of damage, and prepare for recovery.

Key Actions for Investigation:

1. **Analyze Logs and Alerts:**
   o   Review system logs, **security information and event management (SIEM)** tools, and intrusion detection alerts. Look for suspicious activity that could indicate the **attack vector** (e.g., unauthorized login attempts, unusual file transfers, etc.).
   o   For example, if a **phishing attack** occurred, check for **unusual email patterns**, such as phishing emails sent to many employees or opened attachments containing malware.
2. **Identify the Attack Vector:**
   o   Determine how the attackers gained access to your systems. Was it through **phishing**, a **vulnerable application**, a **brute-force attack**, or **insider threats**?
   o   Track the attacker's path through your network by investigating lateral movements. This can help you identify which systems or data were impacted.
3. **Assess Data Compromise:**
   o   Identify whether any sensitive data was stolen or exposed. If the breach involves **customer data** (e.g., **PII** or **payment information**), assess the severity and prepare for **regulatory reporting** (GDPR, CCPA, etc.).

o   Evaluate the **full impact** of the attack. Did the attackers modify or delete files? Was there any exfiltration of data?
4. **Containment Review:**
    o   Ensure that all containment actions were effective. Reassess systems to confirm that the threat has been fully contained and that no further damage is being done.

Practical Example:

A **hospital** experienced a **data breach** that was traced back to a **phishing email**. The investigation involved:

- Analyzing email logs to identify the phishing attempt.
- Reviewing system access logs to determine what data was accessed.
- Working with **security experts** to determine if any sensitive **patient data** had been exfiltrated.

Outcome:
The breach was contained quickly, and patient data was not compromised. However, the hospital implemented additional training for staff on phishing and reinforced its email security protocols.

---

3. Recovery: Restore Operations and Strengthen Defenses

Once the incident is understood and the threat has been contained, it's time to move into the **recovery** phase. Recovery is focused on restoring normal operations, ensuring that no threats remain, and preventing future incidents.

Key Actions for Recovery:

1. **Restore Systems from Backups:**
    o   If systems or data were **corrupted** or **lost** (as in the case of **ransomware**), restore them from **clean backups**. Ensure that the backups are not infected by malware before restoring.

o   Test the recovered systems to ensure they are functioning as expected and that they are free of malware or vulnerabilities.

2. **Patch Vulnerabilities:**
   o   If the attack exploited a **known vulnerability** in your systems (e.g., unpatched software), immediately patch the vulnerability and update your software.
   o   Conduct a thorough vulnerability scan to ensure all systems are up-to-date with the latest security patches.

3. **Reset Credentials and Revoke Access:**
   o   Reset passwords for all **compromised accounts** and enforce **multi-factor authentication** (MFA) on critical systems. This ensures that attackers cannot regain access using stolen credentials.
   o   Review access permissions and ensure that employees only have access to the systems and data necessary for their roles.

4. **Monitor Systems for Re-infection:**
   o   Continue to monitor your network for signs of residual malware or ongoing attack activity. Implement **continuous monitoring** for any suspicious activity or potential re-infection.
   o   Regularly run **security scans** to verify that all systems are clean.

5. **Restore Public Trust:**
   o   If sensitive customer data was impacted, **notify affected individuals** and offer credit monitoring or identity theft protection services, as required by relevant regulations (e.g., **GDPR, CCPA**).
   o   If the attack was publicly reported, issue a **press release** or statement detailing what happened, what was done to resolve the issue, and what steps are being taken to prevent future incidents.

Practical Example:

After a **ransomware attack** at a **manufacturing company**, the team took the following recovery steps:

- **Restored systems** from secure, clean backups stored offsite.

- Installed the latest **security patches** for all critical systems to close any exploited vulnerabilities.
- **Reset all passwords** across the network and enforced **multi-factor authentication** on critical systems.
- Issued a public statement and offered **identity theft protection** to customers whose data might have been impacted.

Outcome:

The company was able to restore normal operations within a few days, and customer data was protected. The company also learned valuable lessons that led to strengthening its overall cybersecurity strategy.

Flowchart: Steps to Take During a Cyberattack

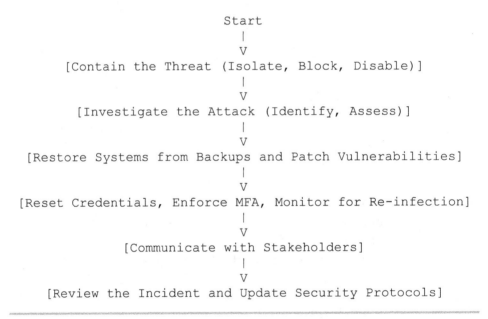

```
                          Start
                            |
                            V
        [Contain the Threat (Isolate, Block, Disable)]
                            |
                            V
          [Investigate the Attack (Identify, Assess)]
                            |
                            V
     [Restore Systems from Backups and Patch Vulnerabilities]
                            |
                            V
      [Reset Credentials, Enforce MFA, Monitor for Re-infection]
                            |
                            V
                [Communicate with Stakeholders]
                            |
                            V
        [Review the Incident and Update Security Protocols]
```

The steps you take during a **cyberattack** can significantly impact the outcome. **Containment, investigation**, and **recovery** are the key phases that guide your response to minimize damage and restore normal operations. By acting quickly, communicating effectively, and following a structured process, you can ensure that your business can recover from a cyberattack with minimal disruption.

10.3: Communicating with Stakeholders After a Cyberattack

Cyberattacks are stressful and disruptive, but how your business communicates during and after an attack is just as critical as how it responds to the threat itself. Effective communication can minimize reputational damage, maintain customer trust, and ensure that all stakeholders are informed and aligned throughout the recovery process. Whether it's updating **employees**, informing **customers**, or reporting to **regulatory bodies**, transparent, timely communication is key to managing a cyberattack effectively.

In this section, we will guide you through best practices for communicating with **internal stakeholders** (employees) and **external stakeholders** (customers, regulatory authorities, and the public) after a cyberattack. We'll discuss when and how to communicate, what information to include, and how to maintain a positive relationship with your stakeholders despite the breach.

1. Internal Communication: Keep Employees Informed and Aligned

Employees are the first line of defense during a cyberattack, and keeping them well-informed ensures they can follow procedures and support the recovery effort. Effective internal communication also helps maintain morale and reduces confusion or anxiety in the workplace.

Key Actions for Internal Communication:

1. **Immediate Notification:**
    o   As soon as a cyberattack is detected and confirmed, **alert employees** to the situation. Make it clear that an incident is underway and that the team is actively responding.

o   Set up a **central communication channel** (e.g., a dedicated email list, Slack channel, or internal webpage) where all relevant updates and instructions can be communicated in real-time.

Example:
A **tech company** experiencing a **ransomware attack** immediately notified all employees, including remote workers, using a secure internal messaging platform. Employees were instructed to stop accessing company systems and were given clear instructions on the next steps.

2. **Guidelines for Employee Actions:**
   o   Provide **step-by-step instructions** on what employees should do during the attack (e.g., disconnect from the network, stop using certain applications, change passwords, etc.).
   o   If the attack involves compromised data or systems, ensure that employees know **how to report suspicious activity** and what actions they need to take to protect company assets.
   o   In some cases, employees may need to temporarily change their work habits. For example, restrict email usage if the attack involves **phishing** or **malware**.
3. **Regular Updates:**
   o   Keep employees informed throughout the incident and recovery process. Provide **regular status updates**, even if there is no new information. It helps to build trust and ensures that employees stay on the same page.
   o   Update your internal communication as the situation develops, especially after containment, recovery efforts, and lessons learned.

Practical Tip:
Set a regular interval (e.g., **every 2 hours**) to update employees, even if it's just to acknowledge that the response team is still working on the incident. This prevents speculation and ensures everyone knows they're being kept in the loop.

4. **Post-Incident Debrief:**

- Once the incident is resolved, conduct a **post-mortem meeting** with all employees to discuss what happened, how it was handled, and what steps will be taken to prevent future incidents. This should include feedback on communication practices, as employees will often have valuable insights.

Example:
After a **phishing attack**, a **financial institution** gathered feedback from employees on the incident, focusing on how communication could be improved in the future. They then updated their **employee training** and **communication plan** accordingly.

2. External Communication: Engaging with Customers and the Public

Clear communication with **external stakeholders**, particularly **customers**, is vital for maintaining trust after a cyberattack. How you handle this can make the difference between a long-term relationship with your customers or a permanent loss of business.

Key Actions for External Communication:

1. **Initial Customer Communication:**
   - As soon as the breach is identified, notify customers about the situation. Acknowledge the breach, provide **basic details** about what happened, and reassure them that steps are being taken to resolve the situation.
   - Be **honest** but avoid overloading them with technical details. Focus on what's important for them to know (e.g., **whether their data was compromised, what actions they need to take**, etc.).

Example:
A **retail company** that had a data breach informing customers within hours with a message like:
"We recently experienced a cybersecurity incident, and we want to let you know that your account information may have been

compromised. We are taking immediate action and have implemented enhanced security measures. Please change your password and watch for any unusual activity on your account."

2. **Ongoing Updates:**
   - Provide customers with regular **status updates** as the situation evolves. They need to know that you're actively working to resolve the issue and prevent further damage. Customers will appreciate transparency and a clear timeline for resolution.
   - This is especially important if you are still in the **investigation** or **containment** phases, as customers will want to know how long the disruption may last.

Practical Tip:
Use a **dedicated webpage** or **FAQ section** to keep customers updated. This way, they can find answers to their questions without having to contact support.

3. **Post-Incident Communication (Recovery Phase):**
   - After the incident is resolved, inform your customers of what you've done to rectify the situation, and outline what steps you're taking to prevent future incidents.
   - Offer **compensation**, such as **credit monitoring** or **free security services**, if necessary, especially if sensitive customer data like **credit card details** was involved in the breach.
   - Issue a **formal apology** for any inconvenience caused, and focus on how you're improving security to prevent such breaches from happening again.

Example:
A **bank** that suffered a data breach sent a letter to impacted customers explaining the nature of the breach, the immediate actions taken, and the measures being introduced to improve security. They also offered **free credit monitoring** for affected customers.

4. **Public Statement and Press Release:**
   - If the cyberattack is high-profile or could affect your business's reputation, issue a **public statement** or **press**

release. Be transparent about the situation and focus on what's being done to protect stakeholders moving forward.

- o Addressing the incident in a **calm and professional manner** will demonstrate to the public that your business is handling the situation responsibly.

Example:
A **global e-commerce platform** impacted by a **data breach** issued a **public statement** saying:
"We are aware of the cybersecurity incident that has affected our platform. We are taking immediate action to secure our systems and investigate the matter. We are committed to safeguarding customer information and are enhancing our security measures to prevent future incidents."

5. **Regulatory Notification:**
   - o In some jurisdictions, you are **legally obligated** to report a breach to regulatory bodies within a certain time frame (e.g., **72 hours** under **GDPR**).
   - o Ensure that you comply with **all legal obligations**, providing all required details to authorities and affected parties.

Example:
Under **GDPR**, a **healthcare provider** reported a **data breach** involving patient information to **regulatory bodies** and directly notified all impacted individuals within the required timeframe, offering compensation as part of the recovery process.

3. Communicating with Regulators and Legal Authorities

Communication with **regulatory bodies** (e.g., GDPR authorities, local data protection authorities, financial regulators) is often a legal requirement following a data breach. Even if the breach didn't involve sensitive customer data, authorities still need to be informed, and you need to be ready to provide clear documentation.

Key Actions for Regulatory Communication:

1. **Report the Incident:**
   o Notify the relevant **authorities** in compliance with local laws (e.g., **GDPR, CCPA, HIPAA**) within the specified time frame. The report should include:
     - **Date of the incident**
     - **Types of data affected**
     - **Steps taken to contain the breach**
     - **Measures in place to prevent future incidents**
2. **Cooperate with Investigations:**
   o Be ready to provide investigators with the data they need to understand the scope of the breach. This could include system logs, incident reports, and any other relevant evidence.

Practical Example:
A **European retailer** hit by a **payment card breach** reported the incident to **GDPR regulators** within **48 hours**, following the required procedures and offering full cooperation in the investigation.

Flowchart: Stakeholder Communication During a Cyberattack

```
                        Start
                          |
                          V
         [Internal Communication: Notify Employees]
                          |
                          V
      [External Communication: Notify Affected Customers]
                          |
                          V
    [Regulatory Communication: Notify Relevant Authorities]
                          |
                          V
        [Ongoing Updates: Keep All Stakeholders Informed]
                          |
                          V
       [Post-Incident: Apologize and Offer Compensation]
                          |
```

```
                          V
   [Press Release or Public Statement (if needed)]
                          |
                          V
   [Rebuild Trust and Improve Security Practices]
```

Effective communication is critical in managing a **cyberattack**. By being transparent and timely in your communication with both internal and external stakeholders, you can not only mitigate the impact of the attack but also maintain trust with your employees, customers, and regulatory bodies.

Remember, your goal is to convey that you are taking the incident seriously, working diligently to resolve it, and putting measures in place to prevent future attacks. How you communicate during and after a cyberattack can determine the long-term impact on your business's reputation and customer loyalty.

Chapter 11: Business Continuity and Disaster Recovery

In the face of cyberattacks, natural disasters, or other unforeseen disruptions, a business must be prepared to maintain its operations and recover swiftly. **Business Continuity Planning (BCP)** and **Disaster Recovery (DR)** are essential frameworks that help organizations minimize downtime and protect critical assets during a crisis. When executed properly, they ensure that your business can continue operating during and after a disruption, allowing you to recover quickly and keep customers and stakeholders informed.

This chapter will guide you through the importance of **Business Continuity Planning**, effective **Disaster Recovery strategies**, and the critical role that **backup systems** play in ensuring recovery. Whether you are a small business or a large corporation, these frameworks are vital in safeguarding your operations.

11.1: Importance of Business Continuity Planning

In today's digital and highly interconnected world, businesses face numerous risks that can disrupt their operations. Whether it's a **cyberattack**, a **natural disaster**, or even a **supply chain failure**, the ability to **continue operations** during and after an event is crucial for long-term success. This is where **Business Continuity Planning (BCP)** comes into play.

Business Continuity Planning is the process of creating systems and strategies to ensure that critical business functions can continue in the face of disruptions. A well-thought-out BCP not only helps businesses survive crises but also ensures that they can recover as quickly as possible.

In this section, we'll explore why Business Continuity Planning is essential, what risks it mitigates, and how businesses can develop a continuity plan that works for them.

Why is Business Continuity Planning Critical?

Business continuity is more than just a "nice-to-have" concept—it's a **necessity** for businesses of all sizes and industries. When disruptions occur, **time** and **resources** are often in short supply. A robust business continuity plan helps minimize these variables, allowing companies to maintain or quickly restore key operations.

1. Minimizing Operational Downtime

Downtime can be a company's worst enemy. Whether due to a cyberattack, a data breach, or a natural disaster, every minute spent inoperable equates to lost revenue, missed opportunities, and a damaged reputation. Business Continuity Planning is designed to **minimize downtime** by ensuring that critical systems and processes can continue or be quickly restored.

- **Example**:
  A **manufacturing plant** loses production for several days due to a fire in the main factory. Without a continuity plan, the plant would have to deal with **delayed orders**, loss of **customer trust**, and additional repair costs. With a continuity plan, however, they can activate backup systems, relocate operations to alternate facilities, and ensure that production continues with minimal disruption.

2. Safeguarding Revenue and Profitability

Every business operation relies on revenue, and disruptions lead directly to **lost income**. If a business cannot serve customers, fulfill orders, or maintain its financial systems, the results can be disastrous.

- **Practical Example**:
  A **retail business** experiences a cyberattack, disabling its online store. The company's revenue drops because it cannot process online transactions. With a **continuity plan** in place, the business

can switch to an alternate sales channel (e.g., manual order processing or temporary website solutions), ensuring continued revenue generation while IT staff works on resolving the issue.

3. Protecting Brand and Reputation

Customers expect companies to be dependable, especially in times of crisis. If a business is unable to deliver on its promises or provide essential services, customer loyalty can quickly deteriorate. **Communication** during a disruption is key, and a well-prepared business can recover customer trust even in the aftermath of a major incident.

- **Example**:
  A **financial services firm** suffers a **data breach** compromising sensitive customer information. Through a clear, proactive communication strategy, the firm informs affected customers, offers support, and implements additional security measures to restore trust. This transparency not only preserves their reputation but helps the company rebuild stronger relationships with its clients.

4. Legal and Regulatory Compliance

Many industries face regulatory obligations related to business continuity. Governments and regulatory bodies often require businesses to have plans in place to protect sensitive data and ensure minimal disruption in the event of a crisis. Failing to meet these requirements can lead to **penalties**, **legal consequences**, and loss of business.

- **Practical Example**:
  A **healthcare provider** faces strict requirements under **HIPAA** to ensure that patient data remains accessible and secure, even during a disaster. Without a proper business continuity plan, the provider risks legal ramifications, including hefty fines for non-compliance.

5. Ensuring Employee Safety and Well-being

Business continuity plans also focus on **employee safety**. In the event of a physical disaster like an earthquake, flood, or fire, businesses need to ensure that their workforce is safe and accounted for. Beyond physical safety, continuity planning addresses **remote work** arrangements in case employees are unable to access the office or work environment.

- **Example**:
  During a **pandemic**, a company with an established business continuity plan can quickly transition its workforce to **remote work**. By having the proper infrastructure, tools, and training, employees can continue working, avoiding the long-term disruption that others may experience.

Key Components of Business Continuity Planning

A Business Continuity Plan (BCP) isn't just a document—it's a structured and actionable strategy that prepares your organization for unexpected events. Here's a breakdown of the key elements involved in creating a BCP:

1. Business Impact Analysis (BIA)

A **Business Impact Analysis** is the foundation of your continuity plan. It involves assessing the potential impact of different threats and disruptions on your business operations. By understanding what functions are critical and what resources are required to support them, you can prioritize which areas need the most attention.

- **Steps to Conduct BIA:**
  1. **Identify Critical Business Functions**:
     Understand what parts of your business are vital for continued operations, such as customer service, order fulfillment, or financial systems.
  2. **Evaluate the Potential Impact**:
     For each function, assess the potential consequences of an interruption. What would happen if that function were unavailable for hours, days, or weeks? How would this affect your customers, revenue, and overall business?
  3. **Determine Recovery Time Objectives (RTO)**:
     Define how long each business function can be down before it starts causing significant damage.

- **Practical Example**:
  A **small business** that relies on an online platform for sales conducts a BIA and identifies that its **e-commerce platform** is critical for generating revenue. The business sets an RTO of **4 hours** to restore this function after an outage.

2. Risk Assessment and Mitigation

Once you've identified your critical functions, the next step is to conduct a **risk assessment**. This involves identifying the potential threats and vulnerabilities that could impact your business.

- **Identify Internal and External Risks**:
  Internal risks might include hardware failure or employee errors, while external risks could include cyberattacks, natural disasters, or supply chain disruptions.
- **Mitigation Strategies**:
  Develop strategies to reduce or eliminate these risks. For example, if a cyberattack is a major concern, you could invest in **firewalls, intrusion detection systems**, and **cybersecurity training** for employees.
- **Practical Example**:
  A **manufacturing plant** assesses its supply chain vulnerabilities and decides to diversify suppliers for critical raw materials. This mitigates the risk of a **supply chain disruption** that could halt production.

3. Establishing Recovery Strategies

Recovery strategies outline how you will restore business operations following a disruption. This involves setting up backup systems, alternate processes, and recovery sites. A **hot site, warm site**, or **cloud-based backup** may be part of your strategy to ensure that business operations can continue if the primary infrastructure is unavailable.

- **Practical Example**:
  A **law firm** implements a **cloud-based backup system** for all client documents and case files. If their physical office is compromised, they can quickly restore access to important files from any location, allowing the business to continue working without delay.

4. Communication Plan

Communication is key during a disruption. Not only must you keep employees informed, but you also need to communicate with customers, partners, and regulatory bodies. Establishing clear channels of communication and defining key messages will help your business manage expectations and minimize confusion.

- **Internal Communication**:
  Develop a system for notifying employees and keeping them informed during the incident. This could include internal emails, text alerts, or automated phone systems.
- **External Communication**:
  Be transparent with customers and stakeholders. Define what information you will share, how you will communicate, and who is authorized to speak on behalf of the company.
- **Practical Example**:
  After a **data breach**, a **tech company** issues a public statement, sends out emails to affected customers, and sets up a helpline to handle inquiries. The clear communication minimizes panic and helps rebuild trust.

5. Testing and Updating the Plan

Your continuity plan should be **dynamic**. Regularly test your plan through drills, tabletop exercises, and simulations to ensure its effectiveness. Update the plan based on feedback and lessons learned from tests or real incidents.

- **Testing Methods**:
  Conduct **tabletop exercises**, which simulate potential disruptions and allow your team to practice responding to the crisis.
- **Post-Incident Review**:
  After an actual incident, review the response to identify gaps in your plan and implement improvements.
- **Practical Example**:
  A **financial institution** conducts annual tests of its **disaster recovery plan**, which includes simulated cyberattacks and network failures. The results help them refine the plan and improve response times.

Flowchart: Business Continuity Planning Process

```
                        Start
                          |
                          V
              [Conduct Risk Assessment & BIA]
                          |
                          V
            [Identify Critical Business Functions]
                          |
                          V
            [Develop Risk Mitigation Strategies]
                          |
                          V
      [Establish Recovery Strategies (Backup, Sites)]
                          |
                          V
        [Create Communication Plan for Stakeholders]
                          |
                          V
            [Test and Update the Plan Regularly]
                          |
                          V
        [Implement the Plan in Case of Disruption]
                          |
                          V
        [Monitor, Evaluate, and Improve the Plan]
```

Business Continuity Planning is not just about surviving a disaster; it's about ensuring that your business can thrive even in the face of adversity. By identifying risks, preparing recovery strategies, and maintaining a focus on clear communication, you can protect your business from the devastating effects of disruptions. Effective BCP not only ensures your business stays operational, but also strengthens your brand, customer trust, and long-term resilience.

11.2: Disaster Recovery Strategies and Solutions

In the face of business disruptions caused by cyberattacks, natural disasters, or even hardware failures, **Disaster Recovery (DR)** is your safety net. While **Business Continuity Planning (BCP)** focuses on ensuring that critical functions continue during a disruption, **Disaster Recovery** focuses specifically on restoring IT systems, data, and technology infrastructure to normal. Without an effective DR strategy, businesses can face significant downtime, data loss, and a long recovery process, all of which can be devastating for customer trust, revenue, and reputation.

In this section, we'll dive deep into **Disaster Recovery strategies**, provide insights into different solutions, and walk you through practical implementations. You'll learn how to design a DR plan that minimizes downtime, recovers essential business functions, and ensures data integrity, all while ensuring business operations get back on track as quickly as possible.

Why Disaster Recovery is Crucial for Your Business

Disasters can take many forms—whether they are **hardware failures**, **cyberattacks**, **data breaches**, or **natural disasters**—and they can strike at any time. Without a robust disaster recovery strategy in place, the consequences can range from financial loss to a complete business shutdown. Here's why DR is so important:

1. Minimize Downtime

In today's competitive landscape, **downtime** is a major concern. Businesses rely on their IT systems to function, and prolonged downtime can affect **customer transactions**, **employee productivity**, and **business profitability**. DR strategies aim to restore operations as quickly as possible to ensure minimal disruption.

2. Protect Critical Data

Data is often a business's most valuable asset. Losing customer data, intellectual property, or financial records can have severe legal and financial consequences. Effective DR ensures that critical data is **backed up**, **encrypted**, and **recoverable**, reducing the risk of permanent data loss.

3. Compliance and Regulatory Requirements

Certain industries, such as healthcare and finance, are subject to stringent regulations that require businesses to have a disaster recovery plan. A **well-prepared DR plan** ensures compliance with regulations like **HIPAA**, **GDPR**, and **PCI-DSS**, avoiding costly fines and penalties.

4. Maintain Customer Trust

If your business experiences an **extended outage**, it can significantly damage your reputation. Customers expect your business to recover swiftly and securely. A clear DR strategy helps you communicate your response and recovery efforts to customers, building trust and demonstrating your ability to handle crises.

5. Cost Savings

While the upfront cost of implementing DR solutions can seem high, the cost of not having a DR strategy in place can be far greater. With a proper plan, your business can recover more quickly, reducing the financial impact of downtime and minimizing potential losses from security breaches or other disasters.

Key Components of a Disaster Recovery Strategy

A disaster recovery plan is not a one-size-fits-all solution. It should be tailored to your business needs, including the type of data you handle, the critical systems you rely on, and the risks you face. The main components of a DR strategy include:

1. Risk Assessment and Business Impact Analysis (BIA)

Before crafting a DR strategy, it's essential to identify the risks your business faces and evaluate the potential impact of a disruption. This includes:

- **Internal and external risks**: Cyberattacks, power outages, hardware failures, natural disasters.

- **Critical business functions**: Which systems, data, and processes are essential for day-to-day operations?
- **Recovery objectives**: How much downtime can your business tolerate for each function? This helps define your **Recovery Time Objective (RTO)** and **Recovery Point Objective (RPO)**.

2. Data Backup and Storage Solutions

Backups are at the core of any disaster recovery strategy. Whether it's **cloud backup**, **on-premise backups**, or a **hybrid approach**, ensuring that your data is safely stored and can be quickly recovered is essential.

- **Frequency of backups**: Set up **automated daily or weekly backups** depending on your business needs.
- **Offsite storage**: Use **cloud-based solutions** or **remote data centers** to store backups in different geographic locations, reducing the risk of data loss during local disasters.

3. Disaster Recovery Sites: Hot, Warm, and Cold Sites

Disaster recovery sites provide alternate locations where your IT systems and operations can be restored.

- **Hot Sites**: These are fully equipped recovery sites that mirror your primary systems. They allow you to resume operations almost immediately. While they provide the quickest recovery time, they are typically the most expensive option.
- **Warm Sites**: A warm site is partially equipped with the necessary infrastructure (e.g., servers, storage). It takes a bit more time to get up and running than a hot site, but it's more cost-effective.
- **Cold Sites**: These sites are basic facilities with minimal infrastructure. They're the least expensive but require a full setup before you can start operations. Recovery can take a long time, as everything needs to be brought online.

4. Recovery Time Objective (RTO) and Recovery Point Objective (RPO)

These are key metrics in disaster recovery planning:

- **RTO (Recovery Time Objective)**: This defines the maximum allowable downtime for critical systems and operations before they impact the business.
- **RPO (Recovery Point Objective)**: This is the maximum acceptable amount of data loss. For example, if you perform hourly backups, your RPO is one hour, meaning you could lose up to an hour of data in the event of a disaster.

5. Communication Plan

During a disaster, clear communication is crucial. Your team, customers, partners, and regulatory bodies must be kept informed. A DR communication plan should outline:

- **Who will communicate**: Assign roles for internal and external communication.
- **What information will be communicated**: Regular updates on the status of recovery efforts and expected timelines.
- **How communication will take place**: Email, phone calls, automated systems, and social media updates should be set up to keep all stakeholders informed.

6. Testing and Drills

It's essential to **test** your DR plan to ensure it works as intended. Regularly schedule **disaster recovery drills** to simulate potential incidents and evaluate the response. This helps identify weaknesses in your plan and ensures that your team knows their roles in a crisis.

- **Tabletop exercises**: Involve key personnel in a simulated disaster scenario and assess how well the plan is executed.
- **Full-scale tests**: Simulate a real disaster and test the entire recovery process, including backup systems, communication, and data restoration.

Disaster Recovery Solutions and Tools

There are several technologies and tools available to businesses to implement their disaster recovery plans. Here's a breakdown of some of the most common DR solutions:

1. Cloud-Based Disaster Recovery (DRaaS)

Cloud-based solutions, or **Disaster Recovery as a Service (DRaaS)**, provide a flexible, cost-effective way to implement DR. By utilizing cloud-based storage and processing power, businesses can quickly restore operations after a disaster.

- **Benefits**: Low cost, scalability, and rapid recovery. With DRaaS, businesses don't need to maintain expensive offsite facilities.
- **Providers**: Popular DRaaS providers include **Amazon Web Services (AWS)**, **Microsoft Azure**, and **Google Cloud Platform**

2. Backup and Recovery Software

Many businesses use backup software to automate data backups and enable fast restoration. Backup solutions offer features such as incremental backups, encryption, and scheduling to ensure data is protected and easily recoverable.

- **Popular Backup Solutions**:
  - **Veeam**: Comprehensive backup and recovery solutions for virtual, physical, and cloud environments.
  - **Acronis**: A reliable tool for data backup and disaster recovery, offering cloud integration and encryption.
  - **Datto**: Specializes in backup and recovery services for small businesses with automated solutions and cloud storage.

3. Network Failover Solutions

Network failover solutions ensure that in the event of a failure, your systems can automatically switch to an alternative network route, minimizing downtime and keeping operations running.

- **Failover Clustering**: Ensures that critical systems like databases remain available even if one server or system fails. **Microsoft**

SQL Server and Oracle RAC are examples of failover clustering technologies.

- **Load Balancers**: Distribute traffic across multiple servers or networks, ensuring that if one server fails, the load is automatically shifted to a backup.

Practical Example: A Healthcare Provider Implements a DR Strategy

The Challenge:
A **healthcare provider** with thousands of patient records needed a disaster recovery strategy that ensured data availability and compliance with **HIPAA** regulations. They were concerned about the risk of downtime due to cyberattacks, hardware failure, or natural disasters.

The Solution:

- **Cloud Backup and DRaaS**: The provider adopted **cloud-based disaster recovery** for all their patient data and operational systems. They chose a **DRaaS provider** with **HIPAA compliance** to ensure regulatory requirements were met.
- **RTO and RPO**: The healthcare provider set an **RTO of 4 hours** and **RPO of 15 minutes**, ensuring that they could quickly recover systems and minimize data loss in case of a disaster.
- **Hot Site**: They also set up a **hot site** for their critical medical systems, ensuring that patient care could continue uninterrupted, even if their primary data center went offline.

Outcome:
When a cyberattack disrupted their primary systems, the healthcare provider was able to restore operations within hours. They successfully avoided prolonged downtime, maintained patient trust, and met HIPAA compliance standards.

Flowchart: Disaster Recovery Strategy Implementation

```
Start
```

```
                        |
                        V
          [Conduct Risk Assessment and BIA]
                        |
                        V
      [Define RTO and RPO for Critical Systems]
                        |
                        V
      [Implement Backup and Recovery Solutions]
                        |
                        V
      [Set Up Recovery Sites (Hot, Warm, Cold)]
                        |
                        V
   [Develop Communication Plan and Testing Protocol]
                        |
                        V
        [Conduct Regular DR Drills and Tests]
                        |
                        V
         [Activate DR Plan During Crisis]
                        |
                        V
        [Evaluate and Improve DR Strategy]
```

Disaster recovery is a critical aspect of any business's risk management strategy. By implementing effective **DR strategies**, such as cloud-based solutions, backup systems, and failover technologies, businesses can ensure minimal downtime and data loss during a disaster. Regular testing and refinement of the plan will allow you to recover quickly and keep your operations intact, even in the face of a crisis.

11.3: Backup Systems and Their Role in Recovery

In the modern digital landscape, **data** is the lifeblood of business operations. Whether it's customer records, intellectual property, financial data, or operational plans, losing access to critical information can be catastrophic. That's where **backup systems** come into play. A reliable backup system ensures that your data is safely stored and can be restored quickly in the event of a disaster—whether due to a cyberattack, hardware failure, or natural disaster.

In this section, we'll explore the critical role that backup systems play in disaster recovery, discuss the different types of backups available, and provide practical advice on how to implement a robust backup strategy that aligns with your business needs.

Why Backup Systems are Crucial for Recovery

1. Data Protection and Availability

Data loss can happen unexpectedly, whether through **hardware failure**, **human error**, or **cyberattacks** (such as **ransomware**). Backups ensure that your business can recover critical information quickly, minimizing downtime and data loss.

Example:
A **law firm** that handles sensitive client information experienced a **hardware failure** on their primary storage device. Without backups, they would have been unable to access critical case files. However, since they had automated backups to the cloud, the firm was able to recover all their data within hours, allowing them to continue serving clients without significant disruption.

2. Compliance and Regulatory Requirements

Certain industries, such as **finance**, **healthcare**, and **government**, face strict regulatory requirements around data protection. For example, healthcare providers must ensure that **patient data** is backed up and recoverable under **HIPAA** regulations. Failure to meet these compliance requirements can result in significant fines and reputational damage.

Example:
A **financial institution** was audited and found to have inadequate backup procedures, which exposed them to potential **regulatory violations**. In response, they implemented robust cloud-based backup solutions to meet compliance standards and prevent data loss.

3. Reducing Downtime

The ability to **quickly recover data** and restore systems to normal is crucial for minimizing downtime. Downtime can result in lost revenue, customer dissatisfaction, and damage to your brand's reputation. Backup systems are designed to reduce recovery time and get businesses up and running as quickly as possible.

Practical Implementation:
A **retail chain** implemented a daily backup schedule that automatically uploads sales data to the cloud. When their on-premise servers failed due to a power surge, they were able to restore the sales data from the previous day within **30 minutes**, preventing delays in transactions and minimizing lost sales.

4. Disaster Recovery Readiness

Backups are a critical component of your **disaster recovery (DR)** plan. In the event of a disaster, whether it's a cyberattack, fire, or flood, your ability to restore business operations quickly is highly dependent on having reliable backup systems in place.

Example:
During a **ransomware attack**, a **manufacturing company** was able to restore key production data from its **cloud-based backups**. The backup systems allowed them to avoid paying the ransom and resume operations with minimal downtime.

Types of Backup Systems

To build a strong backup strategy, it's important to understand the different types of backup systems available. The right choice depends on your business's needs, such as how much data you need to back up, how quickly you need to restore it, and your budget.

1. Full Backups

A **full backup** copies all data, including files, applications, and system configurations. It's the most comprehensive backup method but also the most time-consuming and resource-intensive.

Advantages:

- **Complete data protection**.
- **Simple to restore**—only one set of backup data needs to be restored.

Disadvantages:

- **Time-consuming** and requires more storage space.
- Not ideal for businesses that generate large amounts of data daily.

Practical Example:
A **corporate law firm** conducts **weekly full backups** of all their documents, contracts, and case files. While the process takes several hours, the firm is able to recover completely in the event of a data breach, as everything is contained in one backup.

2. Incremental Backups

An **incremental backup** only saves the data that has changed since the last backup. This method is faster and requires less storage space than full backups, but it can take longer to restore, as you need to combine the last full backup with all subsequent incremental backups.

Advantages:

- **Faster backup process** compared to full backups.
- **Less storage** required.

Disadvantages:

- **Slower restore times**, as multiple backups need to be restored in sequence.

Practical Example:
A **digital marketing agency** performs **daily incremental backups** of their client databases. Each day, only the data that has changed (such as new client content or analytics) is backed up. This method allows them to back up large volumes of data without overwhelming storage capacity, but restores can take slightly longer.

3. Differential Backups

A **differential backup** copies all data that has changed since the last **full backup**. Unlike incremental backups, it doesn't rely on a chain of previous backups to restore data, making it faster to recover but requiring more storage than incremental backups.

Advantages:

- **Faster restore times** compared to incremental backups, as only the last full and the latest differential backups need to be restored.
- **No need for a series of backups** to restore data.

Disadvantages:

- **Requires more storage** compared to incremental backups.

Practical Example:
A **software company** uses **differential backups** to back up source code and project files. Every night, the system copies the changes made since the last full backup, enabling faster recovery of the most up-to-date data without the need for sequential restores.

4. Cloud-Based Backups

Cloud backups store data offsite in remote servers, which can be accessed over the internet. Cloud backup solutions offer scalability, remote accessibility, and flexibility, making them ideal for businesses with multiple locations or remote workforces.

Advantages:

- **Offsite storage** offers protection against local disasters (fires, floods, etc.).

- **Access from anywhere**, making it ideal for remote teams and multi-location businesses.
- **Scalable**—you only pay for the storage you need.

Disadvantages:

- **Dependence on internet connectivity**—data recovery may be slow if your internet connection is unreliable.
- Ongoing **subscription fees** for cloud storage.

Practical Example:
A **global e-commerce platform** uses a **cloud backup solution** to ensure their customer orders, inventory, and transaction data are always protected. Cloud storage enables them to access and restore data from any location, and they can scale storage as needed during peak seasons.

5. Hybrid Backup Solutions

A **hybrid backup** combines both **on-premise** and **cloud-based backups**. This strategy provides the speed and control of local storage with the security and redundancy of cloud storage.

Advantages:

- **Redundancy**—data is backed up in two places, ensuring higher security and reliability.
- **Faster access** to backups stored locally, with cloud as a backup.

Disadvantages:

- **Complexity** in managing two different systems.

Practical Example:
A **consulting firm** uses a **hybrid backup solution**, with critical client files stored on local NAS (Network Attached Storage) devices for quick access, while all data is also backed up daily to the cloud. This ensures that if their local systems fail, data can still be restored from the cloud without significant delays.

Best Practices for Backup Systems

To ensure your backup systems are effective, it's important to follow these best practices:

1. Follow the 3-2-1 Backup Rule

The **3-2-1 rule** is a widely accepted best practice in backup strategy:

- **3 copies** of your data (the original data and two backups).
- **2 different media types** (e.g., one on-premise and one cloud storage).
- **1 off-site backup** (to protect against local disasters like fires or floods).

2. Automate Backups

Automating the backup process ensures that backups are completed regularly and consistently without human intervention. Set your backup systems to automatically perform daily or weekly backups, depending on the frequency of data changes.

3. Regularly Test Restores

Testing restores ensures that your backups are actually usable and reliable. Perform regular **restore tests** to ensure you can recover data quickly when needed. A backup is only valuable if it can be restored successfully.

4. Encrypt Backups

To protect sensitive data, ensure all backups—whether stored locally or in the cloud—are **encrypted**. This ensures that even if a hacker gains access to your backup storage, they cannot read your data.

5. Keep Backups for a Defined Period

Define how long backups will be retained. Depending on your business needs and regulatory requirements, you may need to keep backups for a certain period (e.g., 30 days, 6 months, or 1 year). Set up retention policies to ensure that outdated backups are removed to save storage space.

Flowchart: Backup Strategy Implementation

```
                          Start
                            |
                            V
          [Conduct Risk Assessment & Data Analysis]
                            |
                            V
      [Select Backup Type (Full, Incremental, Differential)]
                            |
                            V
         [Implement 3-2-1 Backup Rule (Cloud, On-Premise)]
                            |
                            V
            [Automate Backup Process & Scheduling]
                            |
                            V
              [Test Backup Integrity Regularly]
                            |
                            V
             [Encrypt Backups for Data Protection]
                            |
                            V
             [Define Retention and Recovery Periods]
                            |
                            V
              [Monitor and Update Backup System]
```

Case Study: A Manufacturing Company Implements Backup Systems

The Challenge:
A **manufacturing company** that relies on real-time data for inventory management, supply chain coordination, and production schedules was at risk of downtime due to aging backup systems. They experienced periodic system failures, which made it difficult to recover data quickly.

The Solution:

- The company implemented a **hybrid backup system**, storing critical data both on local servers and in the cloud.

- They adopted the **3-2-1 backup rule** to ensure redundancy and flexibility.
- **Automated nightly backups** were configured to ensure that all production data, order information, and inventory records were securely backed up.

Outcome:

When a **server failure** occurred, the company was able to restore the entire system from their **cloud backup** within **30 minutes**, minimizing downtime and allowing operations to resume quickly. The business was able to continue fulfilling orders and processing inventory without losing any data.

Part 4: Specialized Cybersecurity Concerns (Compliance and Regulations)

Chapter 12: Navigating Compliance with Cybersecurity Regulations

In the world of cybersecurity, **compliance** is not just a legal obligation—it's also a critical component of a robust security strategy. As organizations handle more sensitive data, they must navigate a complex landscape of regulations designed to protect that data and ensure the privacy and security of individuals. These regulations, such as the **General Data Protection Regulation (GDPR), Health Insurance Portability and Accountability Act (HIPAA), and California Consumer Privacy Act (CCPA)**, are not just about following the law—they are also about maintaining trust with customers, ensuring the integrity of business operations, and avoiding significant financial and reputational risks.

This chapter will explore the key cybersecurity regulations you need to understand, provide practical steps for achieving compliance, and help you understand the consequences of non-compliance, along with strategies to avoid them.

12.1: Understanding Cybersecurity Regulations (GDPR, HIPAA, CCPA)

Introduction:

In today's digital landscape, **data privacy** and **cybersecurity regulations** are more important than ever. With businesses collecting and processing vast amounts of sensitive information, it's crucial to follow regulatory standards designed to protect that data. Compliance with laws such as the **General Data Protection Regulation (GDPR), Health Insurance Portability and Accountability Act (HIPAA), and California Consumer Privacy Act (CCPA)** is not just about avoiding penalties—it's about ensuring trust, safeguarding your reputation, and fostering long-term business success.

In this section, we will break down these three major cybersecurity regulations and what they mean for your business. We'll dive into their core principles, key requirements, and practical steps for implementation.

1. General Data Protection Regulation (GDPR)

The **General Data Protection Regulation (GDPR)** is a data privacy law enacted by the **European Union (EU)** in 2018. It applies to all businesses, regardless of location, that process the personal data of individuals within the EU. GDPR is considered one of the most comprehensive data protection regulations globally, and it has a far-reaching impact on businesses worldwide.

Key Principles of GDPR:

1. **Data Protection by Design and by Default:**
   - **What it means**: GDPR requires businesses to incorporate data protection into their processes from the outset. This principle ensures that privacy is considered in the design of systems and workflows, not just as an afterthought.
   - **Practical Example**: A **cloud service provider** ensures that its systems are built with **encryption** and **access controls** as part of the design process, ensuring data protection is a core feature of their services.
2. **Consent:**
   - **What it means**: Businesses must obtain clear, unambiguous consent from individuals before collecting or processing their data. The consent must be freely given, specific, informed, and revocable at any time.
   - **Practical Example**: A **newsletter subscription form** must have a checkbox where users actively consent to receiving marketing emails, and they must also be able to easily withdraw consent by unsubscribing.
3. **Right to Access and Data Portability:**
   - **What it means**: Individuals have the right to access their personal data and request copies in a commonly used

electronic format that can be transferred to another service provider.
- o **Practical Example**: A **fitness app** must allow users to request a copy of their data (e.g., workout history, goals, etc.) in a downloadable format like CSV or JSON.

4. **Right to be Forgotten:**
   - o **What it means**: Individuals can request the deletion of their data if it is no longer necessary for the purposes it was collected for, or if they withdraw consent.
   - o **Practical Example**: An **e-commerce store** must delete a customer's account and all associated data upon request if the customer no longer wishes to use their services.

5. **Data Breach Notification:**
   - o **What it means**: If a data breach occurs, businesses must notify the relevant authorities within **72 hours** and inform affected individuals if there's a high risk to their rights and freedoms.
   - o **Practical Example**: A **social media platform** must alert users and authorities within three days if there's a breach involving their personal data, such as email addresses and passwords.

Practical Implementation:

To ensure GDPR compliance, a **global marketing company** conducted a full audit of its data processing practices, implemented clear **opt-in consent** forms for all email communications, and set up a system to respond to **data access requests** and **data deletion requests**. They also updated their privacy policy to clearly outline how personal data is collected, used, and stored.

Outcome:
By ensuring transparency and giving users control over their data, the company avoided potential fines and enhanced customer trust.

2. Health Insurance Portability and Accountability Act (HIPAA)

HIPAA is a U.S. law that governs the protection of **health information**. It applies to **covered entities** such as healthcare providers, insurance companies, and business associates who handle protected health information (PHI). HIPAA ensures that individuals' health data is kept private and secure while being processed or stored by healthcare organizations.

Key Aspects of HIPAA:

1. **Privacy Rule:**
   - **What it means**: The Privacy Rule sets standards for how healthcare organizations must handle and protect PHI. It limits who can access and share PHI and requires that patients give written consent before their information is shared.
   - **Practical Example**: A **doctor's office** must obtain a patient's signed authorization before sharing their medical records with another healthcare provider.
2. **Security Rule:**
   - **What it means**: This rule requires healthcare organizations to implement safeguards to protect electronic PHI (ePHI). These include administrative, physical, and technical safeguards to ensure data is secure from breaches, theft, or loss.
   - **Practical Example**: A **hospital network** encrypts all patient data stored in their electronic medical record (EMR) system and ensures that only authorized personnel can access it through multi-factor authentication.
3. **Breach Notification Rule:**
   - **What it means**: If a data breach involving PHI occurs, healthcare organizations must notify affected individuals, the Department of Health and Human Services (HHS), and sometimes the media, depending on the size of the breach.
   - **Practical Example**: A **health insurance provider** must notify customers within 60 days if their personal health data has been exposed or compromised due to a security breach.
4. **Business Associate Agreements (BAA):**
   - **What it means**: If an organization outsources certain tasks involving PHI (e.g., to a cloud provider or data processor), they must have a **Business Associate Agreement (BAA)** in

place, ensuring the third party also complies with HIPAA standards.
- o **Practical Example**: A **billing company** contracted by a hospital must sign a BAA, ensuring they follow HIPAA-compliant practices when handling patient data.

Practical Implementation:

A **healthcare clinic** conducted a **HIPAA compliance audit**, implemented **data encryption** for all patient records, and trained employees on proper handling of **ePHI**. They also ensured all third-party vendors handling patient data signed **BAAs**.

Outcome:
The clinic ensured compliance with HIPAA regulations and reduced the risk of data breaches while improving patient confidence in their data protection practices.

---

3. California Consumer Privacy Act (CCPA)

The **CCPA** is a California state law that provides privacy rights to residents of California. It is designed to give consumers more control over their personal data, including the ability to know what data is being collected, request its deletion, and opt out of the sale of their data. While the CCPA primarily targets businesses that collect data on California residents, its scope can extend to companies outside California that meet certain criteria.

Key Aspects of CCPA:

1. **Consumer Rights:**
   - o **What it means**: The CCPA gives California residents the right to:
     - ▪ **Access** their personal data.
     - ▪ **Request deletion** of their personal data.
     - ▪ **Opt-out** of the sale of their personal data to third parties.
   - o **Practical Example**: A **consumer electronics company** provides California residents with an easy-to-use portal

where they can view the data the company has collected, request its deletion, or opt-out of third-party data sharing.

2. **Data Disclosure and Transparency:**
   - o **What it means**: Companies must provide a **privacy policy** that explains what personal data they collect, why they collect it, and who they share it with.
   - o **Practical Example**: A **social media platform** updates its **privacy policy** to disclose the types of personal data it collects from users, how that data is used, and whether it shares the data with any third-party advertisers.

3. **Penalties and Enforcement:**
   - o **What it means**: Non-compliance with the CCPA can result in substantial penalties, including fines up to **$2,500 per violation** or **$7,500 per intentional violation**.
   - o **Practical Example**: A **retail website** receives a fine after failing to implement an opt-out mechanism for users who wish to prevent the sale of their personal data.

Practical Implementation:

A **tech company** based in California implemented an automated system for consumers to easily request **data access**, **deletion**, and **opt-out** of data sales. They also updated their **privacy policy** to clearly explain how data is collected and used.

Outcome:
The company not only ensured compliance with CCPA but also enhanced customer trust by providing transparency and control over personal data.

Comparison: GDPR, HIPAA, and CCPA

Regulation	Scope	Penalties for Non-Compliance	Key Focus
GDPR	EU businesses and any business processing EU data	Fines up to 4% of annual revenue or €20 million, whichever is higher	Data protection, privacy rights, consent

Regulation	Scope	Penalties for Non-Compliance	Key Focus
HIPAA	U.S. healthcare providers and their business associates	Fines up to $50,000 per violation, with a maximum of $1.5 million	Protection of health information (PHI)
CCPA	California residents and businesses processing CA data	Fines up to $7,500 per intentional violation, $2,500 per other violations	Consumer privacy, transparency, and rights

Flowchart: Understanding Cybersecurity Regulations

```
                        Start
                          |
                          V
            [Identify Applicable Regulation(s)]
                          |
                          V
   [Understand Key Requirements (Consent, Access, Deletion)]
                          |
                          V
            [Implement Data Protection Measures]
                          |
                          V
         [Ensure Transparency with Privacy Policies]
                          |
                          V
     [Monitor for Compliance and Implement Regular Audits]
                          |
                          V
          [Provide Easy Access to Consumer Rights]
                          |
                          V
       [Handle Data Breaches and Violations Promptly]
                          |
                          V
             [Maintain Ongoing Compliance]
```

Understanding and complying with **GDPR**, **HIPAA**, and **CCPA** is crucial for any organization that handles sensitive personal data. These regulations are designed to protect individuals' privacy, ensuring businesses process their data securely and responsibly. By implementing data protection measures, obtaining clear consent, and enabling consumer rights such as data access and deletion, your business can not only ensure compliance but also build trust with customers and avoid significant penalties.

12.2: Practical Steps for Achieving Compliance

Achieving and maintaining compliance with cybersecurity regulations is a critical component of any modern business strategy. Whether you're adhering to GDPR, HIPAA, CCPA, or a combination of multiple regulations, the process can seem overwhelming. However, with a clear, systematic approach, businesses can navigate the complexities of compliance effectively and ensure they meet all necessary legal requirements while safeguarding data and building trust.

In this section, we'll guide you through **practical steps** to ensure compliance with these cybersecurity regulations. These steps are designed to be actionable, scalable, and tailored to businesses of all sizes. By following this guide, you can create a compliance framework that is not only efficient but also sustainable in the long term.

1. Conduct a Comprehensive Data Audit

The first step to achieving compliance is understanding what data your business collects, how it is processed, where it is stored, and who has access to it. A thorough data audit lays the foundation for compliance by identifying gaps and areas that need improvement.

How to Conduct a Data Audit:

- **Map Your Data Flow**:
  Identify where sensitive data originates (e.g., customer information, health records, payment data) and trace its movement

throughout your organization. Consider how it is collected (forms, websites, emails), stored (on-premise servers, cloud), and shared (third-party vendors, affiliates).

- **Identify Sensitive Data**:
  Understand what qualifies as sensitive or personal data under the applicable regulations. For instance, under **GDPR**, sensitive data could include racial or ethnic data, political opinions, and health information.
- **Evaluate Data Storage and Access**:
  Review where the data is stored and who has access to it. Are there adequate controls in place to ensure that only authorized individuals can access sensitive information?
- **Create a Data Inventory**:
  Develop a comprehensive inventory of all data assets. This should include:
  - The type of data.
  - The source and destination of the data.
  - Storage methods (cloud, on-premise).
  - Retention policies (how long the data is stored).

Practical Example:

A **financial services company** conducted a data audit to comply with **GDPR**. They mapped the customer data lifecycle, from collection at the point of account creation to sharing with third-party services like credit agencies. This audit helped them identify where personal data was being stored and who had access to it, ensuring GDPR requirements for data access and storage were met.

Outcome:
The company was able to implement tighter access controls, encrypt sensitive data, and adjust their data retention policies to meet regulatory standards.

---

2. Implement Strong Data Protection Measures

Data protection is at the heart of regulatory compliance. Whether you're complying with **GDPR**, **HIPAA**, or **CCPA**, your business must implement robust security controls to protect sensitive data from unauthorized access, breaches, or loss.

Key Data Protection Measures:

- **Encryption**:
  Encrypt data both at rest (when stored) and in transit (when transmitted). This ensures that if data is intercepted or accessed without authorization, it remains unreadable.
- **Access Controls**:
  Implement **role-based access controls (RBAC)** to ensure that only authorized personnel can access sensitive data. Ensure that employees only have access to the data necessary for their role.
- **Multi-Factor Authentication (MFA)**:
  Use **MFA** to add an extra layer of security to systems containing sensitive data. This can significantly reduce the risk of unauthorized access.
- **Data Masking**:
  Mask data to hide certain parts of sensitive information, such as credit card numbers, while still allowing the system to function normally.
- **Backup and Disaster Recovery Plans**:
  Regularly back up your data and implement disaster recovery protocols to ensure that in case of data loss, you can restore the system with minimal downtime.

Practical Example:

A **healthcare provider** dealing with patient health records implemented **HIPAA-compliant encryption** for all ePHI. They also set up **role-based access control (RBAC)** to restrict access to medical records to only those healthcare providers who needed it for patient care.

Outcome:
The provider met **HIPAA** compliance and minimized the risk of a data breach by protecting sensitive patient data with encryption and access controls.

---

3. Obtain Clear and Explicit Consent

Regulations such as **GDPR** require that businesses obtain **clear and explicit consent** from individuals before collecting, processing, or sharing their personal data. This means consent must be informed, unambiguous, and freely given.

How to Obtain Consent:

- **Clear Opt-in Mechanisms**:
  Use checkboxes or forms that allow individuals to actively agree to the collection of their personal data. Avoid pre-checked boxes, as these do not meet the explicit consent requirement under GDPR.
- **Provide Clear Information**:
  Be transparent with individuals about how their data will be used. This includes explaining the purpose of data collection, how it will be stored, and with whom it will be shared.
- **Allow Easy Withdrawal of Consent**:
  Provide individuals with an easy mechanism to withdraw their consent at any time, such as an unsubscribe link in emails or a data management portal where users can delete or update their data.

Practical Example:

A **retail company** operating in the EU updated their online form to include a **GDPR-compliant consent checkbox**. Customers were required to explicitly agree to their data being processed for marketing purposes before they could complete the purchase.

Outcome:
The company ensured GDPR compliance by obtaining valid consent and providing users with an option to revoke consent at any time.

---

4. Create and Update Privacy Policies

A **privacy policy** is a legal document that explains how your business collects, processes, and protects personal data. It must be clearly written, accessible, and regularly updated to reflect changes in data processing practices.

Key Elements of a Privacy Policy:

- **What data is being collected**: Clearly outline the types of personal data your business collects (e.g., name, address, email, financial information).
- **Why the data is being collected**: Explain the purposes for which the data will be used (e.g., marketing, product improvement).
- **Data sharing practices**: Indicate if you will share data with third parties and under what circumstances.
- **Data retention policies**: Specify how long data will be retained and when it will be deleted.
- **User rights**: Describe the rights users have under applicable regulations (e.g., GDPR's right to access, delete, or correct data).

Practical Example:

A **global tech company** updated its **privacy policy** to reflect GDPR compliance. They included sections on data access rights, outlined the retention policy, and explained how customers could request data deletion or transfer.

Outcome:
This transparent approach not only ensured compliance with GDPR but also built customer trust by clearly communicating how their data was being handled.

---

5. Implement Data Subject Rights Procedures

Regulations like GDPR and CCPA grant individuals specific rights over their personal data. It's important to have processes in place to enable individuals to exercise these rights.

Key Data Subject Rights:

- **Right to Access**: Users have the right to access their personal data upon request.
- **Right to Rectification**: Users can request corrections to inaccurate or incomplete data.

- **Right to Deletion**: Users can request their data be erased, commonly known as the "right to be forgotten."
- **Right to Restrict Processing**: Users can limit the way their data is used.
- **Right to Data Portability**: Users can request their data in a machine-readable format to transfer to another service provider.

Practical Example:

A **financial institution** sets up an automated system that allows customers to submit data access or deletion requests via an online portal. The company commits to responding to these requests within the timeframes required by **CCPA** and **GDPR**.

Outcome:
The financial institution ensured full transparency and streamlined the process for customers to exercise their data rights, ensuring compliance and improving customer satisfaction.

---

6. Monitor and Maintain Compliance

Achieving compliance is not a one-time task; it's an ongoing process. Businesses must continuously monitor their practices, update their procedures, and adapt to new legal requirements.

Ongoing Compliance Steps:

- **Regular Audits**: Conduct regular audits to assess compliance with regulations. These audits help identify gaps in data protection and ensure that you're adhering to policies.
- **Employee Training**: Continuously train employees on data protection principles, security protocols, and the latest legal updates.
- **Stay Updated**: Laws and regulations change over time. Stay informed about regulatory changes to ensure your business remains compliant with new rules.

Practical Example:

A **healthcare provider** implements an annual **HIPAA compliance audit** to review their handling of patient data. They also conduct quarterly **training sessions** for employees to ensure they are aware of the latest privacy laws and data protection practices.

Outcome:
The healthcare provider remains consistently compliant with HIPAA requirements, minimizing the risk of violations and improving overall security.

Flowchart: Practical Steps for Achieving Compliance

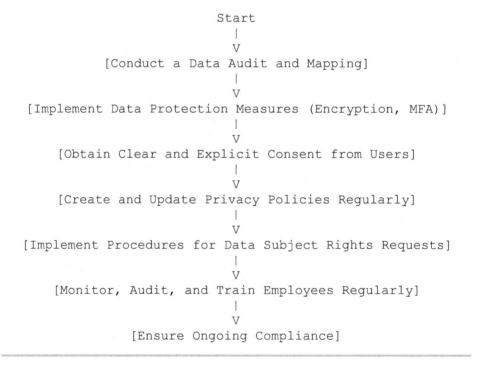

```
                           Start
                             |
                             V
                [Conduct a Data Audit and Mapping]
                             |
                             V
        [Implement Data Protection Measures (Encryption, MFA)]
                             |
                             V
             [Obtain Clear and Explicit Consent from Users]
                             |
                             V
             [Create and Update Privacy Policies Regularly]
                             |
                             V
        [Implement Procedures for Data Subject Rights Requests]
                             |
                             V
            [Monitor, Audit, and Train Employees Regularly]
                             |
                             V
                  [Ensure Ongoing Compliance]
```

Achieving and maintaining compliance with cybersecurity regulations requires a strategic, methodical approach. By conducting comprehensive data audits, implementing strong data protection measures, and ensuring transparency through clear privacy policies, businesses can not only meet regulatory requirements but also enhance customer trust and minimize legal risks. These practical steps help create a sustainable compliance framework that ensures long-term success in a highly regulated digital world.

12.3: Consequences of Non-Compliance and How to Avoid Them

In today's regulatory landscape, **compliance with cybersecurity regulations** is not just a legal obligation but also a **business necessity**. Whether it's complying with **GDPR, HIPAA, CCPA**, or other similar regulations, the consequences of non-compliance can be severe. These include **heavy fines**, **reputational damage**, and even **legal action**. However, achieving compliance is not a one-off task—it requires continuous effort, monitoring, and adapting to new regulations and industry standards.

This section will outline the potential **consequences of non-compliance**, including financial, legal, and operational risks. Additionally, we will explore practical steps businesses can take to **avoid** these penalties and ensure they remain in compliance with applicable cybersecurity regulations.

1. Financial Penalties and Fines

The most immediate and well-known consequence of non-compliance is **financial penalties**. Regulatory bodies enforce strict fines to ensure that businesses take their data protection responsibilities seriously.

How Fines are Imposed:

- **GDPR**:
  Under GDPR, businesses can face fines of up to **€20 million** or **4% of annual global turnover**, whichever is higher, for the most severe violations. Lesser violations can result in fines of up to **€10 million** or **2% of annual turnover**.

- **HIPAA**:
  Non-compliance with HIPAA can lead to fines ranging from **$100 to $50,000 per violation**, depending on the severity and level of negligence. Annual penalties can reach up to **$1.5 million**.
- **CCPA**:
  The CCPA imposes fines of **$2,500 per violation** or **$7,500 per intentional violation**. Additionally, businesses that fail to comply with CCPA regulations may also face class-action lawsuits.

Real-World Example:

A **social media platform** was fined **€50 million** by the **French Data Protection Authority (CNIL)** for failing to meet GDPR consent requirements. The company did not obtain explicit consent for personalized ads, resulting in one of the largest GDPR fines to date.

Outcome:
The company was not only fined heavily but also faced a massive public relations hit. Their user base decreased, and their reputation as a data handler took a severe blow.

---

2. Reputational Damage and Loss of Consumer Trust

Reputational damage is another significant consequence of non-compliance. When customers entrust businesses with their personal data, they expect it to be handled securely and ethically. A data breach or regulatory violation can result in a **loss of customer trust**, which is often difficult to recover from.

How Reputational Damage Happens:

- **Data Breaches**:
  A data breach that exposes customer data, such as **names**, **emails**, **credit card information**, or **medical records**, can severely damage a company's reputation. Customers may feel their personal information is at risk, leading to mistrust.
- **Transparency Issues**:
  If a company fails to be transparent about its data practices or

doesn't communicate breaches effectively, customers may view the company as unreliable or untrustworthy.

Practical Example:

A **global retailer** suffered a **data breach** that exposed the personal data of millions of customers. While the company was eventually found to be compliant with some data protection laws, its **lack of transparency** in informing customers led to a **public backlash**. The incident resulted in lost sales, a decrease in customer loyalty, and **negative press coverage**.

Outcome:
The retailer took significant steps to recover from the breach, including improving data protection protocols and launching customer communication campaigns. However, the financial impact was felt for months, as customers chose to shop with competitors who were perceived as more secure.

---

3. Legal Consequences and Lawsuits

Failure to comply with regulations can lead to **legal consequences** beyond regulatory fines. Businesses can face **lawsuits** from customers, employees, or partners who believe their data privacy has been violated.

Potential Legal Risks:

- **Class-Action Lawsuits**:
  Under laws like the **CCPA**, individuals whose data is compromised can file lawsuits, potentially resulting in class-action lawsuits that could cost millions.
- **Customer Lawsuits**:
  Customers whose personal data is mishandled or exposed may choose to file lawsuits for damages, leading to significant legal fees and potential settlements.
- **Regulatory Legal Action**:
  Regulatory bodies, like the **FTC** (Federal Trade Commission) in the U.S., can file legal action against businesses that fail to comply with data protection laws, resulting in penalties and required corrective actions.

Real-World Example:

A **credit reporting agency** faced a class-action lawsuit after a massive data breach exposed the personal information of 147 million people. The company settled the lawsuit for **$700 million** in compensation, which included providing identity theft protection services to affected consumers.

Outcome:
The company not only paid a large settlement but also suffered significant damage to its reputation, facing ongoing scrutiny from regulators and customers alike.

---

4. Operational Disruptions

Non-compliance can also lead to **operational disruptions** that hinder a business's ability to function efficiently. These disruptions can occur when data is lost, systems are compromised, or when businesses are forced to spend time and resources addressing regulatory issues.

Examples of Operational Disruptions:

- **System Downtime**:
  When a company faces a **data breach** or is investigated for non-compliance, it may need to shut down systems or services temporarily to prevent further damage or to address security gaps.
- **Forced Corrective Actions**:
  Regulatory authorities can demand that businesses implement corrective actions, such as strengthening data protection measures or changing data-handling practices. This can divert valuable resources and cause delays in normal operations.

Practical Example:

A **payment processing company** was forced to halt operations temporarily due to non-compliance with **PCI-DSS** (Payment Card Industry Data Security Standard) requirements. The company had to rebuild its security infrastructure to meet the required standards, leading to operational delays and loss of revenue during the downtime.

Outcome:
The company faced financial losses and reputational damage, which took months to recover from as they scrambled to address compliance gaps.

---

5. How to Avoid the Consequences of Non-Compliance

While non-compliance can lead to severe consequences, businesses can take proactive steps to **avoid** these penalties and safeguard their operations. Here are the key steps to ensure your business remains compliant:

1. Stay Informed About Regulatory Changes:

- **Why it matters**: Cybersecurity regulations evolve frequently. Staying informed ensures that your compliance efforts are up-to-date and aligned with current laws.
- **How to do it**: Subscribe to regulatory newsletters, attend webinars, and regularly consult legal experts to stay ahead of changes in data protection laws.

2. Implement a Comprehensive Data Protection Strategy:

- **Why it matters**: Implementing strong data protection measures, such as **encryption**, **access controls**, and **regular audits**, helps reduce the risk of non-compliance.
- **How to do it**: Use tools like **SIEM (Security Information and Event Management)** to monitor data security and **encryption software** to protect sensitive data both in transit and at rest.

3. Regularly Audit and Test Compliance:

- **Why it matters**: Regular audits and **stress tests** ensure that your business's systems are working as expected and that compliance gaps are identified before they lead to problems.

- **How to do it**: Schedule **quarterly compliance audits** and perform **penetration tests** to ensure that your security systems are robust.

4. Provide Employee Training on Data Privacy:

- **Why it matters**: Employees play a vital role in ensuring data protection. Regular training helps staff understand their responsibilities regarding data privacy and security.
- **How to do it**: Offer **annual training sessions** on data privacy regulations and best practices, and ensure employees are aware of their roles in maintaining compliance.

5. Work with Legal and Cybersecurity Experts:

- **Why it matters**: Consulting with experts can help navigate the complexities of compliance and ensure that your policies align with legal and regulatory standards.
- **How to do it**: Hire a **compliance officer** or work with legal advisors who specialize in data privacy laws to review and update your compliance strategies.

6. Implement Data Management and Documentation Systems:

- **Why it matters**: Maintaining accurate and accessible records is a key requirement of many regulations, such as **GDPR** and **HIPAA**.
- **How to do it**: Use **data management software** to track data access, modifications, and deletions. Maintain logs to show compliance with retention and access policies.

Flowchart: Steps to Avoid Non-Compliance

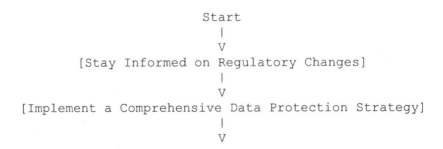

```
                    Start
                      |
                      V
        [Stay Informed on Regulatory Changes]
                      |
                      V
   [Implement a Comprehensive Data Protection Strategy]
                      |
                      V
```

```
        [Regularly Audit and Test Compliance]
                         |
                         V
     [Provide Employee Training on Data Privacy]
                         |
                         V
      [Work with Legal and Cybersecurity Experts]
                         |
                         V
 [Implement Data Management and Documentation Systems]
                         |
                         V
             [Ensure Ongoing Compliance]
```

Non-compliance with cybersecurity regulations can result in significant penalties, reputational harm, legal repercussions, and operational disruptions. However, by taking proactive steps—such as conducting data audits, implementing strong data protection measures, and staying informed about regulatory changes—businesses can avoid these risks and ensure long-term success.

Chapter 13: Cybersecurity for Remote Work and Cloud Solutions

The modern workforce is evolving. With the rise of **remote work** and **cloud solutions**, organizations are finding new ways to increase flexibility and accessibility. However, along with these advantages comes the need to adopt **strong cybersecurity practices** to protect sensitive data and systems from potential threats.

Remote work environments and cloud platforms pose unique challenges to cybersecurity. In this chapter, we'll explore how businesses can secure their remote work environments, protect data in the cloud, and implement best practices for managing remote access and Bring Your Own Device (BYOD) policies.

By the end of this chapter, you'll have a solid understanding of how to safeguard your remote workforce and cloud-based infrastructure, ensuring your organization remains protected in today's dynamic digital landscape.

13.1: Securing Remote Work Environments

As the world moves towards a more **remote-first workforce**, ensuring the **security of remote work environments** has never been more crucial. Employees working from home or other remote locations are often accessing sensitive business data from unsecured networks and personal devices. These conditions create ample opportunities for cybercriminals to exploit vulnerabilities, resulting in potential data breaches, financial losses, and damage to a company's reputation.

In this guide, we will explore **key strategies and best practices** for securing remote work environments. From **network security** to **device**

management, we'll cover how businesses can ensure their remote workforce is both productive and safe.

---

1. Use Virtual Private Networks (VPNs)

A **Virtual Private Network (VPN)** is a critical tool for securing remote work environments. It creates an encrypted tunnel through which employees can securely access corporate networks and systems over the internet, even when using potentially insecure public Wi-Fi networks.

How VPNs Enhance Security:

- **Encrypts Data**: VPNs encrypt the data being transmitted between the remote employee's device and the corporate network. This prevents hackers from intercepting and reading sensitive data, even if they manage to gain access to the network.
- **Masks IP Address**: By masking an employee's IP address, a VPN helps obscure the device's location, further securing the network against cyber threats.
- **Access Control**: VPNs can be configured to ensure only authorized users can access the company's internal network.

Best Practices for VPN Usage:

- **Ensure All Remote Workers Use VPNs**: Make it a company policy that every employee accessing the network remotely must use a VPN.
- **Use Strong Encryption**: Choose a VPN service that uses high-level encryption (e.g., AES 256-bit encryption) to protect your data.
- **Regularly Monitor VPN Connections**: Regularly monitor the usage and performance of your VPN to ensure it is functioning properly and that no unauthorized access is taking place.

Practical Example:
A **law firm** with remote employees ensured that all of its attorneys and administrative staff used a **VPN** to access client records securely from home. They used **MFA (Multi-Factor Authentication)** for an added layer

of protection and encrypted all files being transferred between remote devices and company servers.

Outcome:
The law firm successfully mitigated the risk of unauthorized access to confidential client data, ensuring compliance with privacy regulations like **GDPR**.

---

2. Enforce Strong Authentication Practices

To secure remote access, it's crucial that businesses use **strong authentication** to verify the identity of users attempting to access company systems. **Password-based authentication** alone is often not enough, especially when employees are accessing company resources from potentially insecure locations.

Two-Factor Authentication (2FA) and Multi-Factor Authentication (MFA)

- **Two-Factor Authentication (2FA)**: Requires users to authenticate their identity using two separate forms of identification, typically something they know (password) and something they have (a code sent to their phone).
- **Multi-Factor Authentication (MFA)**: An extension of 2FA that may require additional forms of verification, such as biometrics (fingerprint or face recognition), smart cards, or tokens, to provide an even higher level of security.

Why It Matters:

Even if a cybercriminal manages to steal a user's password, they will be unable to access the network without the second factor of authentication.

Best Practices for Authentication:

- **Require MFA for All Remote Access**: Ensure that all remote access to company systems requires MFA.

- **Use Password Managers**: Encourage employees to use password managers to store and generate strong, unique passwords for each service.
- **Enforce Regular Password Changes**: Implement policies that require employees to update their passwords regularly to reduce the risk of compromised accounts.

Practical Example:
A **global software development company** implemented **MFA** for all remote access to their code repository and project management tools. This added an extra layer of security to their sensitive intellectual property, which was frequently accessed by remote developers.

Outcome:
The company significantly reduced the risk of unauthorized access to their systems, even when employees used devices outside the company network.

---

3. Use Endpoint Security Solutions

The devices that remote employees use to access company systems (laptops, smartphones, tablets) are often the most vulnerable entry points for cyberattacks. These devices can be lost, stolen, or infected with malware, making them prime targets for cybercriminals.

Endpoint Protection Solutions:

Endpoint security tools protect remote devices from threats such as malware, ransomware, phishing, and other malicious attacks. These tools monitor device activity and apply security policies to prevent unauthorized actions.

Key Features of Endpoint Protection:

- **Real-time Malware Detection**: Detect and block malware in real-time as it attempts to infiltrate the device.
- **Device Encryption**: Encrypt data on remote devices to ensure that even if a device is lost or stolen, the data remains inaccessible.

- **Remote Wipe Capability**: In the event of a device being lost or stolen, remote wipe allows IT teams to delete sensitive data from the device, preventing unauthorized access.

Best Practices for Endpoint Security:

- **Deploy Endpoint Protection Software**: Implement **antivirus software**, **firewalls**, and **malware protection** on all devices used by remote workers.
- **Encrypt Devices**: Require full disk encryption on all devices that access corporate systems, ensuring that sensitive information is protected if a device is lost.
- **Regular Device Scans**: Schedule regular scans to detect vulnerabilities, malware, or outdated software on remote devices.

Practical Example:
A **marketing agency** required all of its remote workers to install an endpoint security solution on their laptops and smartphones. They also enforced **automatic device encryption** and enabled the **remote wipe feature** to ensure no data could be accessed if a device was lost.

Outcome:
The agency protected client data and internal communications, ensuring that even if a device was compromised, sensitive information would remain secure.

---

4. Secure Communication Channels

Remote work often involves communication through various channels, such as email, chat apps, video conferencing, and file-sharing platforms. Each of these tools can become a vulnerability if not properly secured.

Encrypted Communication:

Ensure that all communication tools used by remote workers, such as **email**, **video conferencing**, and **file sharing**, are **encrypted**. This ensures that sensitive conversations or documents cannot be intercepted during transmission.

- **End-to-End Encryption (E2EE)**: For services like **video calls** or **instant messaging**, use platforms that provide **end-to-end encryption** to ensure that only authorized users can access the content.
- **Secure Email**: Use email encryption tools to prevent unauthorized users from accessing the content of sensitive emails.

Best Practices for Secure Communication:

- **Use Secure Communication Tools**: Encourage employees to use platforms with built-in encryption, such as **Slack**, **Zoom**, and **Microsoft Teams**, that provide secure communication for remote teams.
- **Educate on Phishing and Social Engineering**: Train employees on how to spot phishing attempts and fraudulent communications. Make sure they know never to share passwords or sensitive data through unsecured channels.

Practical Example:
A **tech startup** switched to using a **secure file-sharing platform** that offered **end-to-end encryption** for all files exchanged among remote employees. They also provided regular phishing awareness training to ensure that employees recognized and reported suspicious emails.

Outcome:
The startup reduced the risk of data leaks and unauthorized access by securing communication channels and increasing awareness of social engineering tactics.

---

5. Monitor Remote Access and Network Activity

Continuous monitoring of remote work environments is essential for detecting suspicious activity and responding to security incidents quickly. By monitoring network traffic, system logs, and user activities, businesses can identify potential threats before they cause harm.

Key Monitoring Practices:

- **Log Management**: Use log management tools to track user activities, such as login attempts, file access, and system changes. Regularly review these logs to detect unusual or unauthorized behavior.
- **Intrusion Detection Systems (IDS)**: Use IDS to monitor network traffic for potential attacks, such as malware or unauthorized access attempts.
- **Behavioral Analytics**: Implement tools that track user behavior to detect anomalies, such as an employee accessing systems or files they wouldn't normally use.

Best Practices for Monitoring:

- **Real-time Alerts**: Set up real-time alerts for suspicious activities, such as multiple failed login attempts, large data transfers, or access to sensitive files by unauthorized users.
- **Audit Remote Connections**: Regularly audit remote connections to ensure that only authorized devices and users are accessing the network.

Practical Example:
A **financial institution** deployed an **IDS system** to monitor network traffic and detect any unauthorized access attempts. They also set up **real-time alerts** for any suspicious behavior, such as attempts to access high-risk accounts outside of normal working hours.

Outcome:
By continuously monitoring and detecting unusual activity, the institution was able to respond to potential security threats quickly, preventing data breaches and ensuring compliance with financial regulations.

Flowchart: Securing Remote Work Environments

```
                      Start
                        |
                        V
          [Use VPN for Secure Connections]
```

```
                        |
                        V
        [Enforce Multi-Factor Authentication (MFA)]
                        |
                        V
         [Deploy Endpoint Security on All Devices]
                        |
                        V
          [Ensure Secure Communication Channels]
                        |
                        V
        [Monitor Network Traffic and User Activity]
                        |
                        V
       [Train Employees on Security Best Practices]
                        |
                        V
           [Continuous Review and Improvement]
```

Securing remote work environments is a multi-faceted challenge that requires a combination of technology, policies, and employee awareness. By implementing **VPNs**, **MFA**, **endpoint protection**, **secure communication channels**, and **continuous monitoring**, businesses can significantly reduce their vulnerability to cyberattacks while allowing employees to work securely from any location.

13.2: Protecting Data in Cloud Platforms

Cloud platforms have revolutionized the way businesses store, manage, and process data. From **flexible storage solutions** to **cost-effective scalability,** cloud services like **Amazon Web Services (AWS)**, **Microsoft Azure**, and **Google Cloud Platform** have become essential for modern organizations. However, as more sensitive data is stored and accessed in the cloud, the security challenges also increase.

In this guide, we will explore how businesses can **protect their data in cloud platforms**. We will cover the key concepts of cloud security, best practices for data protection, and actionable steps to safeguard your data while benefiting from cloud services. Additionally, we will discuss how businesses can comply with relevant regulations, such as **GDPR** and **CCPA**, when using cloud solutions.

---

1. Understand the Shared Responsibility Model

Before diving into security practices, it's important to understand the **shared responsibility model** for cloud security. This model defines the security responsibilities of both the cloud service provider and the customer.

What is the Shared Responsibility Model?

- **Cloud Provider's Responsibility**: Cloud providers are responsible for the security **of** the cloud infrastructure. This includes the physical security of data centers, network security, and securing the hypervisor layer (the virtualized infrastructure).
- **Customer's Responsibility**: The customer is responsible for securing **in** the cloud. This includes securing data, managing user access, configuring security settings, and ensuring compliance with data protection laws.

Example:

For instance, **AWS** provides physical security, network security, and encryption for data at rest. However, as the customer, it's your responsibility to **manage encryption keys**, configure access controls, and ensure the security of applications running in the cloud.

Why It Matters:

Understanding this model helps organizations understand their specific security obligations. For example, while a provider ensures the physical security of cloud servers, the responsibility for securing sensitive data, such as customer information, lies with the business.

---

2. Data Encryption: A Non-Negotiable Security Measure

Data encryption is one of the most effective methods for protecting sensitive information stored in the cloud. It ensures that data is unreadable without the correct decryption key.

Types of Encryption:

- **Encryption at Rest**:
  This refers to encrypting data that is stored on cloud servers (e.g., databases, file systems, and backups). This ensures that if the cloud infrastructure is compromised, attackers cannot access the data in its raw form.
- **Encryption in Transit**:
  This refers to encrypting data that is being transmitted between your devices and the cloud service (e.g., via HTTPS, SSL/TLS). It ensures that data is protected during transfer and cannot be intercepted by third parties.

Best Practices for Encryption:

- **Use strong encryption standards**: Implement **AES-256** encryption for data at rest and **TLS 1.2 or higher** for data in transit.
- **Manage encryption keys securely**: Use services like **AWS Key Management Service (KMS)** or **Azure Key Vault** to manage encryption keys securely.
- **Implement end-to-end encryption**: Ensure that data is encrypted throughout its entire lifecycle, from creation to storage to transmission.

Practical Example:
A **retail company** storing customer payment information on **Google Cloud** ensured that all sensitive data was encrypted at rest using AES-256 and used **TLS encryption** to secure transactions between their online store and cloud storage.

Outcome:
The company minimized the risk of data exposure, even if attackers gained access to their cloud infrastructure.

---

3. Access Management and Identity Controls

Controlling who can access your cloud resources is critical for maintaining security. Proper **Identity and Access Management (IAM)** can help ensure that only authorized users can access sensitive data and perform critical actions.

Key IAM Practices:

- **Principle of Least Privilege**:
  Ensure that users only have the permissions they absolutely need to perform their job. This minimizes the attack surface in case an account is compromised.
- **Role-Based Access Control (RBAC)**:
  Implement RBAC to assign permissions based on job roles. For example, **admins** can manage cloud resources, while **end-users** only have access to certain files.
- **Multi-Factor Authentication (MFA)**:
  Enforce MFA for all users accessing the cloud platform. This provides an additional layer of security beyond just a username and password.
- **Regular Audits**:
  Regularly review and audit user access and permissions to ensure they are still aligned with job roles.

Practical Example:
A **financial services firm** using **AWS** implemented **RBAC** to give its team access only to the cloud services necessary for their role. They required **MFA** for all users accessing sensitive data and conducted quarterly audits of user access to detect any unauthorized changes.

Outcome:
The firm ensured that only authorized personnel had access to financial data, reducing the risk of insider threats or unauthorized access.

4. Backup and Disaster Recovery

Cloud platforms offer **redundant** infrastructure, which helps protect against data loss. However, it's still essential for businesses to have **backup and disaster recovery (DR)** strategies in place to protect against accidental deletion, cyberattacks, or system failures.

Best Practices for Backup and DR in the Cloud:

- **Automated Backups**: Set up automated backups of critical data to cloud storage solutions (e.g., **AWS S3**, **Azure Blob Storage**). Regularly schedule backups to ensure the most up-to-date data is always available.
- **Geographically Redundant Backups**: Store backups in multiple geographic locations to ensure data is protected against regional failures (e.g., server outages, natural disasters).
- **Test Your Recovery Plan**: Regularly test your disaster recovery plan to ensure that data can be restored in the event of a system failure or data breach.

Practical Example:
A **media company** using **Microsoft Azure** implemented automated backups for their video content and media libraries. The backups were stored in **multiple regions** to ensure high availability and fault tolerance. They also conducted quarterly **disaster recovery drills** to ensure that they could quickly restore content in case of a cloud service outage.

Outcome:
The media company minimized the risk of data loss, ensuring that their valuable content remained available even during system failures or cloud disruptions.

5. Compliance and Regulatory Requirements

As cloud platforms handle a large volume of sensitive data, organizations must ensure they comply with relevant data protection regulations, such as

GDPR, **HIPAA**, **CCPA**, and others. Non-compliance can lead to hefty fines and reputational damage.

How to Ensure Compliance:

- **Choose Compliant Cloud Providers**:
  Select cloud providers that comply with industry-specific regulations (e.g., **ISO 27001, SOC 2, HIPAA, GDPR**). Ensure they offer security features like data encryption, access controls, and regular security audits.
- **Data Localization**:
  For organizations under strict compliance regulations (e.g., **GDPR**), ensure that data is stored within the required geographic regions. Cloud providers like **AWS**, **Azure**, and **Google Cloud** offer services with region-specific data storage options.
- **Documentation and Audits**:
  Maintain documentation of all cloud security practices and perform regular audits to ensure your practices align with regulatory requirements.

Practical Example:
A **healthcare provider** using **AWS** for storing patient data ensured that their cloud setup adhered to **HIPAA** compliance by using **AWS HIPAA-eligible services** and implementing strict access controls. They also kept logs of all user activities to comply with **data access** and **audit trail** requirements.

Outcome:
The healthcare provider remained compliant with HIPAA, ensuring the security and confidentiality of patient data while avoiding potential fines.

---

6. Monitor and Detect Threats in the Cloud

Threat detection and continuous monitoring are crucial to identify and respond to cyber threats before they cause significant harm. Cloud platforms provide tools to help monitor cloud resources and detect suspicious activity.

Key Tools and Practices:

- **Cloud Security Posture Management (CSPM)**:
  Use CSPM tools to continuously monitor your cloud environment for misconfigurations, vulnerabilities, and non-compliance with security policies. These tools provide real-time alerts and automated remediation.
- **Cloud-native Security Tools**:
  Platforms like **AWS**, **Azure**, and **Google Cloud** offer native security tools, such as **AWS CloudTrail** and **Google Cloud Security Command Center**, to monitor cloud resources for threats and ensure the integrity of cloud services.
- **Threat Intelligence Integration**:
  Integrate threat intelligence services into your cloud environment to stay updated on emerging threats. These tools provide context and insights into potential vulnerabilities and attacks.

Practical Example:
A **technology company** used **AWS CloudTrail** to monitor all API calls and activity within their AWS environment. This helped them identify unusual behavior, such as unauthorized access to sensitive files, and take quick action to prevent a potential breach.

Outcome:
The company was able to detect suspicious activity in real time, allowing them to mitigate the risk of data breaches and secure their cloud infrastructure.

Flowchart: Protecting Data in Cloud Platforms

```
                    Start
                      |
                      V
      [Understand the Shared Responsibility Model]
                      |
                      V
    [Implement Data Encryption (at Rest & In Transit)]
                      |
                      V
            [Control Access Using IAM and MFA]
                      |
```

```
                              V
        [Set Up Backup and Disaster Recovery Plans]
                              |
                              V
           [Ensure Compliance with Regulations]
                              |
                              V
      [Monitor Cloud Resources for Suspicious Activity]
                              |
                              V
      [Regularly Review and Update Security Practices]
                              |
                              V
             [Ensure Ongoing Cloud Security]
```

Protecting data in cloud platforms requires a strategic approach to security, combining encryption, access management, monitoring, compliance, and backup strategies. By understanding the **shared responsibility model** and applying best practices in these areas, businesses can leverage cloud solutions safely and efficiently while minimizing risks.

As cloud adoption continues to grow, the need for robust cloud security will remain a top priority. By staying proactive, businesses can ensure that their cloud environments are secure, compliant, and ready to meet the challenges of the modern digital landscape.

13.3: Best Practices for Remote Access and BYOD (Bring Your Own Device) Policies

In today's business landscape, remote work is no longer a trend—it's become the norm for many organizations. With the rise of **Bring Your Own Device (BYOD)** policies, employees often use their personal devices (laptops, smartphones, tablets) to access corporate resources. While this flexibility offers many benefits, it also presents significant cybersecurity challenges. Organizations must balance **security** with **employee**

convenience to ensure data protection, regulatory compliance, and efficient operations.

In this section, we'll dive deep into best practices for managing **remote access** and **BYOD policies**. We'll explore how to secure remote work environments, protect corporate data, and ensure compliance with industry regulations while allowing employees to use their own devices for work.

---

1. Define Clear Remote Access Policies

One of the most crucial steps in securing remote work environments is to have clear, **comprehensive remote access policies**. This policy should outline the rules and guidelines for accessing corporate resources from remote locations.

Key Elements of a Remote Access Policy:

- **What is Allowed and What's Not**: Define which systems, data, and applications employees are permitted to access remotely. Determine whether they can access **sensitive data**, such as customer information, intellectual property, or financial records, and under what conditions.
- **VPN Requirement**: Mandate the use of a **VPN** for all remote access. The VPN should use strong encryption protocols (e.g., **AES-256**), ensuring that the data is securely transmitted.
- **MFA Requirement**: **Multi-Factor Authentication (MFA)** should be enforced for all remote access. This ensures that even if credentials are compromised, an attacker cannot gain access without passing additional layers of security.
- **Device Restrictions**: Specify which devices are allowed to access corporate networks. Employees should only be permitted to connect using **company-approved devices** or **secure personal devices** with appropriate security measures in place.
- **Access Time Restrictions**: Consider imposing **time-based access** controls. For example, remote access may be allowed only during specific working hours, or access to sensitive data may be limited to certain locations or regions.

Best Practices for Creating Remote Access Policies:

- **Be Clear and Specific**: Avoid vague language. Define the exact systems and services employees can access remotely, and under what conditions.
- **Regularly Review and Update**: As new threats emerge and business needs change, remote access policies should be updated regularly to ensure they remain relevant and effective.

Practical Example:
A **global consulting firm** implemented a remote access policy that required **VPN** usage for all remote work and **MFA** for logging into corporate systems. They restricted access to financial data to only senior finance team members, who were required to use company-issued laptops with full disk encryption.

Outcome:
This policy effectively secured the company's data while still allowing employees the flexibility to work remotely, improving productivity and maintaining high security standards.

---

2. Implement Strong BYOD (Bring Your Own Device) Security Measures

Allowing employees to use their **personal devices** for work (BYOD) offers flexibility, but it can also create significant security risks if not properly managed. Organizations need to establish clear guidelines and deploy the right tools to ensure that personal devices do not become weak links in the security chain.

Key BYOD Security Best Practices:

- **Mobile Device Management (MDM)**:
  Use **MDM software** to manage and secure employees' personal devices. MDM allows organizations to enforce security policies, such as encryption, strong password requirements, and remote wipe functionality in case of loss or theft.

- **Device Encryption**:
  Ensure that all personal devices accessing corporate data are **encrypted**. This prevents unauthorized access to sensitive information if the device is lost or stolen.
- **Separation of Work and Personal Data**:
  Implement a **containerization** approach to separate work-related data and personal data on employees' devices. This ensures that work data is protected and is not mixed with personal apps or data.
- **App Control and Whitelisting**:
  Restrict which applications can be installed on personal devices. By only allowing **approved apps** and using app whitelisting, you reduce the risk of malware or unauthorized apps gaining access to your corporate network.
- **Remote Wipe Capability**:
  Enable the ability to remotely wipe devices if they are lost, stolen, or if an employee leaves the company. This ensures that sensitive corporate data is erased from the device and cannot be accessed by unauthorized individuals.

Best Practices for BYOD:

- **Set Clear Device Requirements**: Establish guidelines for what constitutes an acceptable device (e.g., operating system version, security software) and require employees to register their devices with IT before they can access corporate resources.
- **Educate Employees**: Make sure employees are aware of the security risks involved in using personal devices for work and provide regular training on best practices.

Practical Example:
A **marketing agency** implemented an MDM solution to manage employees' personal smartphones and tablets. Employees were required to download the MDM app before accessing company email and file-sharing platforms. The company also enforced **strong password policies** and **remote wipe** functionality in case a device was lost.

Outcome:
The agency was able to secure sensitive client data while allowing employees the flexibility to use their personal devices for work, ensuring compliance with internal security standards.

3. Ensure Secure Communication Channels

In a remote work environment, employees are communicating more frequently via **email**, **video calls**, and **instant messaging**. Securing these communication channels is critical to maintaining data privacy and protecting sensitive information.

Best Practices for Secure Communication:

- **Encrypted Email**:
  Use **email encryption tools** to ensure that sensitive messages and attachments are protected. This can prevent hackers from intercepting emails during transmission.
- **Secure Messaging Platforms**:
  Use secure **instant messaging** and **video conferencing** platforms that offer **end-to-end encryption (E2EE)**. E2EE ensures that only the sender and the recipient can read the content of the message or conversation, even if it is intercepted.
- **File Sharing Security**:
  When employees share files, ensure they are using secure cloud-based platforms (e.g., **Google Drive**, **Dropbox**, **OneDrive**) that offer encryption and access controls.
- **Virtual Private Networks (VPNs)**:
  Encourage employees to use a VPN when accessing communication platforms from public or unsecured networks, ensuring that data in transit remains encrypted and secure.

Practical Example:

A **software company** switched to using **Zoom** with **end-to-end encryption** for all team meetings and client consultations. They also encouraged employees to use **encrypted email services** when sending sensitive documentation.

Outcome:
This approach protected both internal and client communications, ensuring privacy even when employees were working from unsecured or public networks.

4. Conduct Regular Security Awareness Training

One of the most effective ways to mitigate risks associated with remote work and BYOD policies is through **ongoing security awareness training**. Human error remains one of the biggest threats to cybersecurity, so it's important to educate employees on how to recognize and prevent common threats like **phishing**, **social engineering**, and **malware**.

Key Components of Security Awareness Training:

- **Phishing Awareness**:
  Train employees to recognize phishing emails, suspicious links, and fraudulent requests for personal or financial information. Provide examples of common phishing tactics and how to respond to suspicious emails.
- **Password Security**:
  Educate employees on the importance of using strong, unique passwords for each account and the risks of password reuse. Encourage the use of **password managers** to securely store credentials.
- **Safe Browsing Practices**:
  Encourage safe browsing practices, such as avoiding public Wi-Fi for work-related tasks, and using **VPNs** to secure data when accessing the internet remotely.
- **Data Protection**:
  Provide training on how to handle and store sensitive data, both on personal devices and in the cloud. Teach employees about the **principles of least privilege** and how to securely share files.

Practical Example:
A **healthcare organization** implemented quarterly **security training sessions** for remote workers, covering topics such as phishing, safe use of personal devices, and HIPAA compliance. They also ran simulated phishing campaigns to test employee awareness and responsiveness.

Outcome:
Employees became more vigilant against cybersecurity threats, significantly reducing the risk of phishing attacks and data breaches.

5. Regularly Review and Update Policies

As the landscape of remote work and cloud solutions evolves, it's essential to regularly **review and update** your remote access and BYOD policies. This ensures that your organization remains compliant with regulations and adapts to emerging security threats.

Key Areas to Review Regularly:

- **Security Tools**: Ensure that your MDM, VPN, and encryption tools are up-to-date and meet the latest security standards.
- **Access Controls**: Periodically review user permissions and remote access configurations to ensure that only authorized employees can access sensitive data.
- **Compliance Requirements**: Stay informed about changes in data protection laws (e.g., **GDPR, CCPA**) and ensure that your policies align with the latest requirements.

Practical Example:
A **law firm** reviewed their remote access and BYOD policies every six months to ensure compliance with **GDPR** and **HIPAA**. They updated their VPN configuration, encryption methods, and access permissions to address new security concerns and regulatory changes.

Outcome:
The firm maintained a secure environment for both employees and clients while staying compliant with legal and regulatory obligations.

Flowchart: Best Practices for Remote Access and BYOD Policies

```
                        Start
                          |
                          V
          [Create Clear Remote Access Policies]
                          |
                          V
```

```
       [Enforce VPN, MFA, and Device Restrictions]
                          |
                          V
          [Implement BYOD Security Measures (MDM)]
                          |
                          V
       [Ensure Secure Communication (Email, Messaging)]
                          |
                          V
          [Conduct Regular Security Awareness Training]
                          |
                          V
      [Review and Update Remote Access Policies Regularly]
                          |
                          V
              [Ensure Ongoing Compliance]
```

Securing remote access and managing BYOD policies are critical aspects of maintaining a secure, flexible, and compliant workforce. By implementing strong security practices, providing employee education, and continuously reviewing your policies, you can protect your organization's sensitive data while enabling employees to work remotely using their own devices.

As the nature of work continues to evolve, these best practices will help your organization stay ahead of potential threats and ensure that your remote work environment remains both productive and secure.

Part 5: Continuing Your Cybersecurity Journey (Ongoing Improvements)

Chapter 14: Monitoring, Auditing, and Improving Your Cybersecurity

Cybersecurity is not a one-time setup; it's an ongoing process. As technology evolves and new threats emerge, your business must remain vigilant to safeguard sensitive data and systems. Continuous monitoring, regular security audits, and timely updates to your cybersecurity measures are essential to maintain a strong defense against cyberattacks.

In this chapter, we'll dive into the critical components of **continuous monitoring**, **security audits**, and **vulnerability testing**, and explore how businesses can stay proactive in adapting to new threats. By the end of this chapter, you'll have the tools and strategies to ensure your cybersecurity measures are always up to date and effective.

14.1: The Importance of Continuous Monitoring

In the fast-paced world of cybersecurity, threats evolve constantly, and new vulnerabilities appear every day. This makes it increasingly difficult to rely on one-time security measures or static defenses. **Continuous monitoring** provides the proactive oversight needed to keep systems secure in an ever-changing environment. Think of it as your organization's "security heartbeat"—constantly checking and reacting to potential risks before they escalate into full-blown security incidents.

In this section, we will explore why continuous monitoring is essential for modern cybersecurity, how it works, and the best practices for implementing it in your organization.

What is Continuous Monitoring?

Continuous monitoring is the real-time tracking of your organization's security environment to detect, analyze, and respond to potential security threats, breaches, or vulnerabilities. Unlike periodic checks or audits, which happen at set intervals, continuous monitoring is an ongoing process that involves the automated collection, analysis, and reporting of security data at all times.

In simpler terms, continuous monitoring allows you to spot security issues **as they arise** rather than waiting for a routine audit to uncover problems.

Why is Continuous Monitoring Important?

1. **Proactive Defense**:
   With the increasing sophistication of cyber threats, a reactive approach to security (waiting until a breach occurs) is no longer enough. Continuous monitoring helps organizations stay ahead of threats by detecting malicious activities or vulnerabilities in real-time. By catching issues early, companies can mitigate the damage before it escalates into a serious breach.
2. **Increased Visibility**:
   Continuous monitoring provides **constant visibility** into your IT environment. This means that you can track all activities—whether it's a failed login attempt, suspicious network traffic, or access to sensitive files—and analyze them for potential risks.
3. **Regulatory Compliance**:
   Many industries require organizations to continuously monitor their systems for compliance purposes. For example, **HIPAA**, **GDPR**, and **PCI-DSS** demand that businesses constantly monitor access to sensitive data to ensure privacy and security. Continuous monitoring helps demonstrate compliance by maintaining detailed logs and enabling real-time reporting.
4. **Incident Response Readiness**:
   With continuous monitoring in place, your organization can respond to security incidents faster. Automated alerts and real-time data give security teams the insight they need to take action immediately, whether it's blocking malicious IP addresses, disabling compromised accounts, or isolating infected systems.

Key Components of Continuous Monitoring

1. **Network Monitoring**:
   Network monitoring tracks all traffic within and outside your network to detect anomalies, such as unusual data flow or unauthorized access attempts. This is vital in identifying cyberattacks like **Distributed Denial of Service (DDoS)**, **brute force attacks**, or **data exfiltration**.
   - **Best Practice**: Use network monitoring tools like **Wireshark** or **SolarWinds** to detect unusual traffic patterns and unauthorized devices trying to connect to your network.

2. **Endpoint Monitoring**:
   Every device connected to your network—laptops, smartphones, workstations, etc.—is a potential entry point for attackers **Endpoint monitoring** ensures that devices comply with security policies, run updated antivirus software, and are free from malware.
   - **Best Practice**: Implement **Endpoint Detection and Response (EDR)** solutions like **CrowdStrike** or **Carbon Black** to continuously monitor device health, detect threats, and respond swiftly to security events.

3. **User Behavior Monitoring**:
   User behavior analytics (UBA) track how users interact with systems, files, and applications. This is particularly useful for detecting **insider threats**—employees or contractors who misuse their access privileges.
   - **Best Practice**: Use **UBA tools** like **Splunk** or **Sumo Logic** to analyze normal user behavior patterns and flag anomalies, such as an employee accessing files outside their typical scope of work.

4. **Application Monitoring**:
   Monitoring the performance and behavior of applications—especially those that handle sensitive data—is crucial for spotting vulnerabilities or signs of an attack, such as unauthorized data access or SQL injection attempts.
   - **Best Practice**: Use **Web Application Firewalls (WAFs)** and **Application Performance Monitoring (APM)** tools like **New Relic** to monitor the security and functionality of applications in real-time.

5. **Log Management and Analysis**:
   Logs are a vital source of information about the health and security of your systems. Continuous monitoring collects and analyzes logs to detect events like unauthorized access, malware infections, and policy violations.
   - o **Best Practice**: Leverage **SIEM (Security Information and Event Management)** systems such as **Splunk** or **Elastic Stack** to aggregate and analyze logs from different sources (network devices, servers, applications) and generate real-time alerts.

How Continuous Monitoring Works

Continuous monitoring relies on **automation** and **real-time data analysis** to spot suspicious activities as they happen. Here's how it typically works:

1. **Data Collection**:
   Continuous monitoring tools gather data from various sources, including network traffic, user actions, endpoint devices, logs, and applications. This data is continuously fed into a monitoring system for analysis.
2. **Data Correlation**:
   The monitoring tools analyze the data and correlate it with known patterns, threat intelligence feeds, and security rules. For example, if there's an increase in login attempts from an unfamiliar location or multiple failed logins, the system may flag this as a potential **brute force attack**.
3. **Alert Generation**:
   Once the monitoring tools detect an anomaly or potential threat, they generate an **alert** that is sent to the security team. These alerts can be configured based on severity levels, so your team can prioritize critical incidents and investigate others later.
4. **Incident Response**:
   In the event of a confirmed security incident, continuous monitoring tools help guide the incident response by providing real-time data, including the affected systems, users, and activities. Security teams can then take immediate action, such as isolating compromised systems or blocking malicious IP addresses.

Best Practices for Continuous Monitoring

1. **Set Up Automated Alerts**:
    Automated alerts allow security teams to quickly respond to threats. Create threshold-based alerts for high-risk events like multiple failed logins, unauthorized access to sensitive data, or unusual network activity.
2. **Implement a Centralized Monitoring System**:
    Use **SIEM** tools to collect data from across the network, applications, and endpoints. This provides a unified view of your security posture and allows for better correlation and faster identification of threats.
3. **Integrate Threat Intelligence**:
    Leverage **threat intelligence feeds** to keep your monitoring systems updated with the latest attack methods and emerging threats. Integrating threat intelligence ensures that your monitoring systems are proactive and responsive to the newest tactics used by cybercriminals.
4. **Regularly Review and Update Monitoring Parameters**:
    The threat landscape evolves, and so should your monitoring parameters. Regularly assess and adjust your monitoring configurations to ensure they remain relevant to current threats and technologies.
5. **Perform Continuous Vulnerability Scanning**:
    Continuously scan your infrastructure, applications, and endpoints for vulnerabilities. Use automated tools to identify unpatched systems, misconfigured services, or exposed ports that could be exploited by attackers.

Case Study: Continuous Monitoring in Action

Let's look at an example of how **continuous monitoring** worked in a real-world scenario.

Company: A **global e-commerce business** with a large customer base and an online store.

Challenges:

The company faced frequent cyberattacks, including **brute force login attempts**, **malware infections**, and **unauthorized access to customer data**. With customers relying on the platform for secure transactions, maintaining data security was crucial.

Solution:

The business implemented a **continuous monitoring system** with the following features:

- **Network traffic analysis** to detect unusual spikes in activity that could indicate DDoS attacks.
- **MFA and behavior analytics** to detect abnormal login patterns, such as logins from new locations or devices.
- **Real-time alerts** and **SIEM integration** to provide immediate insight into security incidents and incidents related to customer data.

Outcome:

Within three months, the company identified and stopped an ongoing **credential stuffing attack** attempting to gain unauthorized access to user accounts. The attack had originated from a compromised third-party service used by many of their customers. With continuous monitoring, the company was able to block the attack in real-time, preventing data breaches and protecting customer information.

Flowchart: Continuous Monitoring Process

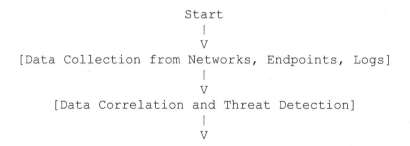

```
                        Start
                          |
                          V
        [Data Collection from Networks, Endpoints, Logs]
                          |
                          V
            [Data Correlation and Threat Detection]
                          |
                          V
```

```
        [Automated Alert Generation]
                    |
                    V
    [Incident Response (Isolation/Blocking)]
                    |
                    V
          [Post-Incident Analysis]
                    |
                    V
  [Review and Update Monitoring Parameters]
                    |
                    V
         [Ensure Ongoing Monitoring]
```

Continuous monitoring is a crucial component of any robust cybersecurity strategy. By actively tracking network traffic, user behavior, application activity, and endpoints, organizations can detect and respond to threats in real-time, minimizing potential damage. Implementing continuous monitoring, along with automated alerts and real-time incident response, not only improves security but also ensures regulatory compliance and better business continuity.

14.2: Regular Security Audits and Vulnerability Testing

In today's digital age, organizations face an ever-growing array of cyber threats. From malware and ransomware attacks to insider threats and phishing schemes, the need to stay ahead of these risks is paramount. One of the most effective ways to do this is through **regular security audits** and **vulnerability testing**. These practices provide proactive measures to identify weaknesses in your systems and processes before they are exploited by attackers.

In this section, we'll dive deep into the significance of security audits and vulnerability testing, the types of tests and audits organizations should perform, and how to implement them effectively to safeguard your business.

What Are Security Audits and Vulnerability Testing?

1. Security Audits:

A **security audit** is a comprehensive evaluation of your organization's security policies, procedures, and infrastructure. Its goal is to assess how well your current security controls are working and whether they align with best practices and industry standards.

Types of Security Audits:

- **Internal Audits**: These are conducted by your in-house security team or external consultants who evaluate internal systems and policies.
- **External Audits**: External auditors assess your security posture from an outsider's perspective, identifying vulnerabilities you may have missed.
- **Compliance Audits**: Specific to industry regulations, compliance audits verify that your organization is adhering to laws like **HIPAA, GDPR**, and **PCI DSS**.

2. Vulnerability Testing:

Vulnerability testing identifies weaknesses within your system that could be exploited by attackers. Vulnerability testing goes beyond identifying surface-level issues to uncover deeper security flaws that could potentially lead to significant breaches.

Types of Vulnerability Testing:

- **Automated Vulnerability Scanning**: This involves using tools like **Nessus, Qualys**, or **OpenVAS** to automatically scan your systems for known vulnerabilities and misconfigurations.
- **Penetration Testing (Pen Testing)**: Ethical hackers simulate cyberattacks to identify vulnerabilities in a controlled environment. Pen testing often includes manual techniques that automated scans might miss.

- **Web Application Testing**: Focused on web apps, this testing identifies issues such as **SQL injection**, **cross-site scripting (XSS)**, and **cross-site request forgery (CSRF)**.
- **Network Testing**: This tests for issues within the network infrastructure, including open ports, weak firewalls, and insecure protocols.

Why Regular Security Audits and Vulnerability Testing Are Essential

1. **Identify Security Gaps**:
   Regular audits and testing help identify vulnerabilities that could otherwise remain hidden, preventing them from being exploited by cybercriminals. For example, missing security patches, outdated software, and misconfigured network settings are common gaps that can easily be fixed before they're used as attack vectors.
2. **Stay Ahead of Emerging Threats**:
   Cyber threats evolve rapidly. Vulnerability testing helps your organization stay up-to-date with the latest threats by identifying newly discovered vulnerabilities. This ensures that your organization is proactive in addressing vulnerabilities before they're exploited.
3. **Regulatory Compliance**:
   Security audits are a critical component of many compliance frameworks, including **HIPAA**, **GDPR**, and **PCI DSS**. Regular audits help ensure that your organization remains compliant with industry regulations, reducing the risk of fines, penalties, or legal consequences.
4. **Improve Incident Response**:
   By identifying and fixing vulnerabilities, audits and testing improve your organization's ability to respond to incidents. A thorough understanding of your systems and weaknesses allows your security team to react quickly and effectively in the event of an attack.
5. **Building Trust**:
   For businesses handling sensitive data—such as in finance, healthcare, or e-commerce—demonstrating a proactive approach to cybersecurity builds trust with clients, partners, and stakeholders.

Regular audits and testing show that you are committed to protecting their data and privacy.

How to Perform Regular Security Audits

Performing security audits involves a combination of automated tools, manual checks, and adherence to industry standards. Here's how to effectively conduct an audit:

1. Identify Audit Scope and Objectives

Before starting an audit, define the scope and objectives. What are you trying to accomplish? Are you checking compliance, assessing vulnerabilities, or improving internal security policies?

Steps to Take:

- Define which systems, networks, and data you want to evaluate.
- Determine whether the audit will focus on a specific area, such as **network security**, **cloud infrastructure**, or **user access controls**.

2. Evaluate Security Policies and Procedures

A security audit begins with a review of your organization's **security policies** and **procedures**. This includes assessing how well your existing policies align with industry standards and whether they are followed in practice.

What to Review:

- **Access Control Policies**: Who has access to what data and resources? Are user roles and permissions appropriately defined?
- **Incident Response Procedures**: How well-prepared is your team to respond to a security incident?
- **Security Awareness Training**: Do employees undergo regular security awareness training to recognize phishing attempts, social engineering, and other threats?

3. Assess Technical Infrastructure and Systems

The next step involves analyzing the technical infrastructure. This is where you review systems for misconfigurations, vulnerabilities, and weak spots. Common areas to evaluate include:

- **Firewalls**: Are firewalls configured correctly to block unauthorized access?
- **Encryption**: Is sensitive data encrypted in transit and at rest?
- **Patch Management**: Are all systems and software regularly updated with security patches?

4. Conduct Interviews and Surveys

Talking to employees is a key aspect of the audit. Interviewing key personnel can uncover issues that aren't easily detected through technical scans. For instance, you might learn that certain employees aren't following security best practices or that security tools are underused.

What to Ask:

- How often do employees use strong passwords?
- Do they use multi-factor authentication (MFA) for accessing sensitive systems?
- Are there any manual processes that need to be secured or automated?

How to Perform Vulnerability Testing

Vulnerability testing typically involves the following steps:

1. Conduct Automated Vulnerability Scanning

Start by running automated vulnerability scanning tools on your network, applications, and systems. These tools will flag potential security issues like outdated software versions, exposed ports, or weak passwords.

Tools to Use:

- **Nessus**: A popular vulnerability scanner that checks for known vulnerabilities in systems.
- **OpenVAS**: Another comprehensive tool for scanning networks and systems for vulnerabilities.
- **Qualys**: A cloud-based vulnerability scanning tool used for automated scanning of web applications and network infrastructures.

2. Perform Penetration Testing (Pen Testing)

Penetration testing is the process of actively attempting to exploit identified vulnerabilities in a system. Ethical hackers simulate real-world attacks to see how easily an attacker could gain unauthorized access.

Types of Pen Testing:

- **External Penetration Testing**: Testing the outside perimeter of your network (e.g., firewalls, public-facing applications) for vulnerabilities.
- **Internal Penetration Testing**: Testing from the inside, simulating an attack by a compromised employee or insider threat.
- **Web Application Pen Testing**: Focuses specifically on identifying vulnerabilities in web applications.

3. Test Web Application Security

Web applications are often the primary target for cybercriminals due to their role in handling sensitive data. Regular testing should identify risks such as **SQL injection**, **XSS**, and **CSRF**.

Tools to Use:

- **OWASP ZAP**: A popular open-source tool for detecting web application vulnerabilities.
- **Burp Suite**: Another tool for testing web applications for security flaws, including automated vulnerability scanning and manual testing features.

4. Network Testing and Assessment

Network security is a foundational aspect of overall cybersecurity. Running network tests helps identify weak points, such as exposed ports or improperly configured routers, that could provide an entry point for attackers.

Tools to Use:

- **Wireshark**: An open-source network protocol analyzer that can capture and inspect network traffic in real-time.
- **Nmap**: A tool used for network mapping and vulnerability scanning.

Best Practices for Conducting Regular Security Audits and Vulnerability Testing

- **Schedule Regular Audits**: Perform audits at least **quarterly** or **annually** depending on your organization's needs and the sensitivity of your data.
- **Automate Where Possible**: Use automated tools for vulnerability scanning and logging to make the audit process more efficient.
- **Use External Experts for Pen Testing**: Consider hiring external security experts or ethical hackers for penetration testing to get an unbiased assessment of your systems.
- **Act on Audit Findings**: Prioritize the findings from audits and vulnerability tests based on risk. Address high-priority issues (e.g., data breaches or exposed access points) first.
- **Document and Report Findings**: Create detailed reports for audit and test findings, including recommendations for remediation and action plans.

Case Study: Security Audit and Vulnerability Testing at a Financial Institution

Company: A **financial institution** that handles sensitive customer data, including banking details and credit card information.

Challenges:

The institution was concerned about its ability to detect insider threats and wanted to ensure compliance with **PCI DSS** requirements for protecting cardholder data.

Solution:

The institution conducted the following:

- **Regular internal audits** to assess compliance with PCI DSS and other financial regulations.
- **Penetration testing** to identify potential vulnerabilities in their online banking platform.
- **Automated vulnerability scans** using Nessus and Qualys to identify any security flaws in their network.

Outcome:

The audit revealed several areas of improvement, including outdated software versions and weak access controls on internal systems. Penetration testing uncovered a vulnerability in the login process that could have allowed unauthorized access to sensitive accounts. As a result, the institution implemented stronger **access control policies** and **updated their patch management** process, preventing potential security breaches.

Flowchart: Conducting Regular Security Audits and Vulnerability Testing

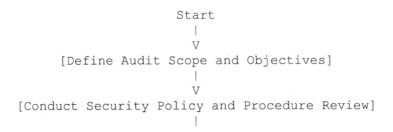

```
                    Start
                     |
                     V
        [Define Audit Scope and Objectives]
                     |
                     V
    [Conduct Security Policy and Procedure Review]
                     |
```

```
                              V
        [Evaluate Technical Infrastructure and Systems]
                              |
                              V
          [Perform Automated Vulnerability Scanning]
                              |
                              V
        [Conduct Penetration Testing (Pen Testing)]
                              |
                              V
         [Test Web Applications and Network Security]
                              |
                              V
       [Identify Vulnerabilities and Develop Action Plan]
                              |
                              V
       [Remediate Vulnerabilities and Strengthen Security]
                              |
                              V
              [Conduct Follow-up Testing]
                              |
                              V
          [Ensure Ongoing Security Improvements]
```

Regular security audits and vulnerability testing are essential practices for any organization that wants to maintain a strong security posture and protect its assets. By proactively identifying and addressing vulnerabilities, businesses can significantly reduce the risk of cyberattacks and ensure that they remain compliant with regulatory standards. These proactive measures also enhance incident response capabilities, making it easier to detect and respond to potential threats before they become major issues.

14.3: Adapting to New Threats and Updating Security Measures

In the world of cybersecurity, **change is constant**. New threats emerge daily as cybercriminals develop more sophisticated methods to exploit vulnerabilities. As a result, your security measures must continuously evolve to stay ahead of these threats. If you fail to adapt and update your security practices, your organization could become a target for devastating attacks that compromise sensitive data, harm your reputation, and disrupt operations.

In this section, we'll explore the importance of **adapting to new threats**, **updating security measures**, and the best practices for keeping your organization's defenses strong in a constantly changing cyber threat landscape. We'll also provide real-world examples of how businesses have successfully adapted to new threats and the lessons they learned along the way.

Why Adapting to New Threats is Crucial

The threat landscape evolves rapidly, with new attack methods, malware variants, and exploitation techniques emerging frequently. Cybercriminals are constantly innovating, and **what worked in the past may no longer be effective** against the attacks of today or tomorrow. This is why adapting to new threats and regularly updating your security measures is not just a good practice—it's a necessity.

1. Emerging Cyber Threats

Some of the most significant emerging threats in the cybersecurity space include:

- **Ransomware**: Attackers lock or encrypt a victim's data and demand payment (typically in cryptocurrency) to restore access. Ransomware-as-a-service platforms have made it easier for even non-technical individuals to launch attacks.
- **Fileless Malware**: Instead of installing files on a victim's computer, fileless malware runs directly in memory, making it harder to detect by traditional antivirus programs.
- **Phishing 2.0**: Cybercriminals have perfected social engineering tactics, creating more convincing and sophisticated phishing emails that are harder to spot and can trick even the most cautious employees.
- **Insider Threats**: These can come from disgruntled employees or contractors who misuse their access to steal or damage sensitive

data. With remote work on the rise, insider threats are increasingly difficult to detect.

- **IoT Vulnerabilities**: As businesses adopt more **Internet of Things (IoT)** devices, hackers are exploiting vulnerabilities in these often unsecured devices to gain access to corporate networks.

2. The Dangers of Falling Behind

If you fail to update your security measures and respond to new threats, you open the door for attackers to exploit vulnerabilities in your system. Falling behind can lead to:

- **Data Breaches**: Exposing customer, employee, or company data, which can lead to financial loss, reputational damage, and legal consequences.
- **System Downtime**: Cyberattacks such as DDoS attacks or ransomware can lock down operations and lead to significant business disruption.
- **Reputation Damage**: Consumers trust businesses with their data. If that trust is broken due to outdated security, you risk losing customers and market share.

3. How Adapting Can Mitigate Risks

Adapting to new threats involves continuously monitoring the cybersecurity landscape, updating defense strategies, and being proactive. This approach helps identify new vulnerabilities, strengthens your existing defenses, and reduces the overall risk of attacks.

How to Adapt to New Threats and Update Security Measures

To ensure your business stays protected in the face of evolving threats, follow these key strategies for adapting and updating security measures:

1. Stay Informed About Emerging Threats

The first step in adapting to new threats is **staying informed**. The cyber threat landscape is constantly changing, and to effectively defend against new attacks, you need to understand what you're up against. Regularly monitoring threat intelligence feeds, attending industry conferences, and participating in cybersecurity webinars are essential to keep up with the latest trends.

Sources for Threat Intelligence:

- **Cybersecurity Blogs and Websites**: Websites like **KrebsOnSecurity**, **DarkReading**, and **ThreatPost** provide regular updates on the latest cybersecurity threats and breaches.
- **Threat Intelligence Services**: Subscribe to threat intelligence services like **FireEye** or **CrowdStrike**, which offer real-time data about emerging threats.
- **Industry Sharing Groups**: Participate in industry-specific sharing groups (e.g., **FS-ISAC** for financial institutions) to learn about threats targeting your sector.

Best Practice: Set up alerts or subscribe to threat feeds that deliver information directly to your security team, so you can react quickly to any new developments.

---

2. Implement a Layered Security Strategy

A **defense-in-depth** approach ensures that even if one security measure fails, there are others in place to stop an attack. It's essential to regularly review and **enhance your security layers** to stay ahead of attackers.

Key Security Layers to Implement:

- **Firewalls**: Ensure firewalls are up to date and configured to block any traffic that might be suspicious or unauthorized.
- **Endpoint Security**: Use **Endpoint Detection and Response (EDR)** tools to protect devices like laptops, smartphones, and IoT devices from malware, ransomware, and other threats.

- **Application Security**: Regularly test and patch applications for known vulnerabilities, such as **SQL injection**, **cross-site scripting (XSS)**, and **buffer overflow attacks**.
- **Network Segmentation**: Divide your network into smaller, isolated segments to prevent an attacker from gaining acccss to the entire system in case of a breach.
- **Encryption**: Use strong encryption to protect sensitive data, both **at rest** and **in transit**. This helps safeguard against **data breaches** or **intercepted communications**.

Practical Example: A **global e-commerce company** adopted a defense-in-depth approach by implementing firewalls at the perimeter, using **EDR tools** for endpoint protection, and applying **web application firewalls (WAFs)** to secure their online store from common vulnerabilities.

Outcome:
When a new **ransomware attack** targeted the e-commerce sector, the company was able to block the attack at multiple points—preventing it from reaching critical systems and protecting customer data.

---

3. Regularly Update and Patch Systems

Keeping your systems up to date is one of the simplest yet most effective ways to protect your organization from emerging threats. New vulnerabilities are discovered regularly, and **patching** is your first line of defense.

Best Practices for Patch Management:

- **Automate Patching**: Set up automated patch management systems to apply patches as soon as they're released. **Windows Server Update Services (WSUS)** and **SCCM** can automate this process for Microsoft environments.
- **Prioritize Critical Updates**: Focus on high-priority patches for critical infrastructure, such as web servers, databases, and any publicly exposed services.
- **Test Before Deploying**: Ensure patches are tested on non-production systems before being rolled out to production environments to avoid disruptions.

Practical Example:
A **healthcare provider** implemented an automated patch management solution for all its critical systems. By prioritizing patches for systems that stored patient health records, they were able to block **ransomware attacks** that targeted known vulnerabilities in unpatched systems.

Outcome:
The healthcare provider maintained a strong security posture and remained compliant with **HIPAA** by ensuring that all patient data was stored securely and updated regularly.

---

4. Use Threat Simulation and Red Teaming

Red teaming involves simulating real-world attacks to evaluate your organization's ability to withstand and respond to threats. This can help identify weaknesses that regular vulnerability testing might miss.

Steps to Implement Red Teaming:

- **Engage Ethical Hackers**: Hire ethical hackers or external cybersecurity firms to conduct penetration tests and simulate attacks based on current threats.
- **Scenario-Based Exercises**: Use **tabletop exercises** or **real-world attack simulations** to test your team's incident response capabilities and readiness for specific types of attacks (e.g., DDoS, insider threat, or supply chain attacks).
- **Continuous Improvement**: After each simulation or test, analyze the results and update your security protocols, training, and response strategies accordingly.

Practical Example: A **large financial institution** regularly conducts **red teaming exercises** to simulate various types of cyberattacks, from insider threats to external breaches. They also perform **blue team** exercises to ensure their defense measures can identify and stop attacks in real-time.

Outcome:
The institution was able to refine its incident response plan, uncover gaps in security, and improve its overall defense mechanisms by learning from these simulated attacks.

5. Employee Training and Awareness

Your employees are often the first line of defense against new threats. **Social engineering** tactics like **phishing** or **spear-phishing** attacks are on the rise, and employees need to be trained to recognize and respond appropriately.

Training Best Practices:

- **Regular Phishing Simulations**: Conduct simulated phishing attacks to teach employees how to recognize suspicious emails, links, and attachments.
- **Security Awareness Campaigns**: Launch ongoing campaigns to educate employees about the latest threats, such as **ransomware** or **business email compromise (BEC)**.
- **MFA Adoption**: Train employees to use **multi-factor authentication (MFA)** for accessing sensitive systems and accounts.

Practical Example:
A **law firm** launched a security awareness training program that included monthly workshops on identifying phishing attempts and other common social engineering attacks. They also ran **simulated phishing exercises** to test employee readiness.

Outcome:
The law firm significantly reduced the number of successful phishing attacks and educated employees on best security practices.

Flowchart: Adapting to New Threats and Updating Security Measures

```
                    Start
                      |
                      V
        [Stay Informed on Emerging Threats]
                      |
                      V
```

```
[Implement Defense-in-Depth Strategy]
                |
                V
[Regularly Update and Patch Systems]
                |
                V
[Use Red Teaming and Threat Simulations]
                |
                V
[Conduct Ongoing Employee Security Training]
                |
                V
[Analyze and Act on Testing Results]
                |
                V
[Adapt and Improve Security Measures]
                |
                V
[Ensure Continuous Monitoring]
```

Adapting to new threats and updating security measures is an ongoing effort that requires vigilance, flexibility, and proactive action. By staying informed about emerging threats, implementing layered security strategies, regularly updating and patching systems, and using red teaming, businesses can keep their cybersecurity defenses robust and responsive.

Chapter 15: Engaging External Experts and Resources

In the complex world of cybersecurity, no one expects you to be an expert in every field. As the threat landscape grows more sophisticated, there comes a point where **external expertise** is no longer optional but essential. Whether you're looking for specialized knowledge, handling complex security issues, or scaling your security capabilities, **engaging external experts** and **leveraging external resources** can be game-changers.

In this chapter, we will explore when and how to hire **cybersecurity consultants**, understand the role of **Managed Security Service Providers (MSSPs)**, and provide guidance on **learning resources** to foster continuous cybersecurity improvement within your organization. These insights will help you build a robust, well-rounded cybersecurity strategy while making the most of external expertise.

15.1: When to Hire Cybersecurity Consultants

Cybersecurity is a critical component of any business, but it's not always feasible for every organization to have a full-time, in-house cybersecurity team, especially when you're just starting out or facing specific, complex security challenges. This is where **cybersecurity consultants** come in. They offer specialized expertise, help navigate security issues, and provide fresh perspectives to improve your organization's security posture.

But when should you **hire a cybersecurity consultant**? What kind of situations demand external expertise? In this guide, we'll explore when and why you might need a consultant, how to find the right one, and how to leverage their expertise effectively. We'll also look at real-world examples to help you understand the value consultants can bring to your organization.

1. When You Lack In-House Expertise for Specific Security Challenges

Cybersecurity is a vast and specialized field. While your internal team may be capable of handling routine tasks, some security challenges require specific expertise—especially when dealing with sophisticated cyber threats or advanced technologies.

What It Looks Like:

- You need assistance with specialized areas, such as **penetration testing**, **cloud security**, **risk assessments**, or **compliance**.
- Your in-house team is overwhelmed with regular tasks and needs external help to address more complex challenges.

Practical Example: A **mid-sized tech company** wanted to migrate their services to the cloud but lacked the expertise to ensure the migration was secure. They hired a **cloud security consultant** who designed the entire migration process, ensured compliance with relevant regulations (e.g., **GDPR**), and implemented secure configurations for cloud infrastructure.

Outcome: The company was able to migrate smoothly without exposing sensitive data to risks, ensuring both security and compliance while avoiding potential regulatory penalties.

2. After a Cybersecurity Incident or Breach

One of the most pressing reasons to hire a cybersecurity consultant is after a **cyberattack** or **data breach**. When your business is compromised, the first priority is to understand the extent of the damage, mitigate the attack, and ensure that it doesn't happen again. A consultant with experience in **incident response** can help you manage the crisis efficiently.

What It Looks Like:

- A ransomware attack encrypts your data and demands payment.

- Sensitive customer data has been exposed in a data breach.
- Your systems are showing signs of **malware** or **unauthorized access**.

Practical Example: A **financial institution** was hit by a ransomware attack that compromised access to critical client data. The internal IT team was unable to restore the systems quickly and assess the full extent of the attack. They hired a **cybersecurity consultant** specializing in **incident response** to contain the breach, assess the impact, and guide them through the recovery process.

Outcome: The consultant helped the firm recover the data, strengthen their defenses, and rebuild customer trust. They also helped the organization create a **robust incident response plan** to handle future threats more effectively.

3. When You're Trying to Meet Industry-Specific Compliance Requirements

Compliance with data protection regulations is critical for many businesses, particularly those in regulated industries such as **finance**, **healthcare**, **e-commerce**, and **education**. Navigating complex legal frameworks like **GDPR**, **HIPAA**, or **PCI DSS** often requires external expertise to ensure full compliance and avoid penalties.

What It Looks Like:

- Your organization needs to ensure compliance with industry regulations like **GDPR** for handling EU customer data or **HIPAA** for managing healthcare data.
- You're preparing for an external audit and need to ensure your security measures meet regulatory standards.
- Your internal team lacks deep knowledge of these specific requirements.

Practical Example: A **healthcare provider** needed to comply with **HIPAA** regulations and protect sensitive patient information. The in-house IT team was focused on daily operations and lacked the specialized knowledge required to meet compliance standards. They hired a **cybersecurity consultant** who reviewed their security practices, implemented necessary changes to meet HIPAA requirements, and prepared the company for the upcoming audit.

Outcome: The company achieved HIPAA compliance, avoided potential fines, and strengthened their overall data protection practices. The consultant also provided training for staff to ensure ongoing compliance.

---

4. When Your Organization Is Scaling Rapidly

As your organization grows, so do the complexities of managing security. Scaling your infrastructure, increasing the number of employees, or expanding to new regions often requires **advanced security frameworks** and tools that an in-house team may not be equipped to handle.

What It Looks Like:

- Your business is moving from a small, local operation to a **global enterprise** and needs to ensure your cybersecurity practices can scale with the increased complexity.
- You're expanding into cloud infrastructure, mobile platforms, or IoT devices and need to implement a security architecture that accommodates these new technologies.

Practical Example: A **global e-commerce company** had been growing quickly and moving into new international markets. As they expanded, they realized their existing security infrastructure was insufficient to handle increased traffic, new payment methods, and customer data storage requirements. They brought in a **cybersecurity consultant** to assess and design a scalable security infrastructure that could handle the demands of their expanding business.

Outcome: The consultant helped them implement a **scalable, secure infrastructure** that supported their international growth and ensured sensitive customer data was always protected, regardless of where it was stored or accessed.

5. When You Need a Fresh, Unbiased Perspective

Internal teams often become "too close" to the systems and processes they manage, leading to blind spots in security. Hiring an external consultant can provide an **unbiased** evaluation of your current security posture and offer **fresh insights** that might not be apparent to your internal team.

What It Looks Like:

- Your team has been managing security for a while, but they're unsure if there are hidden vulnerabilities or areas for improvement.
- You've implemented security measures but haven't had an external review in years.

Practical Example: A small manufacturing company had been handling their own cybersecurity for years without a major breach. However, as their company grew and adopted new technologies, they began to worry about their ability to stay ahead of evolving threats. They hired a consultant for a **comprehensive security audit**, which identified outdated security tools, weak passwords, and an under-utilized firewall.

Outcome: The consultant's recommendations led to major improvements in their security infrastructure, reducing the company's exposure to cyberattacks and ensuring that they were better prepared for future threats.

---

6. When You Need Specialized Expertise for Certain Tools or Technologies

As technology continues to advance, many organizations adopt **specialized security tools** or **emerging technologies** that require expert knowledge to implement and configure effectively. Cybersecurity consultants are highly skilled in using and managing these tools, offering guidance on everything from **firewall management** to **threat intelligence** and **cloud security**.

What It Looks Like:

- Your business is adopting new technologies (e.g., **cloud platforms**, **AI-driven security tools**, or **security automation**) and needs help to configure, implement, and manage them securely.
- You're considering a **security information and event management (SIEM)** solution but need guidance on selecting, implementing, and customizing it.

Practical Example: A **financial services company** wanted to implement an **advanced SIEM system** to improve threat detection and response times. They lacked the expertise to integrate it into their existing systems and set it up to meet their specific security needs. A **cybersecurity consultant** helped them choose the right SIEM solution, integrate it with their existing systems, and configure it for **real-time threat monitoring**.

Outcome: The company significantly improved their ability to detect and respond to threats, increasing overall security while reducing manual workload.

How to Hire the Right Cybersecurity Consultant

1. Define Your Needs and Scope

- What specific problems are you facing (e.g., breach recovery, compliance, risk assessment)?
- Do you need a consultant for a one-time project or on an ongoing basis?

2. Check Credentials and Experience

- Look for certifications like **CISSP, CISM, CEH**, or **CompTIA Security+**, which demonstrate expertise in cybersecurity.
- Ask for references or case studies of past work, especially within your industry.

3. Ensure Cultural and Communication Fit

- A consultant should be able to clearly communicate complex technical concepts to non-technical team members.
- They should align with your company culture and be able to work well with your internal teams.

4. Establish Clear Expectations and Outcomes

- Set measurable goals and timelines for the consultant's engagement.
- Ensure there is a clear understanding of deliverables, such as reports, audits, or security improvements.

Flowchart: When to Hire a Cybersecurity Consultant

```
                        Start
                          |
                          V
    [Lack of In-House Expertise?] -- Yes --> [Consultant for
                  Specialized Knowledge]
                          |
                          V
    [After a Cybersecurity Incident?] -- Yes --> [Incident
                  Response Consultant]
                          |
                          V
    [Need Compliance Assistance?] -- Yes --> [Consultant for
                  Regulatory Compliance]
                          |
                          V
    [Scalability and Infrastructure Challenges?] -- Yes -->
            [Consultant for Security Architecture]
                          |
                          V
      [Seeking Unbiased, External Evaluation?] -- Yes -->
            [Comprehensive Security Audit Consultant]
                          |
                          V
    [Need Help with New Technology?] -- Yes --> [Consultant for
                  Specific Tools or Technologies]
                          |
                          V
                    Hire Consultant
```

Hiring a cybersecurity consultant is a valuable investment for many organizations, especially when faced with specific challenges or complex issues that require specialized expertise. Whether you need help with **incident response, compliance**, or **security architecture**, a consultant can provide critical insights, fast-tracked solutions, and hands-on support to strengthen your cybersecurity posture.

15.2: Overview of Managed Security Service Providers (MSSPs)

Cybersecurity is a critical function that requires constant attention, specialized expertise, and access to advanced tools. As the cyber threat landscape continues to grow more complex, many organizations find it difficult to keep up with the latest security challenges, technologies, and best practices. This is where **Managed Security Service Providers (MSSPs) come in.** MSSPs are third-party companies that provide outsourced security services, offering 24/7 monitoring, threat detection, incident response, and other cybersecurity functions.

In this section, we will provide a comprehensive overview of MSSPs, including their services, benefits, how they can help businesses improve security, and how to choose the right MSSP for your organization.

What is an MSSP?

A **Managed Security Service Provider (MSSP)** is a company that delivers outsourced cybersecurity services to businesses. The goal of an MSSP is to help organizations **manage and mitigate security risks** by providing expertise, monitoring, and support in areas such as threat detection, vulnerability management, incident response, and compliance.

MSSPs typically offer a **full spectrum of security services**, ranging from day-to-day monitoring to strategic consulting. They help organizations protect sensitive data, comply with regulatory requirements, and respond to cybersecurity incidents, often through a combination of **human expertise** and **automated tools**.

Key Services Provided by MSSPs

MSSPs provide a wide range of cybersecurity services designed to reduce risk and improve an organization's security posture. These services can be customized based on the specific needs of a business.

1. 24/7 Monitoring and Threat Detection

MSSPs typically provide around-the-clock monitoring of your organization's network, endpoints, and infrastructure. They use advanced **Security Information and Event Management (SIEM)** tools to analyze data from various sources and identify potential threats in real-time.

- **Threat detection**: MSSPs monitor for suspicious activity, including unauthorized access attempts, unusual data traffic, malware infections, and system anomalies.
- **Alerting**: When a potential threat is detected, MSSPs issue alerts to your internal team or directly respond to mitigate the risk.

Practical Example:
A **global retailer** hired an MSSP to provide 24/7 monitoring of their e-commerce platform. The MSSP detected an attempted **SQL injection attack** targeting the company's database. The MSSP immediately alerted the company and implemented a patch to block the attack.

Outcome:
The retailer avoided a potential data breach and was able to secure customer information before any harm was done.

2. Vulnerability Management

MSSPs perform regular vulnerability assessments and provide recommendations for remediation. This proactive service helps identify and address weaknesses in your organization's infrastructure, applications, and networks before they can be exploited by attackers.

- **Vulnerability scanning**: MSSPs run automated scans to identify vulnerabilities in operating systems, software applications, and network configurations.
- **Patch management**: MSSPs ensure that patches and updates are applied to systems in a timely manner, reducing the risk of exploits.

Practical Example:
A **financial services firm** used an MSSP to regularly scan their systems for vulnerabilities. The MSSP identified several outdated plugins on their public-facing website, which could have been exploited in a cyberattack. They worked with the firm's IT team to update and secure the website.

Outcome:
The company's web application was safeguarded against known exploits, and they were able to maintain compliance with **PCI DSS** regulations.

3. Incident Response and Remediation

In the event of a security breach or cyberattack, MSSPs play a key role in **incident response**. They help organizations contain and remediate threats quickly, minimizing the damage and restoring business operations.

- **Incident identification and containment**: MSSPs can quickly detect and contain a breach to prevent further damage.
- **Root cause analysis**: After an incident, MSSPs analyze the attack to understand how it occurred and recommend corrective actions.
- **Remediation**: MSSPs help organizations recover from incidents, whether it involves restoring data, rebuilding systems, or improving security measures.

Practical Example:
A **manufacturing company** experienced a **ransomware attack** that encrypted several of their critical systems. The MSSP immediately took steps to contain the attack, isolating affected systems, and worked with the company's internal team to restore data from backups.

Outcome:
The company was able to minimize downtime and data loss, allowing them to resume operations quickly after the attack.

4. Compliance and Regulatory Support

MSSPs help businesses comply with industry regulations by ensuring that systems are properly secured and regularly audited. This includes helping organizations adhere to frameworks such as **GDPR**, **HIPAA**, and **PCI DSS**.

- **Security audits**: MSSPs can conduct security audits to identify compliance gaps.
- **Documentation**: MSSPs provide detailed reports and documentation that help demonstrate compliance during audits.
- **Ongoing support**: MSSPs ensure that compliance requirements are met on an ongoing basis, particularly for industries that face frequent regulatory changes.

Practical Example:
A **healthcare provider** partnered with an MSSP to help meet **HIPAA** requirements for patient data security. The MSSP conducted regular audits of the provider's systems, helping them update security practices and submit necessary documentation for HIPAA compliance.

Outcome:
The provider was able to pass HIPAA audits and avoid penalties, ensuring that sensitive patient data was securely handled.

5. Managed Firewall and Endpoint Security

MSSPs can manage and monitor firewalls, intrusion prevention systems (IPS), and endpoint protection tools. They ensure that these defenses are always up to date and properly configured to protect against the latest threats.

- **Firewall management**: MSSPs configure, monitor, and manage firewalls to block unauthorized access and allow legitimate traffic.
- **Endpoint protection**: MSSPs deploy and manage endpoint security tools like antivirus software, device encryption, and mobile security to protect your organization's endpoints from malware and data theft.

Practical Example:
A **retail chain** hired an MSSP to manage their endpoint security. The

MSSP deployed **advanced antivirus software** across all employee devices and provided 24/7 monitoring to prevent malware infections from affecting critical systems.

Outcome:
The company significantly reduced its risk of data breaches and malware infections, particularly from employees accessing public Wi-Fi networks.

As technology continues to shape the world, **cybersecurity** will remain at the heart of digital success. The steps you take today to strengthen your cybersecurity will pay off in the long run by protecting your reputation, data, and business continuity. Embrace **vigilance, education**, and **proactive defense**, and you'll be better prepared to navigate the challenges of tomorrow's digital world. Secure your future today by committing to **continuous improvement** in your cybersecurity practices.

Why Choose an MSSP? The Benefits

1. Access to Advanced Security Tools

MSSPs often use state-of-the-art security tools that many organizations can't afford to implement in-house. This includes **SIEM systems, threat intelligence feeds**, and **advanced malware detection systems**.

2. Cost-Effective Solution

Outsourcing your security to an MSSP can be more cost-effective than hiring an internal cybersecurity team, especially for small to medium-sized businesses. MSSPs provide access to high-level security expertise at a fraction of the cost of building and maintaining an in-house team.

3. 24/7 Monitoring and Response

MSSPs offer continuous, around-the-clock monitoring, ensuring that your organization is protected from threats at all times. This is particularly crucial for businesses that operate outside regular working hours or have a global presence.

4. Scalability and Flexibility

As your business grows, your security needs evolve. MSSPs can scale their services to meet your changing requirements, whether you're expanding to new markets, integrating new technologies, or handling more data.

How to Choose the Right MSSP

Selecting the right MSSP is a critical decision that will impact your organization's security and compliance posture. Here are some factors to consider when choosing an MSSP:

1. Service Offerings

Make sure the MSSP offers the services that align with your business needs, whether it's **24/7 monitoring**, **incident response**, **vulnerability management**, or **compliance support**.

2. Reputation and Experience

Look for MSSPs with a solid reputation in the cybersecurity industry. Check their track record with previous clients, read case studies, and ask for referrals. Also, ensure they have experience in your industry, as different industries have unique security needs.

3. Technology and Tools

Ensure that the MSSP uses modern, reliable tools and technologies. You want an MSSP that invests in the latest security platforms to keep up with evolving threats.

4. Response Times and SLAs

Evaluate their **Service Level Agreements (SLAs)** to understand their response times and escalation procedures in the event of a security incident. It's important that they can respond quickly to prevent or mitigate any damage from a cyberattack.

5. Compliance Expertise

If you're in a regulated industry (e.g., finance, healthcare), ensure the MSSP has experience with the relevant compliance standards (e.g., **HIPAA**, **PCI DSS**, **GDPR**) and can help you maintain compliance.

Case Study: MSSP Success Story

Company: A **global e-commerce company** that operates 24/7 and processes millions of transactions daily.

Challenges:

The company faced increasing threats from **cybercriminals** trying to infiltrate their payment systems and customer data. With a limited internal security team, they lacked the resources to monitor for threats around the clock and respond to incidents quickly.

Solution:

The company engaged an MSSP to manage their cybersecurity needs, including:

- **24/7 network monitoring** for detecting unauthorized access.
- **Endpoint protection** across all employee and customer-facing devices.
- **Compliance management** to ensure adherence to **PCI DSS** standards.

Outcome:

The MSSP detected multiple attempts to breach the company's payment systems, preventing data loss and ensuring uninterrupted service. Their round-the-clock monitoring and proactive response reduced the company's risk of data breaches and helped maintain customer trust.

Flowchart: Selecting the Right MSSP

```
                        Start
                          |
                          V
            [Identify Specific Security Needs]
                          |
                          V
      [Evaluate MSSP's Service Offerings (24/7 Monitoring,
                  Incident Response, etc.)]
                          |
                          V
    [Assess Reputation, Experience, and Industry Expertise]
                          |
                          V
        [Verify Technologies and Tools Used by MSSP]
                          |
                          V
            [Check Response Times and SLAs]
                          |
                          V
      [Ensure Compliance Expertise (if applicable)]
                          |
                          V
                    [Choose MSSP]
```

MSSPs provide an invaluable service by offering comprehensive, round-the-clock cybersecurity coverage that ensures your organization is protected from emerging threats. Whether you need help with **incident response**, **vulnerability management**, or **compliance**, MSSPs bring specialized expertise and advanced tools to the table. By choosing the right MSSP, you can focus on your core business activities, knowing that your cybersecurity needs are in capable hands.

15.3: Learning Resources for Continuous Cybersecurity Improvement

Cybersecurity is not a static field. The landscape is constantly evolving, with new vulnerabilities, threats, and technologies emerging every day. To stay ahead of these changes, businesses need to foster a culture of

continuous learning. Whether you're a cybersecurity professional, an IT administrator, or a business leader, improving your knowledge and skills is essential to defending against the latest cyber threats.

In this guide, we will explore the most valuable **learning resources** that can help you and your team stay informed, up-to-date, and continuously improving your cybersecurity posture. From **online courses** and **certifications** to **websites** and **communities**, these resources will help you enhance your cybersecurity practices and stay ahead of the curve.

---

1. Online Courses and Certifications

One of the best ways to deepen your cybersecurity knowledge and skills is through **structured courses** and **certifications**. These resources are particularly useful for anyone looking to gain a more comprehensive understanding of cybersecurity or specialize in specific areas.

Popular Online Courses:

1. **Coursera**:
   - Coursera offers courses from top universities like **Stanford University, University of Maryland**, and **University of California**. Topics range from **basic cybersecurity fundamentals** to more advanced topics like **cryptography, network security**, and **penetration testing**.
   - **Recommended Course**: *"Introduction to Cyber Security" by NYU Tandon School of Engineering.*
   - **Why It's Valuable**: Coursera's courses are designed by industry experts, and they provide the flexibility to learn at your own pace.
2. **edX**:
   - edX offers a wide variety of cybersecurity courses from universities such as **Harvard, MIT**, and **UC Berkeley**. You can earn certifications that are highly regarded in the industry.
   - **Recommended Course**: *"Cybersecurity for Business" by the University of Colorado.*
   - **Why It's Valuable**: Many courses on edX are part of **professional certificates**, which can help you gain

specialized knowledge in areas like **cloud security**, **data protection**, and **incident response**.

3. **Udemy**:
   - **Udemy** offers a variety of affordable courses that range from beginner to advanced levels. They cover topics such as **ethical hacking**, **network security**, **cyber forensics**, and more.
   - **Recommended Course**: *"The Complete Cyber Security Course" by Nathan House*.
   - **Why It's Valuable**: Udemy's courses are designed to be hands-on and practical, making them great for learners who want real-world skills quickly.

Certifications to Pursue:

1. **CompTIA Security+**:
   - This is one of the most popular entry-level certifications for cybersecurity professionals. It covers foundational concepts like **network security**, **threat management**, and **identity management**.
   - **Why It's Valuable**: It's globally recognized and often required for entry-level cybersecurity positions.
2. **Certified Information Systems Security Professional (CISSP)**:
   - The CISSP certification is one of the most prestigious certifications for experienced cybersecurity professionals. It covers eight domains, including **security and risk management**, **asset security**, and **software development security**.
   - **Why It's Valuable**: It's highly respected in the cybersecurity industry and is often required for senior-level roles.
3. **Certified Ethical Hacker (CEH)**:
   - The CEH certification focuses on penetration testing and ethical hacking techniques, teaching you how to think like a hacker in order to better defend against them.
   - **Why It's Valuable**: It provides the skills needed to identify and address security vulnerabilities proactively.
4. **Certified Information Security Manager (CISM)**:
   - CISM focuses on managing, designing, and assessing an organization's information security program.

- o **Why It's Valuable**: It's ideal for professionals seeking to move into cybersecurity management and leadership roles.

---

2. Blogs, Websites, and News Portals

In the fast-moving world of cybersecurity, **staying up-to-date** with the latest news, vulnerabilities, and threat trends is crucial. There are many cybersecurity blogs and news websites that provide daily or weekly updates on the latest developments in the field.

Popular Cybersecurity Blogs and News Websites:

1. **KrebsOnSecurity**:
   - o Run by investigative journalist **Brian Krebs**, KrebsOnSecurity is a go-to resource for breaking news on the latest cyberattacks, data breaches, and security vulnerabilities.
   - o **Why It's Valuable**: The blog provides in-depth analyses of major security incidents and trends, making it a must-read for anyone interested in cybersecurity.
2. **Dark Reading**:
   - o Dark Reading is one of the most well-respected cybersecurity news sites. It covers topics such as **threat intelligence**, **vulnerability management**, **compliance**, and **security tools**.
   - o **Why It's Valuable**: It's a comprehensive resource for both beginners and experts looking for up-to-date information and in-depth articles on all things cybersecurity.
3. **The Hacker News**:
   - o The Hacker News provides breaking news and updates on the latest hacking techniques, security threats, and vulnerabilities.
   - o **Why It's Valuable**: It offers a wide range of information, from daily news to technical deep-dives, and is updated frequently.
4. **SecurityWeek**:
   - o This website offers a wealth of cybersecurity news, analyses, and research reports, focusing on both **enterprise security** and **emerging cyber threats**.

- o **Why It's Valuable**: SecurityWeek provides useful resources for both businesses and individual cybersecurity professionals, with articles focusing on **business cybersecurity**, **cybercrime**, and **nation-state threats**.

Security Communities and Forums:

1. **Stack Exchange (Information Security)**:
   - o Stack Exchange's Information Security community is a place where cybersecurity professionals ask questions, share answers, and discuss topics ranging from **cryptography** to **incident response**.
   - o **Why It's Valuable**: It's a great place for learning from peers, sharing experiences, and finding solutions to specific cybersecurity problems.
2. **Reddit's r/cybersecurity**:
   - o The r/cybersecurity subreddit offers a community-driven platform to discuss recent security events, share educational content, and ask questions.
   - o **Why It's Valuable**: It's an active community of cybersecurity enthusiasts, professionals, and hackers that regularly shares the latest news, tips, and learning resources.

3. Books and eBooks

Books provide a structured, in-depth way to learn about cybersecurity, often from thought leaders and experts in the field. Many well-established cybersecurity professionals have written books that serve as great learning resources.

Recommended Cybersecurity Books:

1. **"The Web Application Hacker's Handbook" by Dafydd Stuttard and Marcus Pinto**:
   - o A comprehensive guide to web application security, this book covers **penetration testing** techniques for identifying vulnerabilities in web applications.

- o **Why It's Valuable**: It's a detailed, hands-on guide to one of the most important areas of cybersecurity: **web application security**.
2. **"Hacking: The Art of Exploitation" by Jon Erickson**:
   - o This book delves into the technical details of how hacking works, from **buffer overflows** to **network sniffing** and **cryptography**.
   - o **Why It's Valuable**: It provides a deep dive into the mechanics of exploitation, making it essential for anyone interested in ethical hacking.
3. **"The Art of Computer Security" by Mikko Hypponen**:
   - o Mikko Hypponen, a leading expert in cybersecurity, discusses the broad range of topics in modern computer security, including **cybercrime**, **data breaches**, and **global hacking networks**.
   - o **Why It's Valuable**: This book gives a comprehensive overview of modern security issues and real-world attacks, making it a great resource for both professionals and business owners.
4. **"Network Security Essentials" by William Stallings**:
   - o A practical guide to network security concepts, including topics like **firewalls**, **intrusion detection systems**, and **virtual private networks (VPNs)**.
   - o **Why It's Valuable**: This book is a solid choice for those who want to understand the fundamental principles of network security.

---

4. Webinars, Podcasts, and Conferences

Engaging with **webinars**, **podcasts**, and **industry conferences** is an excellent way to stay connected with the cybersecurity community and learn from experts in the field.

Cybersecurity Podcasts:

1. **Security Now**: A podcast hosted by Steve Gibson and Leo Laporte that covers the latest news in cybersecurity and provides expert analysis on key topics.

2. **Darknet Diaries**: This podcast focuses on **real-world cybersecurity stories**, offering a behind-the-scenes look at hacking, breaches, and digital forensics.
3. **The CyberWire Daily Podcast**: Provides a daily digest of the latest cybersecurity news, insights, and expert commentary.

Cybersecurity Webinars and Conferences:

1. **Black Hat**: A leading cybersecurity conference that features world-renowned experts in the field, showcasing the latest research and trends.
2. **RSA Conference**: One of the largest cybersecurity events in the world, RSA provides a platform for security professionals to discuss the latest threats, solutions, and strategies.
3. **SANS Webinars**: SANS Institute offers numerous free webinars on a range of cybersecurity topics, including incident response, malware analysis, and compliance.

---

5. Cybersecurity Simulations and Hands-On Labs

Cybersecurity isn't just about theory—it's about practical, hands-on skills. Engaging in **cybersecurity simulations** and **labs** can give you a chance to test your skills in a real-world, risk-free environment.

Platforms for Hands-On Cybersecurity Learning:

1. **TryHackMe**:
   - A beginner-friendly platform offering virtual cybersecurity labs, challenges, and learning paths for topics ranging from **penetration testing** to **network defense**.
   - **Why It's Valuable**: It's a fun, gamified learning experience that allows you to apply cybersecurity concepts in practice.
2. **Hack The Box**:
   - A platform where cybersecurity enthusiasts can practice penetration testing in a controlled, competitive environment.

- o **Why It's Valuable**: It's a great resource for ethical hackers looking to sharpen their skills and compete with others in solving cybersecurity challenges.
3. **Cyber Ranges**:
    - o Cyber ranges are simulated environments used for practicing cybersecurity skills in real-world scenarios. Examples include **Virtual Battlebox** and **RangeForce**.

Flowchart: Continuous Cybersecurity Learning

```
                         Start
                           |
                           V
   [Identify Learning Goal (Certification, Skill, Compliance)]
                           |
                           V
       [Select Learning Resources (Online Courses, Books,
                        Podcasts)]
                           |
                           V
       [Engage in Hands-On Labs and Simulations to Apply
                        Knowledge]
                           |
                           V
     [Stay Updated on Latest Threats and Trends (Blogs, News
                          Sites)]
                           |
                           V
         [Participate in Cybersecurity Communities]
                           |
                           V
       [Review and Reflect on Learning Progress Regularly]
                           |
                           V
           [Update Skills and Security Practices]
```

Cybersecurity is a rapidly evolving field, and staying ahead of emerging threats requires continuous learning and improvement. By leveraging **online courses, certifications, cybersecurity blogs, hands-on labs**, and **industry events**, you can enhance your skills, stay informed, and ensure that your organization remains resilient against cyberattacks.

Investing in learning resources will not only help you become a more effective cybersecurity professional but will also foster a culture of security awareness throughout your organization, ensuring everyone plays a part in defending against evolving threats.

Conclusion: Securing Your Future in the Digital World

Recap of Key Takeaways

As we reach the conclusion of this book, it's important to reflect on the journey we've taken through the world of **cybersecurity** and recap the **key takeaways** that can help safeguard your business in the digital age.

1. **Cybersecurity is Everyone's Responsibility**: One of the core messages throughout this book is that cybersecurity isn't just the responsibility of the IT department—it's something that needs to be ingrained in the culture of your entire organization. Whether you're a small startup or a global enterprise, **every employee** plays a part in protecting the business from cyber threats.
2. **Understand the Threat Landscape**: The world of cyber threats is constantly evolving. From **ransomware** to **social engineering** and **insider threats**, businesses face a wide range of dangers. The importance of staying informed about emerging threats and adopting strategies to **defend against them** cannot be overstated. Whether it's **phishing** attacks, **data breaches**, or **DDoS** attempts, understanding the **landscape** is the first step in developing a strong defense.
3. **Implement a Defense-in-Depth Strategy**: Throughout this book, we emphasized the importance of adopting a **multi-layered defense strategy**. This involves using a combination of **firewalls**, **endpoint security**, **intrusion detection systems (IDS)**, and **encryption** to protect your systems from various angles. A layered approach ensures that if one defense fails, others will catch the threat. The best way to build your security framework is by thinking about it like a **fortress**, with layers of protection at every critical point.
4. **Security Policies and Employee Awareness**: We've also discussed the critical role of **security policies** in establishing a solid foundation for protecting your business. From **password hygiene** and **authentication procedures** to **remote work guidelines** and **BYOD (Bring Your Own Device)** policies, having clear, enforced policies is essential. Moreover, **training** and

ongoing awareness are just as important as technical measures. **Employees** need to understand the **cybersecurity best practices** and recognize potential threats to prevent human error, the most common cause of security incidents.

5. **Regular Audits and Vulnerability Testing**: Cybersecurity is not a one-time task. It's an ongoing commitment. Regular **audits**, **penetration tests**, and **vulnerability scans** help you identify weaknesses in your system before attackers can exploit them. Just like maintaining a physical building requires regular checks and upgrades, your digital infrastructure needs continuous attention to ensure it remains secure.

6. **Incident Response and Business Continuity**: Despite your best efforts, breaches can still happen. What matters most in those moments is how quickly you can **respond** and **recover**. Developing a comprehensive **incident response plan** and implementing a solid **disaster recovery** strategy is crucial. **Backups, data encryption**, and well-structured **communication plans** will ensure your organization can recover quickly from any cybersecurity incident, minimizing downtime and financial impact.

7. **Engage External Experts When Necessary**: While it's important to build internal capabilities, **external expertise** is also invaluable. Whether it's a **cybersecurity consultant**, a **Managed Security Service Provider (MSSP)**, or a **specialized training resource**, engaging external experts can bring **specialized knowledge** and **best practices** that can strengthen your security defenses and help you address gaps that internal teams might overlook.

8. **Continuous Learning and Improvement**: The cybersecurity landscape evolves rapidly, and so must your skills and practices. To stay ahead of cyber threats, make learning an ongoing habit. Whether it's through **courses, certifications**, or **reading up on the latest security news**, continuous improvement should be at the heart of your cybersecurity strategy. Embrace a mindset of **proactive defense**, rather than reacting after an attack has occurred.

Encouraging Ongoing Vigilance and Improvement in Cybersecurity Practices

As we look ahead to the future, one thing is clear: **cybersecurity is a continuous journey**, not a destination. The digital world is evolving at breakneck speed, and so are the methods that cybercriminals use to infiltrate systems. Therefore, businesses that want to stay secure must constantly adapt, learn, and grow.

To truly **secure your future in the digital world**, ongoing vigilance is essential. It's not enough to implement a few security measures and assume everything is protected. Just as a business evolves, so too must its cybersecurity posture. Here are a few key principles for maintaining long-term security:

1. Stay Agile and Flexible

Cyber threats are highly dynamic. What works today might not be effective tomorrow. Stay agile by constantly assessing your defenses and adapting to new threats. Regularly review your security policies, systems, and response plans. Don't wait for an attack to prompt action. By staying proactive, you can anticipate threats and adjust your defenses accordingly.

2. Foster a Culture of Security

Building a culture where **security is everyone's responsibility** is essential. From leadership to employees, everyone should understand the importance of cybersecurity in their role. This culture can be fostered through regular **training**, **awareness programs**, and **security drills**. When cybersecurity becomes second nature to everyone in the organization, it significantly reduces the risk of human error.

3. Continuously Monitor and Adapt to New Technologies

Technologies like **cloud computing**, **artificial intelligence**, and the **Internet of Things (IoT)** have introduced new attack surfaces. While these technologies offer significant advantages, they also introduce new vulnerabilities. Stay updated on emerging technologies and ensure that your security measures are adapted to protect new environments as they evolve.

4. Invest in Security Tools and Expertise

No matter how large or small your business is, investing in **security tools** and **expertise** is critical. Tools like **intrusion detection systems (IDS)**, **endpoint detection and response (EDR)**, and **SIEM solutions** should be part of your security arsenal. Additionally, continue to invest in **training** and **certifications** for your internal team to ensure they are equipped to handle new challenges.

5. Stay Informed and Networked

Cyber threats are not only technical but also social and political. Join **cybersecurity communities** and participate in industry events, conferences, and forums. By staying connected with others in the field, you can gain valuable insights into the latest threats, solutions, and best practices. Knowledge sharing is one of the most powerful tools in staying ahead of cybercriminals.

6. Learn from Past Incidents

Every incident, whether it's a breach or a near miss, is an opportunity to learn. **Post-incident reviews** and **lessons learned** should be part of your security improvement process. Understand what went wrong, what worked well, and how you can prevent similar incidents in the future. Continuous **self-assessment** is key to strengthening your defenses.

Personal Insights: The Road to Cybersecurity Resilience

In my experience, one of the most important takeaways from working in cybersecurity is the **power of resilience**. No system is 100% foolproof, and cyberattacks will inevitably happen. What truly matters is how you respond, learn, and adapt.

The best cybersecurity strategies are not built on fear, but on a foundation of **continuous improvement**. When you take an active role in learning, adjusting, and fortifying your defenses, you position your organization to not only survive a cyberattack but to emerge stronger. The process of **securing your future in the digital world** is a journey, not a one-time

Appendices

Appendix A: Cybersecurity Terminology Glossary

As you journey through the world of cybersecurity, you will come across many specialized terms. Understanding these terms is crucial to grasping the concepts and practices discussed in this book. Below is a glossary of key cybersecurity terms to help you stay on track and ensure that you're equipped to navigate discussions with confidence.

1. **Authentication**: The process of verifying the identity of a user, system, or device. Common methods include usernames, passwords, and biometric data like fingerprints or facial recognition.
2. **Firewall**: A network security system that monitors and controls incoming and outgoing network traffic based on predetermined security rules. It acts as a barrier between your network and potential threats.
3. **Malware**: Malicious software designed to damage or gain unauthorized access to computer systems. Types of malware include **viruses**, **ransomware**, **spyware**, and **worms**.
4. **Phishing**: A cyberattack that involves tricking individuals into revealing sensitive information, such as usernames, passwords, or credit card numbers, usually via deceptive emails or websites.
5. **Penetration Testing (Pen Test)**: A simulated cyberattack on a system to evaluate its security. Ethical hackers conduct these tests to find vulnerabilities before malicious actors do.
6. **Encryption**: The process of converting data into a code to prevent unauthorized access. Encryption is a fundamental component of data protection in transit and at rest.
7. **Zero-Day Vulnerability**: A flaw in software or hardware that is unknown to the vendor or developer, making it highly vulnerable to exploitation until a patch or fix is released.
8. **SIEM (Security Information and Event Management)**: A set of tools that provide real-time analysis of security alerts generated by applications and network hardware.
9. **Endpoint**: Any device that connects to your network, such as computers, smartphones, tablets, and IoT devices. Securing endpoints is critical in maintaining overall network security.

10. **DDoS (Distributed Denial of Service)**: A cyberattack that aims to overwhelm a network or service by flooding it with traffic, causing it to become unavailable to legitimate users.

Appendix B: Recommended Cybersecurity Tools and Software

To implement the best practices and strategies discussed throughout this book, you will need to have the right tools at your disposal. Below is a curated list of **cybersecurity tools and software** that can help strengthen your organization's defenses.

1. **Antivirus Software**:
   - **Norton Antivirus**: Provides robust protection against malware, ransomware, and other threats.
   - **Bitdefender**: Known for its real-time protection and excellent malware detection capabilities.
2. **Firewalls**:
   - **Cisco ASA**: A trusted enterprise-level firewall solution that offers both hardware and software firewalls to protect against various threats.
   - **pfSense**: A popular open-source firewall solution with features like VPN support and customizable configurations.
3. **Endpoint Protection**:
   - **CrowdStrike Falcon**: A cloud-delivered endpoint protection platform that uses AI to detect and stop breaches before they can cause harm.
   - **Sophos Intercept X**: A leading endpoint protection tool that provides ransomware protection, EDR, and automated response capabilities.
4. **SIEM Solutions**:
   - **Splunk**: A powerful tool that enables you to monitor, analyze, and respond to security threats in real time.
   - **Elastic Stack (ELK)**: An open-source solution for centralized logging and real-time analysis of security events.
5. **Password Management**:
   - **LastPass**: A password manager that securely stores passwords and generates strong, random passwords for all your accounts.

- o **1Password**: Another top-rated password manager with a user-friendly interface and strong security features.
6. **Vulnerability Scanning**:
   - o **Nessus**: A widely used vulnerability scanner that helps identify weaknesses in your network, systems, and devices.
   - o **Qualys**: A comprehensive cloud-based vulnerability management solution that provides real-time visibility into your security posture.
7. **Penetration Testing Tools**:
   - o **Kali Linux**: A popular open-source platform for penetration testing with numerous tools for testing the security of systems and applications.
   - o **Metasploit**: An advanced penetration testing framework used for developing and executing exploit code against remote targets.
8. **Incident Response**:
   - o **TheHive**: An open-source incident response platform that allows security teams to manage and coordinate responses to incidents efficiently.
   - o **Cortex XSOAR**: A security orchestration, automation, and response (SOAR) platform that integrates with existing security systems to streamline incident response.

Appendix C: Creating a Basic Cybersecurity Policy

Creating a clear and concise **cybersecurity policy** is essential for any organization looking to protect its data and systems. Here's a step-by-step guide to creating your first policy:

1. **Define the Scope and Purpose**:
   - o Explain why the policy is important and outline what it will cover. The purpose is to ensure employees and users understand their responsibilities regarding security.
2. **User Access and Authentication**:
   - o Establish rules for user access management. This includes the creation of strong passwords, mandatory use of multi-factor authentication (MFA), and user access controls based on roles.
3. **Data Protection**:

- o Specify how data should be handled, including encryption for sensitive information, safe data storage practices, and methods for securely disposing of outdated data.
4. **Incident Response**:
   - o Develop a clear plan for responding to security incidents, including how employees should report suspicious activities and who is responsible for managing incidents.
5. **Remote Work Security**:
   - o For organizations allowing remote work, provide guidelines on how to secure personal devices, use VPNs, and prevent unauthorized access to company systems.
6. **Software and System Updates**:
   - o Require regular patching and updates for software, operating systems, and applications. Set a schedule for checking for vulnerabilities and installing updates.
7. **Employee Training**:
   - o Ensure employees are regularly trained on security best practices, such as recognizing phishing attempts, using strong passwords, and reporting suspicious activities.
8. **Compliance and Legal Requirements**:
   - o Address how your policy complies with legal and regulatory requirements (e.g., GDPR, HIPAA, PCI DSS) and provide guidelines for ensuring compliance.

Appendix D: Cybersecurity Compliance Frameworks

Compliance with regulatory frameworks is an essential part of ensuring the security of sensitive data and systems. Below is an overview of the most widely recognized cybersecurity compliance frameworks:

1. **General Data Protection Regulation (GDPR)**:
   - o A European Union regulation that protects the personal data of EU citizens. It requires businesses to adopt strong data protection measures and notify authorities of data breaches within 72 hours.
   - o **Key Elements**: Consent management, data subject rights, data encryption, breach notification.
2. **Health Insurance Portability and Accountability Act (HIPAA)**:

- A U.S. law that mandates healthcare organizations to safeguard patient data. HIPAA-compliant organizations must implement stringent controls for data access, storage, and transmission.
- **Key Elements**: Patient consent, data encryption, audit controls, access management.

3. **Payment Card Industry Data Security Standard (PCI DSS)**:
   - A set of security standards for organizations that handle credit card payments. PCI DSS outlines requirements for securing cardholder data.
   - **Key Elements**: Encryption, access control, vulnerability management, regular monitoring.

4. **Federal Information Security Management Act (FISMA)**:
   - A U.S. federal law that requires federal agencies and contractors to secure their information systems. It provides guidelines for information security risk assessments and the establishment of security controls.
   - **Key Elements**: Risk assessments, continuous monitoring, incident response planning, security policies.

5. **ISO/IEC 27001**:
   - A global standard for information security management. ISO/IEC 27001 provides a framework for managing information security risks and ensuring data confidentiality, integrity, and availability.
   - **Key Elements**: Risk management, business continuity, data protection, incident response.

Appendix E: Resources for Cybersecurity Awareness Training

Building a culture of cybersecurity within your organization starts with **employee training**. Here are some resources that provide engaging, comprehensive cybersecurity awareness training:

1. **KnowBe4**:
   - Offers training modules on phishing, password security, and data protection. It includes simulated phishing attacks to help employees recognize real-world threats.
2. **SANS Security Awareness**:

o Provides a range of security awareness training courses that cover topics such as secure communication, data privacy, and incident reporting.
3. **Cofense**:
  o Specializes in **phishing awareness** training, helping employees recognize phishing attempts and reduce the likelihood of falling for cyberattacks.
4. **Cyber Awareness Challenge (DoD)**:
  o A free, government-sponsored resource aimed at improving cybersecurity awareness, including modules on identifying and avoiding common cyber threats.

Appendix F: Cybersecurity Best Practices Checklist

To help ensure your organization is following best practices, use the following checklist as a reference:

- **User Access Control**:
  o Are strong passwords required for all users?
  o Is multi-factor authentication (MFA) enabled for critical systems?
  o Are user access rights regularly reviewed?
- **Data Protection**:
  o Is sensitive data encrypted at rest and in transit?
  o Are secure methods used to dispose of old data (e.g., shredding physical media, secure deletion of digital files)?
- **Incident Response**:
  o Does your organization have an **incident response plan**?
  o Are all employees trained on how to report suspicious activities?
- **Vulnerability Management**:
  o Are all software and systems up to date with the latest security patches?
  o Are regular vulnerability scans conducted on all systems?
- **Training**:
  o Is cybersecurity awareness training provided to all employees?
  o Is phishing simulation performed regularly?
- **Remote Work**:

- o Are remote workers required to use VPNs when accessing the company network?
- o Are personal devices properly secured before accessing sensitive data?

As organizations continue to face evolving cyber threats, ensuring that you have the right knowledge, tools, and resources in place is essential for maintaining a strong security posture. The appendices in this book provide practical tools and resources to help you strengthen your organization's cybersecurity framework, foster a culture of continuous improvement, and build resilience against future cyberattacks.

By using the glossary, tools, templates, and frameworks outlined in the appendices, you can empower your team, improve your security measures, and stay ahead of cybercriminals in this ever-evolving digital world.

www.ingramcontent.com/pod-product-compliance
Lightning Source LLC
LaVergne TN
LVHW080113070326
832902LV00015B/2555

9 798280 335011